Tollygunge to Tollywood

Tollygunge to Tollywood

The Bengali Film Industry Reimagined

Anugyan Nag
Spandan Bhattacharya

Orient BlackSwan

TOLLYGUNGE TO TOLLYWOOD:
THE BENGALI FILM INDUSTRY REIMAGINED

ORIENT BLACKSWAN PRIVATE LIMITED

Registered Office
3-6-752 Himayatnagar, Hyderabad 500 029, Telangana, India
e-mail: centraloffice@orientblackswan.com

Other Offices
Bengaluru, Chennai, Guwahati, Hyderabad, Kolkata,
Mumbai, New Delhi, Noida, Patna

First published by Orient Blackswan Private Limited 2021

ISBN 978-93-5442-034-4

Typeset in
Minion Pro 10.5/12.5 by
Shine Graphics, Delhi 110 094

Printed at
Thomson Press, New Delhi 110 020

Published by
Orient Blackswan Private Limited
3-6-752, Himayatnagar, Hyderabad 500 029, Telangana, India
e-mail: info@orientblackswan.com

For Ritu Da . . .

Rituparno Ghosh (1963–2013)

Contents

List of Figures *ix*
Acknowledgements *xi*
Publishers' Acknowledgements *xiii*

Introduction 1

1. The Transition of the Bengali Film Industry: The Post-Uttam Kumar Era 15

2. The Consolidation of Tollywood and the Logic of Corporatisation: A Case Study of Shree Venkatesh Films (SVF) 57

3. Situating the 'New Parallel' Bengali Cinema: The Logic of Production, Politics of Nostalgia, and Rituparno Ghosh 104

4. Media Convergence and the Discursive Proliferation and Consolidation of Tollywood 150

Conclusion: Tollywood Post-Resurgence 183

Index 207

List of Figures

2.1: YouTube Screen Grab of *Sathi* 59
2.2: Film Poster of *Chirodini Tumi Je Amar* 73
2.3: Production Still of *Chirodini Tumi Je Amar* 74
2.4: Publicity Still of *Chirodini Tumi Je Amar* 75
2.5: Film Poster of *Challenge* 77
2.6: Production Still of *Challenge* 78
2.7: Production Still of *Challenge* 78
2.8: Production Still of *Autograph* 84
2.9: Production Still of *Autograph* 85
2.10: Film Poster of *Dui Prithibi* 89
2.11: Production Still of *Dui Prithibi* 90
2.12: Production Still of *Dui Prithibi* 91
2.13: Production Still of *Dui Prithibi* 91

3.1: DVD Screen Grab of *Unishe April* 106
3.2: DVD Screen Grab of *Dahan* 123
3.3: DVD Screen Grab of *Paromitar Ekdin* 124
3.4: DVD Screen Grab of *Paromitar Ekdin* 124

5.1: DVD Screen Grab of *Jaatishwar* 184
5.2: DVD Screen Grab of *Ichche* 186
5.3: Screen Grab of *Asha Jaoar Majhe* 191
5.4: Screen Grab of *Asha Jaoar Majhe* 191

Acknowledgements

This book has materialised with the constant support, encouragement and guidance of our mentor, Professor Ira Bhaskar. We also extend our gratitude to Professor Ranjani Mazumdar, Professor Bishnupriya Dutt, Dr Kaushik Bhowmik and Dr Veena Hariharan from Jawaharlal Nehru University; Professor Madhuja Mukherjee, Dr Subhajit Chatterjee and Dr Anindya Sengupta from Jadavpur University for giving their valuable time at the initial stages of developing this project; and Professor Shohini Ghosh from Jamia Millia Islamia University. Roopa Sharma, commissioning editor, Orient BlackSwan for believing in our project and consistently engaging with our work over the last few years and Pooja Sanyal for her meticulous editing.

The SPEAR Project fellowship of the School of Arts and Aesthetics, Jawaharlal Nehru University (JNU), New Delhi for our field work in Delhi, Pune and Kolkata.

Most of the research for this book was done at the National Library, Kolkata and Nandan Library and Archive, Bangiya Sathiya Parishad, National Film Archives, Pune and Hitesranjan Sanyal Memorial Collection, Centre for the Study of Social Sciences, Patuli, Kolkata.

We are also indebted to Subrat Dutt, Swara Bhaskar, Abhijit Goswami (Nandan) and Ashis Banerjee (EIMPA) for their help in providing contacts of industry persons. Thanks are also due to those who took out their valuable time in talking to us for long hours, in enriching us with their experiences and anecdotes from Tollywood: Late Anjan Das, Late Bappaditya Bandyopadhyay, Subrata Sen, Swapan Saha, Haranath Chakraborty, Tapan Biswas, Renu Roy, Sandip Sen, Aniruddha Roychowdhury, Ansu Sur, Ranjan Bandyopadhyay, Aniruddha Dhar, Gautam Ghosh, Partha Raha, Shoma A. Chatterji, Ratnottoma Sengupta, Dr Parimal Ghosh, Nilanjan Chattopadhyay, Jayanta Kumar Ghosh, Arijit Dutta, Sagnik Michael Sinha, Shamik Bandyopadhyay, Surya Bandyopadhyay, Indranil Ghosh and

Uttam Kumar Basu, Raj Chakraborty, Pradipta Bhattacharya, Rituparna Sengupta, Buddhadev Dasgupta, Goutam Ghose, Srijit Mukherjee, Swastika Mukherjee, Sreelekha Mitra, Shrikant Mohta, Mahendra Soni, Ashok Dhanuka, Atanu Ghosh, Jagadish Pandey and Subhasish Gangully. A special thank you to Kushali Nag who provided us with invaluable support and contacts throughout the journey of this book.

Friends and colleagues for their love, affection and solidarity: Abhija Ghosh, Agnitra Ghosh, Bindu Menon, Kaustav Bakshi, Radha Dayal, Rajendra Negi, Smita Banerjee, Sumit Dey, Vebhuti Duggal and Deimantas Valanciunas.

Finally, our parents and siblings for their unconditional love and support.

Publishers' Acknowledgements

For granting permission to reproduce copyrighted material in this book, the publishers and authors thank the following:

Shree Venkatesh Films (SVF) Pvt. Ltd, for granting permission for the use of images and posters, in Chapter 2, titled 'The Consolidation of Tollywood and the Logic of Corporatisation: A Case Study of Shree Venkatesh Films (SVF)'.

Journal of Bengali Studies, vol. 1, no. 2 (2012), Janmashtami, 24 Srabon, 1419 Monsoon Issue, *Bengali Cinema: Bengalis and Cinema*, ed., Tamal Dasgupta, asst. ed., Sourav Gupta, Mousumi Biswas Dasgupta and Sujay Chatterjee, for granting permission to reproduce the following two articles in this book as Chapter 1, titled 'The Transition of the Bengali Film Industry: The Post-Uttam Kumar Era' and Chapter 4, titled 'Media Convergence and the Discursive Proliferation and Consolidation of Tollywood', respectively:

Anugyan Nag, 'From Tollygunge to Tollywood: The Transformation of Bengali Film Industry between 1980 and the Present', *Journal of Bengali Studies*, vol. 1, no. 2 (2012), p. 120.

Spandan Bhattacharya, 'Writing a Biography of Bengali Film Publicity: the Logic of Differentiation, and a Journey of Desire', *Journal of Bengali Studies*, vol. 1, no. 2 (2012), p. 87.

Introduction

This book is an attempt to study the emergence of the Bengali film industry in the post-liberalisation period, which is known as Tollywood. Our attempt is to look at the larger changes that have been taking place within the Bengali film industry. We have argued as to how the image of Tollywood gets constructed and reshaped in the consciousness and imagination of the Bengali audience within and outside Bengal through discourse on several media networks and channels. In addition, we dwell on the emergence of the star and celebrity culture, innovative marketing and promotional strategies, the development of diverse film exhibition and distribution models, and most importantly, the corporatisation of film production compounding in reshaping the image of the film industry.

This book's effort has been to look at the transformation of the Bengali film industry, widely referred to as the 'Tollygunge industry' until the 1990s. This was also the period (1980s–90s) that witnessed intense public discourse about the differences between the Bengali *bhadralok*[1] and the mainstream commercial cinema, the reasons for which have been elaborated in the course of this book. This discourse got further complicated during the post-liberalisation period, when the dividing lines between rural and urban locales were gradually blurring in Bengal and elsewhere in India.[2] The book, thus, maps several developments and changes in the industry dynamics, along with media convergence, which pushed Tollywood to reshape itself as an industry in its present form.

We also discuss the post-liberalisation Bengali 'parallel' cinema; the category 'parallel' indicates a distinctive aesthetics, as well the limited distribution and exhibition of these films in relation to West Bengal's mainstream cinema in this period; this was a nostalgic film practice of the Bengali *bhadralok* intelligentsia. We have tried to demonstrate here how an idea of the glorious Bengali cinematic tradition and an attempt to reclaim that lost past became central to this film culture, textually, and also in terms of its production and publicity logic. Central to the study of this parallel cinema's nostalgia discourse is the question of 'good taste', and how this is imagined in continuation with the earlier Bengali cinematic practice. The book aims at problematising the very notion of 'good taste' for this kind of cinema, focusing on how the idea of 'parallel'/'parallelness' itself was generated and got proliferated across film forms, production–distribution chains, specific exhibition sites, media institutions, etc. The book maps the journey of parallel cinema and its nostalgia discourse in post-1990s West Bengal. It also recognises multiple origins in the film society movement, in the overvaluation of realist film practice of this new 'parallel' cinema in the journalistic and academic writings on the late-1970s and 1980s 'crisis narrative' of Bengali cinematic practice, and in the overall *bhadralok* anxiety in post-liberalised Bengal. Relationally, this book discusses how this parallel film culture presupposes a kind of 'cultured Bengaliness' to be performed on film texts and their circulation, and how the informal middle-class intellectual machinery maintains and structures this notion as 'different' from the mainstream model in its networks and regimes of reception.

Subsequently in the year 1998, with the Indian film world being officially accorded the status of an industry, the imbrications of the media and the Hindi film industry, also known as Bollywood, were overtly evident. Following this development, the Bengali film industry, too, initiated an industrial revamp. In the mid-1990s, the Bengali film industry began to adopt corporatisation and maintain close association with the media in order to market and promote itself as Tollywood. In 1996, Shree Venkatesh Films (henceforth SVF) Pvt. Ltd, a corporate film production house, was formed, which, along with Eskay Videos and Surinder Films, introduced several changes into the production, distribution and exhibition systems within the Bengali film industry. This book also takes into account the proliferation of multiplexes, particularly since 2010, which has compelled Tollywood producers and distributors to embrace newer strategies for the marketing and promotion of their films. This has often been similar to the techniques practised by Bollywood producers and distributors. These changes are viewed by the media and industry as responsible for bringing the Bengali middle-class audience 'back to the theatre'. The changes also helped to establish Tollywood as an industry that is 'popular', if not necessarily 'respectable', in the consciousness of the audience within Bengal and beyond. While SVF is credited with the corporatisation of the Bengali film industry, it is also often accused of bringing in absolute monopoly over cinematic processes through vertical integration. This exceptional aspect eventually led to an inflexible style of management control in the entire process of film-making and distribution. This book further attempts to explore the significance of these intersections, the overlapping of production policies, the diversification of the industrial production system, and other such developments within Tollywood.

A Discourse on Bengali Cinema and the Industry

The Bengali film industry is broadly divided into three main phases. First, the Calcutta film studio[3] post-talkies period from the 1930s to the early 1950s is seen as the glorious period of Bengali cinema. The history of several prolific studios, especially the New Theatres Studio, and Calcutta as a centre of film production in India were recognised and acknowledged for quality films, film-makers, actors, writers, lyricists, technicians and musicians. New Theatres made films both in Bengali and other languages, which were highly popular and of equal commercial viability.[4] The second phase is characterised as the golden era of Bengali cinema, and this is the period of the 1950s and 1960s. This is the time that witnessed the tremendous popularity of matinee idol Uttam Kumar and his female lead, Suchitra Sen, along with film-makers like Ajay Kar, Asit Sen and Tapan Sinha, among others. This period was also marked for films largely based on literary works drawn from the vast reservoir of quality Bengali literature. The two decades of the the 1960s and 1970s are significantly associated with the art/parallel cinema movement, primarily because of the works of the greats of Bengali cinema, namely Satyajit Ray, Ritwik Ghatak and Mrinal Sen. The third phase of Bengali cinema is the 1980s, post the death of Uttam Kumar, when the industry faced a massive financial crisis. This crisis led to the rise of a certain kind of cinematic practice that is often described as the 'cheap copy' of 'masala' Hindi films, or it is also referred to as a mere imitation of the one-wall theatre, or *jatra*,[5] by the press and the Bengali *bhadralok*.[6] This phase is also known for its discourse on the 'crisis narrative'. With the liberalisation of the Indian economy in 1991, the Bengali film industry gradually went through diverse changes, as newer groups of producers, directors and film technicians joined in. Simulataneously, Tollywood experienced some business and economic collaborations or joint ventures with investers, producers and other capitalists from Mumbai.[7] All these changes that were coming about received mixed reactions; some were celebratory, while others were critical. Our task here is to closely examine the forces that operate through various circuits within the overall cultural and industrial spectrum of Tollywood.

Most scholarly works and press writings on Bengali cinema have focused on the discourse on 'art films', their auteurs, and generally, the cinema of the 1950s and 1960s. In the popular press and film society writings on the 1980s and 1990s, the recurrent concern that was expressed has been the overall degradation of Bengali films. These writings lament the fact that the films were no longer based on the rich Bengali literature and were quite unlike the films of the golden era, which were marked by realism and were reflective of the wider 'middle-class sentiment'.[8] These discursive responses continued to pour in, along with celebratory works on auteurs like Satyajit Ray,[9] Ritwik Ghatak[10] and Mrinal Sen,[11] largely focusing on the film text and narrative content. During the 1980s and 1990s, many writings on Bengali cinema also expressed concerns about the transition towards 'masala' films that could possibly only appeal to mass audiences.[12] These writings were engaging with the notion of 'crisis' that the middle-class intelligentsia had perhaps constructed.[13] This alleged crisis, according to them, was not economic, but was rather the ever-decaying quality of Bengali cinema.[14] In the writings of the film society members at the time, the division between mainstream popular films and 'quality' films was strictly maintained. Satyajit Ray himself, in his writings, was critical of the quality of average Indian films, pointing fingers towards their 'visual dissonances' and 'lack of maturity'.[15] This idea continued to be followed by the later generation of film society writers in their critique of mainstream cinematic practices.

The second generation of 'art house' film-makers like Goutam Ghose, Buddhadeb Dasgupta, Aparna Sen, Utpalendu Chakraborty and Nabyendu Chatterjee emerged during the Indian New Wave movement of the 1970s. These 'new cinema' directors were hugely influenced by the international art cinema of the 1960s. Many of them were engaged in an alternative film practice that had defined itself in contrast to mainstream cinema.[16] The second generation of 'art house' film-makers radically departed from the idea of the mainstream and the model of popular Indian cinema—both in terms of form and content. They had to rely on state institutions like the Film Finance Corporation (FFC) and other such bodies for the funding and distribution of their films, in many cases.[17]

This period of 'experimental' films in India coincided with the new political phase in West Bengal, when the Left Front came to power and took special interest in developing a refined film culture. Before the formation of the West Bengal Film Development Corporation (WBFDC), the government of West Bengal produced films like *Ganadebata* (*The People*) by Tarun Majumdar in 1979, *Hirak Rajar Deshe* (*In the Land of the Diamond King*) by Satyajit Ray and *Parashuram* (*The Man with the Axe*) by Mrinal Sen in 1980. In 1980, the West Bengal Colour Film and Sound Laboratory Corporation Ltd, which was an independent body, was brought under the ownership and control of the state government. Its objective was to promote and undertake projects for the improvement of cinema in the state. The name of the company was changed to West Bengal Film Development Corporation (WBFDCL), with effect from 1 July 1983. Many remarkable films of the second generation of art house film-makers were produced or co-produced by this organisation on behalf of the government of West Bengal. For example, with *Dakhal* (*The Occupation*) by Goutam Ghose in 1981, *Grihayuddha* (*Crossroads*) by Buddhadeb Dasgupta in 1982, *Chokh* (*The Eyes*) by Utpalendu Chakraborty in 1983, and *Koni* by Saroj Dey in 1986, the West Bengal government showed its intent—both literally and metaphorically—by investing in 'good cinema'. Most of these films, however, failed to reach the audience. The reasons for this failure are attributed both to the lack of proper distribution and popular appeal. Kiranmoy Raha criticises this new phase in Bengali cinema in the following words:

> ... this resurgence, if so it can be called, seen in the eighties has been feeble compared to that of the fifties and the sixties. For one thing

> many of the films the new generation of filmmakers have made or are making are in Hindi. For another, except for Aparna Sen they appear to be overtly concerned with economic and social issues rather than with human ones.[18]

If writers like Kiranmoy Raha blamed their thematic concerns for not being crowd-pullers, others like Someshwar Bhoumik explored the difficulties of state patronage in drawing a larger mass.[19]

However, Shoma A. Chatterji, in her book, recognised a new wave of Bengali films post-1990 with films like *Unishe April* (*Nineteenth April*) (1994) and *Titli* (2002) by Rituparno Ghosh, and *Ek Je Ache Kanya* (*There is a Girl*) by Subrata Sen in 2001.[20] Chatterji states that when the monotony and the lack of art of the mainstream made 'us' disappointed, a 'ray of hope' could be sensed in this new stream of Bengali films, which were 'good films' and were also commercially successful.[21] What Chatterji found 'new' in this stream of (parallel) films was the 'new' point of view towards the 'not so new' subjects of their plots. In an *Anandabazar Patrika* article, Swapan Kumar Ghosh, while recognising this 'departure' of some of these new Bengali films, saw them as carrying the legacy of 'good Bengali' cinema of yesteryears, and described how these films remained 'parallel' to the contemporary mainstream.[22] The art cinema discourse in Bengal, since its origin, has been engaged in the overvaluation of realism associated with 'parallel' or 'serious' cinema and the criticism of the melodramatic form of mainstream films. In film society writings, this idea of polarised forms resulted in constructed boundaries between the two cinemas, which could not be transgressed, and which seemed irreconcilable. Gaston Roberge elaborately discusses this discourse of polarisation in the film society approach to cinema, especially in Chidananda Dasgupta's writings. According to Roberge, Dasgupta has worked out 'the artificial opposition between box-office and art' so fully that 'it is almost impossible for him to say anything significant about the commercial cinema beyond rejecting it'.[23] In the subsequent writings on Bengali cinema, the majority of the writers continued to endorse this split. Moreover, their focus was mostly confined to individual directors and their 'original works', aesthetic sense and auteuristic orientations; also, art cinema's thematics are of mature, intelligent and of adult interest, contrary to the thematics of escapism propagated by commercial film practice.[24] Going beyond this notion of cinema, the book engages with the idea of cinematic practice in its multiple dimensions.

It is relevant here to point out the absolute negation and absence of any serious or critical engagement with the Bengali mainstream cinema practices of the 1980s, which witnessed a major overhaul in terms of industrial dynamics. The only and limited discourse that dominated journalistic works highlighted the crises-ridden conditions of Bengali cinema, almost to the extent of a value-laden assessment. However, in the writings of Sharmishta Gooptu, regarding the shifting trends of mainstream Bengali film narratives in the 1980s, it is argued that the taste of a new class of audience was being targeted through these films. This was the class of audience that had never been considered legitimate viewers of Bengali cinema until the 1970s.[25] This book extends the understanding of Gooptu and lays out other intricate and complex industrial changes that resulted in this transformation, or the change in the aesthetics of narratives of mainstream Bengali films. The success of certain films in this period and the changes in the industry proved to the middle-class intelligentsia that it was not only the paucity of quality films, but also various other factors that were deterring Bengali cinema.[26]

We have attempted to construct this book outside this 'crisis narrative' on the decaying quality of Bengali cinema. We have striven to investigate the transition from the emphasis on Bengali cinema to the Bengali film industry. Our book has been an exploration of Tollywood as a distinct industrial category, as opposed to merely comparing it with corporatised Bollywood, commonly considered to be the standard template for pan-Indian film industries.

Subsequent to the formal recognition of Bollywood as an 'industry' and its developments garnering global popularity especially with Indian and South Asian diaspora, a diverse range of scholarship emerged, which examined Bollywood's industrial merits, a phenomenon and an all-encompassing substitute for Indian cinema, entertainment and culture industries.[27] Tejaswini Ganti's book, *Bollywood: A Guidebook to Popular Hindi Cinema* (2004), is an introduction to the popular Hindi cinema and its production practices. Ganti provides a comprehensive account of the structure and functioning of the Bombay film industry's production and distribution processes and dynamics. Ganti also identifies a formula for popular films, with their distinctive song-and-dance routines, in order to establish their relevance beyond the film narrative and understand their position in the larger socio-cultural scenario. Through an extensive first-hand industry interaction, Ganti offers an anthropological narrative of the Bombay film industry's uniqueness and its evolution into a more global form that is pitted against Hollywood. Ganti's 2012 book, *Producing Bollywood: Inside the Contemporary Hindi Film Industry* further examines the formation of Bollywood as a global phenomenon through a detailed and exhaustive ethnography of the industrial changes that took place during a time when India was experiencing massive changes due to the processes of economic liberalisation. Through the logic of 'gentrification' used metaphorically, the book argues about the restructuring of the Hindi film industry and, in the process, contends the categories of 'good taste' versus films made for the 'masses'. This study has particularly informed our work, providing us with valuable methods to conduct our study on the Bengali film industry.[28] Hence, our book engages in Tollywood from a similar perspective—that of a corporatised industrial form and one that responds to other such formations, especially Bollywood.

It was also important to look at Derek Bose's understanding of Bollywood as a brand; in his work, *Brand Bollywood* (2006), Bose elaborates on how film entertainment in India is no longer just an artistic or creative enterprise, but is also the rapid convergence of various media, such as home videos, satellite television, radio, the internet, animation and gaming. Together, they determine the success or failure of films. In a similar vein, Paul Grainge, in the book, *Brand Hollywood* (2007), discusses the growth in merchandising, product placement, and the rise of movie franchises. He argues that branding has become central to the Hollywood blockbuster economy. Analysing the practice of branding, the poetics of corporate logos, and the industrial politics surrounding the development of branded texts, properties and spaces, Grainge considers the relation of branding to the emergent principle of 'total entertainment'. Considering the above models and studies as templates to look into the media convergence that took place in Bengal's media scenario, Tollywood's formation seems to be very distinctive. It has been our endeavour to examine the overall dynamics of the industry in order to explore whether these processes in the Bengali film industry have ended up producing a clone of Bollywood, or otherwise.

Moinak Biswas has recently focused on a few films from the mid-2000s that draw from the spectacle and sensation of certain political street events, which had direct or indirect implications on popular public imagination. These events inspired directors like Swapan Saha, Haranath Chakraborty and Raj Chakraborty to make films that represented these political expressions.[29] Biswas looks at films like *MLA Fatakesto*, *Minister Fatakesto* and *Tiger* (both films by Swapan Saha, 2006 and 2007, respectively); Haranath Chakraborty's 2007 film, *Tulkalam* (*Chaos*); and the 2008 blockbuster, Raj Chakraborty's *Chirodini Tumi Je Amar* (*You're Mine, Forever*). All of these films present the contemporary political scenario; they are seen as kitschy and distasteful to the *bhadralok* aesthetics of Bengali cinema, as they represent the 'street or mass culture' in and around Bengal.[30] This kind of cinema is also crucial for our book, as these films grossed record revenues at the box office. It was during this period that the so-called commercial mainstream cinema found its way to the multiplexes and launched new stars in Tollywood. The fact that these films were all produced by the two powerful production houses of Tollywood, SVF and Eskay Videos, calls for scrutiny and for an understanding of the changing industrial scenario that Tollywood embodies.

The scholarly writings on Bengali cinema continued to be restricted within the limits of cinematic texts and the quality of the narrative rather than focus on the industrial scenario of Bengali films, with the exception of Someshwar Bhoumik's comprehensive study of the Bengali film industry.[31] In the context of these academic works, our book importantly foregrounds the new industrial formations that led to the emergence of Tollywood beyond the issues of Bengali cinema and its 'Bengaliness'. Central to the issue of industrial formation is an interrelationship between the industry and popular media networks, which are explored in this study, along with an engagement with some of the key films from the leading production houses like SVF and Eskay Videos. The book also signposts the newer experiments with film-making practices and dissemination being carried out within Tollywood post-2012. These new changes and developments have gained an urgency, which this book aims to examine and critically analyse.

Notes and References

1. See Sharmistha Gooptu, *Bengali Cinema: An Other Nation* (New Delhi: Roli Books, 2010), pp. 14–16, where she explains:

   > ... bhadralok to indicate those social classes among the Bengalis who, since the nineteenth century, had been the recipients of some kind of English/western education, were mainly engaged in the professions and services, and found in the cinema a "modern" form which could encapsulate the movement of their lives.... This bhadralok middle class, a varied social group, was the Bengali Film industry's mainstay for the greater part of the period ...

2. This is both in terms of cultural differences and economics. In his article, 'Changing Scenes', Moinak Biswas questions if the *bhadralok* exists in the same form anymore, with the success and popularity of certain kinds of films in Tollywood. At the same time, he also suggests the fading away of the stark difference between *bhadralok* elites and the non-*bhadra* due to the centrality of television in middle- and lower middle-class lives, as well as due to the Bengali language itself getting hybridised mostly by *bhadralok* urban citizens. Moreover, he argues that TV has also picked up this hybridity in the form of language and cultural content. Biswas also draws a parallel with the changes that took place in the then opposition party leader Mamata Banerjee's party, which was accused of being full of hooligans, but transformed as more and more intellectuals joined her protests to fight for a change. Biswas writes:

   > The lyrics of Bangla music band songs, a contemporary development in the vernacular, and newspaper features have come to share an irreverent college canteen idiom that owes its origins partly to the decline in formal skills in the language. It is not a bhadralok idiom formally but is entirely urban. The kind of quasi-English Bengali films that Anjan Dutt makes for urban youth circuits owes a similar debt to the decline of the Bengali language.

   He further argues:

   > Authors like Nabarun Bhattacharya or Gautam Sengupta, on the other hand, write for a serious minority readership and use a hybrid street language to break free of fictional as well as moral conventions. The territory of the image is giving in to unfamiliar people seeking entry. Those who find it wholly unacceptable are likely to turn away from all politics. But signs are clear that the minority culture of distinction has opened its doors to other semiotic neighbourhoods, and has even become dependent on the invasions for survival. We may not like it, but this might serve as an unexpected ground for political change.

Moniak Biswas, 'Changing Scenes', in Monica Narula, Shuddhabrata Sengupta and Jeebesh Bagchi, ed., *Sarai Reader 08: Fear Scared on Screen*, p. 205.

3. A brochure published on the occasion of a screening of selected New Theatres films under the National Film Heritage, a collaborative programme of the Centre for Development of Instructional Technology and the National Film Archive of India, 18–23 February 1985, states:

   > New Theatres, set up in 1930 by Birendra Nath Sircar, played an important role in the creation of the Indian film industry. Functioning from Calcutta, it was not just a well-equipped studio; it was a system, a way of life for the people working with it. Sircar wanted not just cinema halls and a studio; he wanted a system. A pervasive, self-supporting, effectively-managed, supremely equipped, network of men and women and machines, which would sell the celluloid dream like it had never been sold before in the country.

   See also Madhuja Mukherjee, *New Theatres Ltd.: The Emblem of Art, The Picture of Success* (Pune: National Film Archive of India, 2009); and Bhaskar Sarkar, *Mourning the Nation: Indian Cinema in the Wake of Partition* (Durham: Duke University Press, 2009).
4. Gooptu, *Bengali Cinema.*
5. *Jatra* (origin: *yatra*, meaning procession or journey in Sanskrit) is a popular folk theatre form, spread throughout most of the Bengali-speaking areas of the Indian subcontinent, including Bangladesh and the Indian states of West Bengal, Bihar, Assam, Odisha and Tripura. The typical characteristics of *jatra* are its high and excessive melodrama, loud acting, and stereotypical characters, especially that of villains. It is also known for its tacky and trite dialogues, hackneyed plots, and songs, often with lewd or vulgar words. It is interesting to note that newspaper columns, public sphere discussions and part of the film industry called the new popular Bengali films not only 'bad' or 'derogatory', but also described them as an 'art form' that was closer to one-wall theatre (*jatra*) or folk performance than film. Precisely that is why this lack of 'film sense' was talked about when these films were described.
6. The Bengali film magazine, *Anandolok*, between January and May 1995, carried a series of interview-based features titled 'Bengali Films: Why the Crisis?', which presented the views of industry persons like Soumendu Roy, Geeta De, Bibhuti Laha, R. D. Banshal, etc. At the same time, the magazine published some letters from the readers. Both the interviews and the letters expressed dissatisfaction regarding contemporary Bengali films.
7. Yash Chopra, who was the then in-charge of the entertainment wing of cinema attached to the Federation of Indian Chambers of Commerce and Industry (FICCI), led a delegation on its behalf to the then West Bengal Chief Minister, Buddhadev Bhattacharjee, for the revival of the Bengali film industry.

The proposal included the construction of a chain of multiplexes, state-of-the-art entertainment plazas, shopping malls and food rendezvous, which would assure 'a sustainable revenue generation scheme' for the overall entertainment industry in the state; Pradip Biswas, 'Yash Chopra for the Revival of the Bengali Film Industry', *Screen*, 6 December 2002. See also Udit Prasanna Mukherjee, 'Vijay Mallya's Brand to Promote Tollywood'. Vijay Mallya's United Spirits Ltd (the largest Indian-Made Foreign Liquor [IMFL] firm in India) expressed interest in promoting Bengali films through the co-branding of its highest-selling whisky brand, Bagpiper. He started his Tollywood venture with Rituparna Sengupta's debut production; Staff Reporter, '*Patadar Kirti*', *Times City*, *The Times of India*, 10 November 2009, p. 4.

8. Kironmoy Raha, *Bengali Cinema* (Calcutta: Nandan, West Bengal Film Centre, 1991).
9. Surabhi Banerjee, *Satyajit Ray: Beyond the Frame* (New Delhi: Allied Publishers, 1996).
10. Jyotirmoy Basu Roy, *Ritwik Ghataker Chhabi* (*The Films of Ritwik Ghatak*) (Calcutta: Rashbehari Books, 1974).
11. Samik Bandopadhyay, *Mrinal Sen: Sixty Years in Search of Cinema* (Calcutta: Seagull Books, 2003).
12. Somen Ghosh, *Bangla Cinemar Paalabadal* (*The Changing Phases of Bengali Cinema*) (Calcutta: Shyamali Prakashani, 1990), p. 135.
13. Someshwar Bhowmik observed the deterioration of Bengali cinema in the late-1970s with films like *Amanush, Ananda Ashram* or *Baba Taraknath*, arguing that these films were devoid of the 'clean entertainment value' that was a characteristic of Bengali films in the 1950s and the 1960s; Someshwar Bhowmik, 'Sattar Dashaker Bangla Chhabi', in Anil Acharya, ed., *Sattar Dashak* (*The Decade of Seventies*) (Kolkata: Anushtup Publication, 1981), pp. 28–43.

    Somen Ghosh has tried to analyse this 'crisis'-ridden period of Bengali cinema, which was a period, he observes, 'when totally unrealistic, lower standard film made its silver jubilee at the box office, it expressed our shameless nature in our cultural characterless-ness'; Ghosh, *Bangla Cinemar Paalabadal*, p. 135. See also Ghosh, *Prasanga: Bharatiya Chalachchitra* (*Indian Cinema: An In-depth Study*) (Calcutta: Bangabasi Ltd, 1994).

    See also Spandan Bhattacharya, 'The Post Liberalization Bengali "Parallel" Cinema: Bhadralok Nostalgia, the Politics of Past-ness, and the Discourse of "Difference"', Unpublished MPhil Dissertation, The School of Arts and Aesthetics, Cinema Studies, Jawaharlal Nehru University, New Delhi, 2011; Partha Raha, *Bangla Chalachitra Kathakata o Anyanya Prabandho* (Kolkata: Ratna Publications, 2004); Rajat Roy, *Banglar Chalachitra Sanskriti* (Calcutta: Sristi Publication, 2001).
14. In their writings on 1950s and 1960s mainstream Bengali cinema, authors like Rajat Roy and Kiranmoy Raha, and film journalists like Bipra Das,

Ranjan Bandyopadhyay, etc., point out a significant difference between Bengali cinema and other regional cinemas of that period. According to them, unlike other mainstream cinemas, in Bengali mainstream cinematic practice (films featuring the hit pair, Uttam–Suchitra), the mythological narrative and 'vulgar' song and dance took a backseat. This feature, according to them, made this cinema more mature and 'distinct', as compared to the other cinemas of that period. See also Bhattacharya, 'The Post Liberalization Bengali "Parallel" Cinema'.

15. See Satyajit Ray, *Our Films Their Films* (Hyderabad: Orient Longman, 1976), p. 21.
16. See Mira Reym Binford, 'The Two Cinemas of India', in John D. H. Downing, ed., *Film and Politics in the Third World* (New York: Praeger, 1987).
17. It may be noted here that the FFC was founded by the Central Government in 1960, with the aim of extending loans to directors, who wanted to make films outside the commercial circuit. One of its objectives was to support talented and promising directors, who aspired to make socially useful films with small budgets. In 1980, the FFC was merged with the Film Export Corporation to form the National Film Development Corporation (NFDC).
18. See Kiranmoy Raha, *Bengali Cinema* (Kolkata: Nandan, West Bengal Film Centre, 1991), p. 81.
19. See Someshwar Bhoumik, *Bharatiya Chalchchitra: Ekti Arthanaitik Pratibedan* (*Indian Cinema: An Economic Report*) (Calcutta: Papyrus, 1996).
20. See Shoma A. Chattejee, *Cinema Shudhu Cinema Noy* (*Cinema is Not Only Cinema*) (Kolkata: Parumita Publication, 2004).
21. Ibid., p. 11.
22. See Swapan Kumar Ghosh, '*Bangla Chhabite Ekhan Anek Vagavagi*' ('Bengali Cinema Undergoes Rift'), *Anandabazar Patrika*, 4 October 2000, p. 5.
23. See Gaston Roberge, *The Indian Film Theory: Flames of Sholay, Notes and Beyond* (Kolkata: Sampark Publication, 2010), p. 103.
24. See John W. Hood, *The Films of Buddhadeb Dasgupta* (New Delhi: Orient BlackSwan, 2005). See also Shoma A. Chatterji, *Parama and Other Outsiders: The Cinema of Aparna Sen* (Kolkata: Parumita Publication, 2002).
25. Sharmistha Gooptu, 'Changing Contexts, New Texts', in Nalin Mehta, ed., *Television in India: Satellite, Politics and Cultural Change* (New York: Routledge, 2008).
26. Bhattacharya, 'The Post Liberalization Bengali "Parallel" Cinema'.
27. Ashish Rajadhyaksha, '*The "Bollywoodization" of the Indian Cinema: Cultural Nationalism in a Global Arena*', *Inter-Asia Cultural Studies*, Volume 4 (London: Routledge, 2003).
28. Tejaswini Ganti, *Producing Bollywood: Inside the Contemporary Hindi Film Industry* (Durham; London: Duke University Press, 2012).
29. Biswas, *Changing Scenes*, p. 204.

30. See Hemchhaya De, 'Filming Ferment: Tollywood Has a New Buzzword—Political Films that Capture Bengal's State of Political Unrest in Recent Times. Hemchhaya De Goes Behind the Scenes to Find Out What Fuelled the Trend', *The Telegraph Online*, 15 May 2011, available at https://www.telegraphindia.com/7-days/filming-ferment/cid/388625, accessed on 20 April 2012.
31. Someshwar Bhoumik, *Bharatiya Chalchchitra: Ekti Arthanaitik Pratibedan* (*Indian Cinema: An Economic Report*) (Calcutta: Papyrus, 1996).

1

The Transition of the Bengali Film Industry

*The Post-Uttam Kumar Era**

The Bengali film industry in the 1980s was perhaps the most complex in terms of its composition and identity. This period was marked by a transformation that categorically changed the cinematic practices and traditions of Bengali cinema, making way for the emergence of a mainstream cinema that remained in prominence for a long period of time. The transition was marked by a change in the style and content of films commonly referred to as 'masala' or 'formula' films, consisting of elements borrowed from Bombay cinema, such as racy dialogues, stereotypical villainous characters, stylised fights, and song-and-dance sequences. The 1960s and 1970s were a period when West Bengal's social and political scenario underwent drastic changes, with a shift in the political regime. Bengali cinema, alongside Bengali society, experienced a loss in its idealism, and adapted to new ideologies and paradigms.

Until the mid-1970s, Bengali cinema was largely identified by its close association with Bengali literature. The hallmark of this phase was its idea of realism, naturalistic acting style, and the notion of a worldview that was deeply Bengali.[1] In the late-1970s, the film industry was going through a severe economic crisis. Audiences were loving Hindi films for their superior visual quality and other novelty factors. As a result, there was a sharp decline in the number of films being made in Tollygunge. Directors like Anjan Chowdhury, Swapan Saha and Haranath Chakraborty had gradually begun to lose their turf. There came a time when only a handful of 20 or 25 films a

---

* Anugyan Nag, 'From Tollygunge to Tollywood: The Transformation of Bengali Film Industry between 1980 and the Present', *Journal of Bengali Studies*, vol. 1, no. 2 (2012), p. 120.

year were coming out of Tollygunge studios. Single-screen theatres, having incurred heavy financial losses, had begun to pull down their shutters in and around Calcutta. Films were now being released mostly in mofussil (provincial and rural districts) areas. In this chapter, we shall attempt to explore the complex journey of Tollygunge, starting from the 1980s, and leading to the post-liberalisation period of resurgence.

The primary reason was the shift of Bengali audiences towards television, due to the persistently unsatisfactory experience of watching films in deteriorating cinema halls, furthered by the proliferation of Hindi films into Bengali middle-class homes via television and Video Cassette Recorder (VCRs), and also the audiences' preferential leaning towards Hindi films for their superior visual quality and novelty factors, in comparison to their counterparts in Bengal. Post-1970s and post the death of superstar Uttam Kumar, Bengali cinema went through several changes, primarily financial crisis, which reduced the number of films made in Tollygunge. The study of directors like Anjan Chowdhury, Swapan Saha and Haranath Chakraborty is relevant here for the kind of films they made during this period. Their films came under severe criticism from the *bhadralok* intelligentsia for their lack of cinematic formalism and political ideology. However, it paved the way for reorganisation of the film industry, leading to the formation of Shree Venkatesh Films (SVF) in 1996. This production house was to emerge as one of the most formalised and powerful entities of Tollywood.

The Beginning of a New Transition

The research into English and Bengali newspapers that we conducted at the National Library, Kolkata, revealed that there was a constant lament voiced by the press and the industry. The press repeatedly reiterated the vacuum that Uttam Kumar's demise had created in the Tollygunge film industry. Studios had almost stopped functioning, having failed to earn the minimum revenue required to pay salaries to the permanent staff. Established film-makers like Tapan Sinha and Mrinal Sen did not make films that could have absorbed the idle labour force of the Bengali film industry in Tollygunge. However, an exceptional article expressed the state of Bengali cinema and the industry, contrary to the above discourse. This piece refers to the year 1984, specifically in an attempt to draw out an improving and transitioning condition of the industry. Interestingly, this article raised the following relevant questions: Was the death of Uttam Kumar the sole reason for the industry's downfall? And what was the socio-economic and political scenario that sustained West Bengal during the late 1970s and early 1980s?[2] However, around 1984–85, there was a ray of hope that filtered into the darkness with the release of Anjan Choudhury's *Shatru*, which proved to be a big hit commercially. At this point we would like to clarify the claims made towards deducing the success and failures of films through terms like 'hit'/'blockbuster'/'box-office success' and 'flops'/'failures', etc. This book has been collated from press and industry reports, and our conversations with industry insiders (producers, directors, distributors, exhibitors and others), since there is no singular organisation or source that provides accurate statistics on box-office figures and revenues of Bengali films.

The decades spanning the 1980s and 1990s brought in changes through the continuous negotiation and struggle that the industry people went through to cope with and resolve the reasons of its successes and failures. This chapter studies the ushering in of a film tradition by a handful of new directors, who survived harsh criticism from the *bhadralok* class, while at the same time consolidating the tremendous popularity of their films among semi-urban and rural audiences. The end of the 1990s saw new developments in terms of production, distribution and film aesthetics, possibly paving the way for a new beginning.

By the late-1970s, the golden era of Bengali cinema was almost over; the Uttam–Suchitra[3] pair was still a rage, but unfortunately, it failed to generate colossal hits, as it used to earlier. Other actors, namely Supriya Chowdhury, Sabitri Chatterjee and Basanta Chowdhury were seen in selective films, while Uttam Kumar was trying his luck in Bombay. Shakti Samanta made a few bilingual films with Uttam Kumar in the lead. In fact, Samanta's films introduced into Bengali cinema action, romance and fantasy, so far identified quintessentially with Bombay cinema. The Bombay films, targeting a pan-Indian audience, were a remarkable departure from the kind of cinema that the Tollygunge industry had produced till date.

The trend of making films like the ones in Bombay that were popular with audiences robbed Bengali cinema of its uniqueness. Films such as *Anusandhan* (the Bengali version of *Barsaat Ki Ek Raat* [*One Night of Rain*]), and later, *Teen Murthi* (*The Three Musketeers*), starring a host of Bombay stars, set the box-office bell ringing quite piercingly, but the industry barely benefitted from these few films, in terms of benefitting the overall condition of the Tollygunge film industry. This was also the time when Bengali cinema had gradually begun to lose its urban *bhadralok* audiences. Although film production in Tollygunge was in a disappointing state, in 1979, around 32 films[4] were produced and released. However, the biggest challenge that emerged was not related to scripts, actors, stars or budget; it was: 'Where to watch films?' The state desperately required good cinema halls.

Problems of Distribution and Exhibition

In 1979, while the number of films released was 32, the biggest challenge that threatened the Tollygunge industry was the lack of adequate number of cinema halls where these films could be exhibited. Only five Bengali films could be screened simultaneously in Calcutta in the then functioning five chains: Uttara-Purabi-Ujjwala, Minar-Bijolee-Chobighar, Rupobani-Aruna-Bharati, Sree-Indira, and Radha-Purna-Prachi. Many films remained unreleased due to the paucity of cinema halls. Reputed film distributors of that period, such as Chandimata Films, had five movies; and Piyali Films and RB Films had three each, which remained in cold storage.[5] It was obvious that producing good films alone was not enough, if you did not have theatres to release them. Realising the need for more and better theatres, the then Finance Minister called for a press meet, along with the then Information and Broadcasting Minister, Buddhadeb Bhattacharya, to announce a package that would encourage more entrepreneurs to build new cinema halls. Some of the measures announced by the government at that time were:

a) It was willing to give loans at minimum rates of interest, along with incentives, subsidies and tax rebates. Theatre owners who screened a Bengali film produced and financed by the West Bengal Film Finance Corporation (WBFFC) for more than

75 per cent of their total show time were to be fully exempted from any tax.

b) If they devoted 25–50 per cent of their total screening time to Bengali films, the government would provide Rs 25,000–40,000 for the purchase of projection equipment and accessories.
c) The government's plan was to increase the number of cinema halls to a total of 1,000 in the state.
d) In Calcutta, cinema halls ran in 'chains'; the five popular chains were: Uttara-Purabi-Ujjwala, Minar-Bijolee-Chobighar, Rupobani-Aruna-Bharati, Sree-Indira, Radha-Purna-Prachi.
e) Earlier even halls like Basushree-Bina-Mitra would screen Bengali films, but due to the audiences' preferences shifting towards Bombay cinema, they began screening Hindi films.

Despite the government's announcement of various incentives and low-interest loans, no entrepreneur showed any inclination. The possible reasons could be: soaring real estate rates in and around Calcutta; the ever-increasing entertainment tax levied by the government from time to time; the unchecked phenomenon of black marketing of tickets; and the near impossibility of constructing halls within the estimated budget bracket of Rs 12 lakhs that the government promised to provide. The scenario was so bad that even after more than a week of house-full shows, hall owners were struggling to make enough profit so as to be able to pay their employees and manage the maintenance costs.[6] Also, one after another films flopped during this period, forcing the distributors to advance the release dates of many films. This resulted in huge losses for the cinema hall owners. A leading distributor (who insisted on remaining anonymous) of that period revealed that more than 30 films, which were at various stages of production, had to be aborted due to reasons such as no advance money from cinema hall owners and the non-availability of theatre chains in Calcutta. The only option the distributors were left with was to enter the rural territory, where they did not have to depend on these chains. It was felt that at least two more chains were needed in the city to cater to the Bengali-speaking areas.

The Demise of Uttam Kumar: Trouble in Tollygunge

As it is, Tollygunge was grappling with serious issues that threatened its very existence, when the sudden untimely death of matinee idol Uttam Kumar in July 1980 further exacerbated the crisis. He was Bengali cinema's most coveted superstar till then. His death brought in one of the biggest setbacks to the industry. When he died, he was involved in more than six incomplete films. Uttam Kumar had become such a surety for everyone in the business of cinema that for a long time he had been single-handedly ensuring the businesses of Tollygunge studios.

Even today, industry people speak with great emotion and sentiment about those years. They recall how not a single film was produced for the entire year after Uttam Kumar's death, making the industry reach almost the verge of collapse. Until we met these people, it was difficult for us to believe that one person could impact the entire industry to this extent. During our research, we came across a detailed article titled, '*Uttam Kumar er Obhab Tallyganj Para Ekhono Bisesh Ter Paini*' ('Tollygunge Has Not Yet Been Able to Realise the Loss of Uttam Kumar'), written by Bhaskar Choudhury, dated 15 July 1981, in a monthly periodical called *Parivartan*.

In this article, he elaborately writes about how for more than a year after the demise of Uttam Kumar, many cine-goers would exclaim Uttam Kumar's name while watching films, forgetting that all the films released after his death had begun their production while he was alive. People were lamenting his disappearance from the screen. Kumar had been enacting roles in films on a varied range of subjects since the mid-1970s. He had hardly rejected any scripts in the last five years of his career. If people lamented his absence to such an extent, it was an emotion generated out of excessive love and respect for him. There was a strong collective sense of loss and despair among the members of Studio Supply Co-operative, for whom he was such a pillar of strength. Kumar had always supported their cause and given them advice. One such instance was when a studio received a closure notice. The studio employees made an appeal to the government with the help and support of Kumar, preventing the closure. Such was the aura of Uttam Kumar that whichever cause he lent his support to turned out to be a success.

In the year after his death, a total of 28 films were released; 15 during the second-half of 1980, and the remaining in the first-half of 1981. Out of these 28 releases, Uttam Kumar was featuring in three, of which two collapsed at the box office. *Ogo Bodhu Shundari* (*O My Beautiful Wife*) by Salil Dutta in 1981, however, was a record hit. Many argued that the film's success was due to the publicity stills of Uttam Kumar in a shaving sequence, which was widely circulating in newspapers and magazines then. There were others who felt that it had an emotional connect since it was the last film he had done. However, on the other hand, *Raja Shaheb* (*The King*) by Palash Banerjee in 1980, and *Khana Baraha* by Bijoy Bose in 1981, where he played a mythological character, something he had never done before, tanked at the box office. The same year, Tarun Majumdar's 1980 film, *Dadar Kirti* (*Adventures of Big Brother*) witnessed a phenomenal success, despite a cast comprising of mainly newcomers. Press reports of the time suggest that audiences appreciated every component of this film.

The reasons for the failure of *Raja Shaheb* lay in its faulty production value and shoddy look. Also, perhaps the characterisation of Kumar as a merciless corrupt landlord, who goes through a transformation towards the end of the film, was all too hackneyed. There was no novelty in his character, as he had played similar roles before in films like *Rajnandini* (*The Princess*) directed by Sukhen Das in 1980, and *Stree (The Wife)* directed by Salil Dutta in 1972. In *Khana Baraha*, Uttam Kumar played the role of Baraha, depicting deep anguish, pain and sorrow, which were his strengths as an actor. Yet, the film did not appeal to the audience.

In *Ogo Bodhu Shundari*, loosely adapted from George Bernard Shaw's *Pygmalion*, Kumar played a happy-go-lucky lost professor. The film still appealed to the audience for its production value, music and story, although he had played such a character before. During 1980–81, 28 films were released without Uttam Kumar. Nineteen of them were average grossers.[7] In the article mentioned above, Chowdhury also points out that the state government's decision to reduce the ticket price to Re 1 did entice a section of the audience. However, at the same time, there was no guarantee that if these 19 films had featured Uttam Kumar, they would have been successful.

At the time of his death, Uttam Kumar had left 11 films unfinished. The producers and directors of these films became so paranoid that some of them even used dummies of the dead actor to finish their projects on which they had already made significant investments. Some of them resorted to changing scripts and managed to somehow finish them. Five of two such films were even released. The rest remained unfinished and eventually got shelved. In the last one year of his long-spanning career, Kumar had also acted in two Hindi films, which were released after his death. These were *Dooriyaan* (*The Distance*), directed by Bhimsain Khurana in 1979, and *Plot No.: 5* directed by Yogesh Saxena in 1981. Both the films flopped at the box office, although his work was much appreciated by the critics. In this context, the story behind the making of the film *Bancharam er Bagan* (*The Garden of Bancharam*) directed by Tapan Sinha in 1980, is worthy of telling here.

The narrative goes like this: Uttam Kumar had been initially signed for the film to play the role of a *zamindar* (landlord), but owing to his ill-health, he could not do the film. As a result, a comparatively new actor, Dipankar Dey, bagged the role. This infuriated the star and he even went on to file a lawsuit against the director. However, before it could come up for hearing in the court, he passed away. Several newspapers and magazines reported this incident, which annoyed the die-hard fans of Uttam Kumar. Surprisingly, the film did very well at the box office. No one raised objections about Dey.[8] With the success of *Bancharam er Bagan*, Dey became a busy actor, signing the maximum number of films in that year and the year subsequent to that. Other actors of the same film, like Samit Bhanja, Ranjit Mullick and Shantu Mukherjee, too, became popular and bagged a respectable number of offers. Certain directors and producers, who did not have to work hard with Uttam Kumar as a star in their films, were now in great difficulty. They did not announce any film for more than a year after his death.

It was in this situation that the audience and many cinema hall owners, along with the government, came to perceive that film production in Tollygunge was on a decline. The fact was that the number of films being produced during this period had increased. One of the prime reasons for this rise was government funding. This was also the time when numerous new technicians entered studios, alongside established directors. New directors were making more films. Many of them were casting new actors and were experimenting along the lines of the 'art' or 'parallel' film-making practice, in keeping with the impulse of the new wave movement that had emerged during the 1970s. The Indian New Wave movement, a realist project, spearheaded by the likes of Mrinal Sen and Shyam Benegal, was a response to the socio-political issues of the time and also emerged as a counter-movement to the dominant cinematic characteristics of mainstream cinema.[9] As Mira Reym Binford has observed, the 'new wave' aligned itself with a 'serious international artistic enterprise'.[10] The aspects that distinguished the cinematic treatment of the new wave films from the mainstream ones were their excessive emphasis on realism and experimentation with technical form and content. The content of new wave films dealt with subjects like class conflicts, caste inequalities, social injustices and patriarchal repression.[11] In Bengal, this form of cinema found a new face with the establishment of the state-sponsored West Bengal Film Development Corporation (WBFDC), which extended its patronage to certain directors who could carry forward the legacy of the literary and cinematic traditions of Bengal. The press, the state institutions, and the *bhadralok* section of audience also conformed to this new form of cinema for its strong association with ideology, especially Leftist ideology, in the case of Bengal.

Directors like Utpalendu Chakraborty, Buddhadev Dasgupta, Nabyendu Chatterjee, Aparna Sen and Goutam Ghose entered Tollygunge with their vigour and orientation towards the new wave cinema movement. They introduced new actors and kept up the workflow in the studios. However, the biggest challenge that the government and Tollygunge had to confront was the issue of earning revenue from the new wave directors' films. The Calcutta city cinema theatres were already incurring losses and were repeatedly devoting more screening time to Hindi mainstream cinema. The situation was grimmer in small towns and rural areas, where halls had a limited number of seats and where ticket prices were lower. The tax benefits and rebates that the government provided for films produced and financed by the WBFFC were also not lucrative, as these films barely attracted audiences in smaller towns and rural areas, or for that matter, in Calcutta, mainly due to the lack of proper distribution and exhibition.

The competition from commercial mainstream Bombay cinema being relatively high, there were lesser chances of risks being taken by the distributors, and hence, the small and independent films that lacked the elements and attractions of popular cinema were generally avoided by them, thus making it extremely difficult for state-funded films to find screens for exhibition. The government took steps to finance several issue-driven film projects, but failed to wake up to the issue of distribution and exhibition centres that could possibly cater exclusively to this kind of cinema. All the new wave or parallel cinema directors were consistently supported by WBFDC, and later, by the National Film Development Corporation (NFDC) to make films that were different from mainstream cinema.

As Aruna Vasudev points out, this kind of cinema was born out of 'governmental decision', and not merely from 'the impetus of film-makers rebelling against the existing popular cinema'.[12] Critics like Iqbal Masud wrote against this kind of cinema, citing them as 'orthodox' and 'detached' from the average viewers. Also, the class of audience (mainly the bourgeois *bhadralok*) at whom these films were targeted perhaps preferred to sit at home and enjoy television. Films like *Grihayuddha* (*The Crossroads*) and *Charachar* (*The Shelter of the Wings*) directed by Buddhadev Dasgupta in 1982 and 1993, respectively; *Chokh* (*The Eyes*) by Utpalendu Chakraborty in 1983; *Paar* (*The Crossing*) by Goutam Ghose in 1984, in Hindi; and *Koni* by Saroj Dey in 1986 failed to reach the audience. Probably they were too 'ideological' in their form and content. This is evident when Kiranmoy Raha, in his book, *Bengali Cinema*, is critical of the press reports that excessively hailed the 'parallel' or 'good cinema' movement. While Raha criticised the concerns of these films in terms of their form and content, Someshwar Bhoumik also expressed his views about the failure of these films when he wrote, quoting film-maker Goutam Ghose, that the films produced by the state (WBFDC and NFDC) hardly reached the audience outside the circuits of film festivals and film societies.[13]

The regular cinema halls that otherwise mostly screened mainstream cinema, were also not maintained properly, and the situation had deteriorated beyond repair, forcing many producers and distributors to quit the industry. This exodus severely affected the film business in Tollygunge.[14] At the same time, directors and producers who used to make star-centric films were in trouble, such as the ones who were making films with Uttam Kumar. However, this trend began fading after his passing away. It was no longer clear as to what kind of films could be made without him. Uttam Kumar's strongest rival, Soumitra Chatterjee, was not seen in the type of films that Uttam Kumar did or would have done. Besides, he continued to do a maximum of three to four films a year, rejecting several offers that were specifically written for Uttam Kumar.[15] Many successful distributors during the Uttam Kumar phase now took time to comprehend the shifting trends in film-making practices. They could no longer enjoy profits. It was time for the survivors to survey the market seriously, and to understand the art and business of film-making minutely. A large number of film-makers realised that they had to work hard on the script and the screenplay of a film, which were earlier not seen as important. This change was crucial, and the industry had to come to terms with this huge shift from an era that was so strongly dominated and controlled by a star.

Thus, while the industry was trying to tackle the void created by Uttam Kumar and was trying out newer ways of storytelling, it was at the same time getting split into the binaries of parallel and mainstream cinema. Perhaps, this scenario was also responsible for the bifurcation and segmentation of the audience, which drastically affected the overall condition of the Bengali film industry. The Bengali *bhadralok* gradually distanced itself from mainstream cinema that continued to flourish throughout the 1980s. The *bhardralok* instead turned to television that provided them with an opportunity to watch films from the Uttam–Suchitra era, along with the films being made by the parallel cinema directors of the 1970s–80s. The press, too, was very critical of mainstream films. The *bhadralok* community was voicing its vehement criticism against mainstream film-makers and the kind of films they made. Their primary concern was that the Bengali mainstream was imitating popular Hindi cinema aesthetics and form excessively and blatantly. The element of *masala* ('spicy' commercial elements) was not something with which Bengali cinema associated. Therefore, a serious disconnect developed between mainstream Tollygunge cinema and its otherwise most loyal audience base till the 1970s.[16] This period and phenomenon are also termed as the crisis period or the crisis narrative of Bengali cinema. While the industry insiders were struggling to address this crisis, the state government took various steps and initiatives to alter this plummeting state of affairs.

State Government Policies and Initiatives

The state government came up with a law for the resurgence of Bengali cinema and the industry. On 25 June 1981, The Calcutta Information Centre organised a meeting for the first time, with the re-established Film Development Board (FDB) that was attended by 27 of the 40 registered members. Some of the attendees were Mriganka Sekhar Roy, Ramananda Sengupta, Subrata Sensharma, Samarendra Sengupta, Anil Chatterjee, Pantu Nag, Mohit Chatterjee, A. K. Dey, Purnendu Patri, Basanta Choudhury, Hari Dasgupta, Swapan Dutta, Mrinal Gupta, A. N. Bhattacharya, Sishir Sen, Habul Das, D. Majumdar, M. A. Saiyad, Salil Choudhury, D. Mukherjee, Satyen Chatterjee, Soumendu Roy, Bijoy Chatterjee, Indranath Banerjee, Parthasarathi Choudhury, Shibnath Chatterjee, as well as representatives of the Eastern India Motion Pictures Association. The Vice-Chairman, Buddhadeb Bhattacharya, mentioned in his speech that 'the Board approved the state government's position regarding the compulsory screening of Bengali films in cinema houses within West Bengal for a period of 12 weeks in a year'.[17] In response, Subrata Sensharma pointed out that the state government could easily impose this law and call for a renewal of license, without any further delay.

The law had to be drafted in a way that none of the cinema halls could deviate from the terms and conditions. Hence, a section from the Cinematograph Code was incorporated in the draft, which mentioned that:

> ... [t]he State Government may from time to time, issue directions to licensees generally or, if in the opinion of the State Government circumstances so justify, to any licensee in particular, for the purpose of regulating the exhibition of any film or class of films and in particular the exhibition of scientific films, films intended for educational purposes, films dealing with news and current events, documentary films or films produced in India and where any such directions have been issued, these

> directions shall be deemed to be additional conditions and restriction subject to which the license has been granted.[18]

Following this, on 10 July the same year, the Left-ruled government issued a letter with the above-mentioned clauses and the mandate of 12 weeks of compulsory Bengali film-screening to the Home Department Secretary, 11 district offices, the Calcutta Police Commissioner, and cinema hall owners. However, this was a shock to most hall owners. The news created a tremor in Tollygunge studios, in the Dharmatala area of distributors' offices, and especially among cinema house owners who ran Hindi or English films round the year. Simultaneously, several cinema halls were shortlisted by the Calcutta Municipal Corporation (CMC), and a notice was issued to them to immediately amend the hall in order to keep their license intact, as the maintenance standards of these halls were below the quality mark. Cinema theatre owners had earlier avoided the compulsory conversion to air-conditioning on grounds of frequent power-cuts, and a frequent increase in renting, hiring or booking charges.[19]

During the Congress's rule in the 1970s, the Information Minister, Subarata Mukherjee, had raised considerable debate in the Legislative Assembly in favour of the mandatory screening of Bengali films in the state's cinema houses. However, due to various oppositions and the delay in the formation of the policies, the mandate was withdrawn. After the victory of the Left Front in West Bengal, a Bill was passed in the Bidhan Sabha (Legislative Assembly) for the imposition of this law, but the final rule had to be passed by the Centre. The bill was nevertheless rejected after a period of two years, with the logic that it would disrupt national integration.[20] The government was not sure about the repercussions of this law, as there was only one year left for the state assembly elections, and if forced, cinema houses could go to court to challenge this rule.

Basically, the Left government had lost huge sums when they had invested in 13 feature films, along with nine children's films and another 37 feature films that were already under production. The films so far produced by the government had not only incurred losses, but some had also not been released in cinema houses for even a single week's run. Private distributors had not bought most of the government-financed films. Cinema hall owners refused to screen any of these films. Most hall owners earned more profits from the 'black market' by screening Hindi films, and thus, the repeated notices and requests from the government did not affect them. A strong reason for this was that none of the government-funded films were box-office earners. A very limited group came to watch these films. The government was left with no option but to implement the law of compulsory screening of Bengali films. The larger and more pertinent question was—would producers and distributors be able to meet this sudden increase in demand for Bengali films to be run for 12 weeks by all the cinema houses in the state. Only 30 films were being released per year on an average count during the early-1980s. This somehow met the demands of the five prominent chains (cinema houses) in Calcutta.[21]

On an average, these five chains would run new Hindi films for nine months in a year, and for the rest of the year, they would show old Bengali films. Although the number of new films released in a year was 30, there would always be at least more than 10 films at a time that had been certified, but were not eligible for theatrical release due to a lack of cinema halls. A major reason for Bengali films not getting enough halls was the large number of Hindi films that were released and also that major distributors of Bengal exclusively distributing Hindi films would book cinema houses and chains, paying hefty advance amounts to hall owners, who were then contract-bound to show only Hindi films. For instance, halls like Basushree-Bina-Darpana and Priya would earlier show a greater number of Bengali films. However, they chose to stick to only Hindi films from 1981–83. Several others followed the trend. This was a matter of concern because the law the government wanted to impose demanded at least 75 feature films to be produced in Tollygunge.[22] In 1981, West Bengal had a total number of 350 cinema halls that were permanent, and roughly another 210 exhibition sites that were temporary. In order to meet the demands of the cinema halls, a greater number of films would have to be released. The state Tollygunge was in at the time did not permit the production of so many films. The lack of actors, technicians, efficient producers and committed directors was a major drawback, alongside the poor and deteriorating condition of the studios. Although the prices of tickets had been reduced to Re 1, only hall owners who had a hit Bengali film running would make a profit.[23]

The reduced ticket price policy also disturbed the business for new releases, because even old films were being run simultaneously for a Re 1 ticket; this was another source of competition for newly released Bengali films. The films that had already earned substantial profits were facilitating extra returns to the hall owners. However, in this extra profit, producers or distributors had no share. Distributors made good use of this loss by gaining greater control over the rural sector. They took a major portion of profit from small hall owners in rural areas, and in return, gave new releases to them.[24]

On the other hand, the issue that perturbed distributors and hall owners was how they would run Bengali films in areas where the audience was majorly non-Bengali. They would incur huge losses if they had to run Bengali films for 12 weeks in such areas. In such a situation, the government's intervention with the compulsory rule of screening Bengali films for 12 weeks complicated the situation further. Since the government had incurred considerable losses by bringing down the ticket price to Re 1 and financing several feature films that both audience and exhibitors refused to acknowledge, the scenario for Bengali film-makers, distributors, producers and hall owners became acutely tricky and challenging.[25]

The year 1980 was also a turbulent one for the Tollygunge industry, which was triggered by a prolonged strike during September and October by the Bengal Motion Pictures' Employees Union, which demanded an increase in the payment structure and bonus benefits, and by the subsequent lockout declared by the Eastern India Motion Pictures Association. Out of the 400-odd cinema halls in West Bengal, almost all the halls were shut down except for four or five. Hall owners could not meet the demand for a hike in the bonus and salaries of employees. They argued that they had to pay 125 per cent of the ticket price as entertainment tax to the government; thus, they barely earned enough to pay their employees. The strike and lockout caused an estimated loss of Rs 10 to 12 lakhs per day to the industry and of Rs 15 lakhs to the government. This deeply affected the regular cine-goers, especially the audiences for Bengali cinema. The death of superstar Uttam Kumar and the more-or-less weakening condition of the overall Bengali cinema industry created a detachment in the minds of the audiences of Bengali cinema, making the scenario very dismal.

Calcutta as a metropolitan city was also changing—culturally, socially and politically—in the mid-1980s when the Bengali *bhadralok* middle class was familiarising itself with television sets at home, through which they were gaining the privilege of watching films in the comfort of their households. The VCR was also making its entry into the city-dwellers' rooms, which enabled them to watch films of their choice at their discretion, conveniently avoiding the drawbacks of the overall experience of going to the cinema theatres.

Producers and distributors, especially from the 1970s, were anxiously searching for a formula that could reclaim the praise and dedicated viewership that they had enjoyed in the past. Actor-director Sukhen Das started making films that made way for the new genre and aesthetic that Anjan Chowdhury's *Shatru* robustly embodied. Some box-office hits of Das were *Nayan* (*Eye*) in 1977, *Singhaduar* (*Gate*) in 1978, *Maan Abhiman* (*Honour and Sentiment*) in 1978, *Jibon Maran* (*Life and Death*) in 1983, *Milantithi* (*The Hour of Union*) in 1985, *Achena Atithi* (*The Unknown Guest*) in 1973, *Shunoyinee* (*Doe-Eyed*) in 1979, *Rajnandini* (*Princess*) in 1980, and *Pratishodh* (*Revenge*) in 1981. A popular actor of the 1980s and 1990s, Tapas Pal, who acted in several films directed by Das, says in an interview to *Anandalok* magazine that Sukhen Das was like a *gharana*, as in a school unto himself. Pal adds that the kind of films that became popular in the 1980s and 1990s made by directors like Anjan Chowdhury were actually initiated by Sukhen Das. His films also dealt with social and contemporary issues. Most of his films had very successful music tracks and songs. He was a pioneer in bringing talent from Bombay whenever the film needed it. Das had a unique style of storytelling. He gave priority to the story, and the dialogue and drama were the most important aspects of his films. He made way for the voice of the suppressed to be heard and articulated through his films. But he was not free from criticism. There were opinions around his films that termed them regressive, lacking in cinematic sense and high in melodrama, similar to the *jatra*.[26]

Shatru and the Anjan Chowdhury Moment

In 1984, a young scriptwriter from Tollygunge directed his first feature film, *Shatru*, which changed the scenario of Bengali cinema.

Shatru altered the earlier situation of Bengali films running for a maximum of two to three weeks, and then struggling to sustain themselves in the cinema hall chains in Calcutta. It was as if Anjan Chowdhury had discovered the formula that the film industry had been frantically looking for. *Shatru* ran for more than one-and-a-half months with 'house-full' boards in the major cinema halls of Calcutta. Unexpectedly, tickets of *Shatru* were being sold in 'black'. Chowdhury's *Shatru* makes a striking departure from the tradition of the popular genre of romantic films in Bengal. The protagonist is a noble, honest and a dutiful police inspector played by Ranjit Mullick. Before this film, he was mainly identified as a romantic hero. Ranjit Mullick's character of the Officer In-Charge of Haridevpur village lives up to the image of a hero as a fighter who is capable of physical action. The protagonist's figure can be identified with the 'angry-young-man' image of Amitabh Bhacchan in Hindi cinema, which was popular in the 1970s.[27]

Shatru had a mixed ensemble cast, with a corrupt Member of the Legislative Assembly (MLA) played by Manoj Mitra, whose son is a rogue, troubling and eve-teasing the village school-master's college-going daughter. There was another character of a comic and corrupt police sub-inspector played by Anup Kumar, and the figure of a local businessman dealing in illegal country liquor. The film had fight sequences, theatrical comedy, and heavy melodramatic dialogues. *Shatru* ran very successfully in city halls like Radha-Purabi-Ujjwala-Sri for seven weeks consecutively, mostly with 'house-full' boards. This situation of an overwhelming audience response was until then associated with the so-called *bhadralok* cinemas of the 1950s, 1960s, and to an extent, the 1970s. People flooded back to the halls in huge numbers to watch *Shatru*. In an interview to Dipankar Chakraborty of *Anandabazar Patrika*, Anjan Chowdhury mentions the various elements that he incorporated into his scripts for a positive impact on his audiences.[28] Some of these elements were class conflict, emphasis on human emotions and relationships, and the idea of revenge driving the plot and narrative of the film in a racy pace.

For Chowdhury, therefore, the Bengali audience was now that of the class who identified more with the themes and stories of *jatra*. Elements like theatricality, over-the-top dialogue delivery, farcical comedy, and sorrowful or joyful music were essential in his scripts.

Shatru today occupies a distinct position as a significant marker in initiating a new phase in the history of Bengali cinema.[29] A black-and-white film with absolutely no big star cast, how did *Shatru* become a hit?

Chowdhury justified his style of storytelling as a formula, which, if and when not altered by the director or distributor, would ensure success. For instance, in his scripted film, *Prayaschitta* (*Penance*), directed by Arabinda Mukhopadhyay in 1984, according to the script he had written, at the end, the hero (Ranjit Mullick) would die, because the character had committed many mistakes in his life. However, the distributor, Amar Nan, did not agree and wanted the hero to remain alive. The director had to listen to the distributor's demands and to the great dissatisfaction of Chowdhury, the hero had to be kept alive. The final outcome was that the film flopped.

Shatru was received with whistles, hooting and claps at theatres like Ujjwala, Purna and Sri, every time the police officer landed a blow on or kicked the villains. The film had three to four songs, a dance number for which Bombay cinema's Jayshree Talpade was featured and the fight master, and Mr Makravi, too, was brought in from Bombay. Other actors included veteran character actor Bikas Roy, Manoj Mitra, and newcomers like Prosenjit Chatterjee and Shakuntala Barua.

In the 1980s, a large section of the audience avoided going to theatres for films that had too many songs, which were seen as superfluous. A part of the audience walked out of the theatres when the songs began to play because they knew they would not miss out on any important part of the story if they did not watch the song sequence. Chowdhury tried his best to alter this mindset. For him, songs were a very important part of Bengali cinema, and he felt that it was through music and songs that directors expressed their ethical thoughts and sentiments.

Shatru had a song directly commenting on the corruption in the police force, which was written by Chowdhury himself. He kept the suspense flowing through the song, so that no one could leave their seats and go away. Keeping the female audience in mind, Chowdhury kept a song, with the lyrics, '*Hotam khushi tomar majhe maa ke fire pele* ...' ('I would be happy to get back my mother in you ...') where the orphan (whose father is killed because he gets involved with the illegal country liquor-seller of the village) sings the song while embracing the childless widow (Shakuntala Baruah). According to Chowdhury, emotions, sentimentality, motherly care and love are crucial to satisfy the female audience. Chowdhury was also conscious of not giving away too much. Thus, he avoided any chance of a possible romance between the police officer (Ranjit Mullick) and the young widow (Shakuntala Baruah).

Chowdury emerged as one of the busiest scriptwriters and directors of the 1980s. He scripted *Mahamilan* (*The Great Union*) in 1987 for the widely appreciated director, Dinen Gupta. According to Gupta, Chowdhury could incorporate various 'positive aspects' in his script, such as the problems that ail the present-day society. His stories and heroes sold a dream to end social evils. He further added that the old-school way of storytelling was no longer relevant, where films are based on the literary adaptations of writers such as Saratchandra Chattopadhyay and the likes. Also, he felt that the Bengali audience was somewhat bored by the monotonous overdose of Hindi films of that time.[30]

In the 1980s and early-1990s, some of the films that Chowdhury directed were *Bidrohi* (*Rebel*) in 1987, *Gurudakshina* (*Obeisance*) in 1987, *Chhoto Bou* (*Youngest Daughter-in-Law*) in 1988, *Anjali* in 1988, *Bidhilipi* (*Destiny*) in 1991, *Indrajit* in 1992, etc. He also scripted several films like *Aakrosh* (*Rage*) in 1989, *Mangaldip* (*Holy Lamp*) in 1989, *Shatarupa* in 1989, and so on. There was a lot of hope bestowed on Chowdhury for his ability to deliver hits by foregrounding the voice of the oppressed and the subaltern figure, and for highlighting the everyday issues of the common man living in the margins of the city. In an interview to Dipankar Chakraborty, Tollygunge's famous Chhayabani Distributors' proprietor, Nirendranath Shil, said that although he had not seen *Shatru*, he had gathered information that *Shatru* had a lot of sentimental emotions, which might have touched the hearts of the female audiences, as according to him it was the female audience that mainly came to watch Bengali films.

However, we read a different message that Chowdhury tries to deliver in *Shatru*. He actually targets the youth, both the audience and the young talent of the Tollygunge film industry. Haridevpur's law and order is set right, the corrupt MLA and his rogue son are taught the right lesson, the illegal businessman is beaten up by the honest, upright and dutiful police officer who takes off his police cap (a symbol of his official duty of protecting and upholding law and order and justice) and puts it on the head of the orphan, picks him up, looks at the audience (into the camera), and gives a congratulatory smile.

It is important to note here that earlier in the film there was a song sequence written by Chowdhury, where the MLA's son was making fun of the same police cap. The lyrics were: '*ei tupi kake porai*'('who shall I put this cap on?'), and at the end of the film, the same cap is put on the head of the child, when the song sequence goes, '*ey tupi noy shei tupi*' ('this cap is not that cap'), for in Bengali, '*tupi porano*' ('to cap somebody') is used as a phrase that means to fool or cheat someone. Thus, at the end of the film, Chowdhury tries to establish the message that the youth is the future of any developing nation, and that the legacy of power, control and the fight for justice should be passed on to the next generation. The cap symbolically expresses this and perhaps metaphorically gestures to the trend that the then Prime Minister Rajiv Gandhi initiated—that 1985 marked the beginning of a new India—*Yuva Bharat* (an India of the Youth).

Chowdhury's *Shatru* made it possible for the Bengali film industry to fight back and ensure that the production, distribution and exhibition process could continue. Chowdhury became a banner, with two of his films that were released back-to-back becoming super hits. These were *Gurudakhina* in 1987, a musical still remembered for its music and popular songs, and *Chhoto Bou* in 1988 that foregrounded everyday family crises in middle-class, or rather, lower middle-class joint families, and was narrated from the perspective of the female members of the family. Revenge, and opression of the economically poor by rich landlords, and the local businessman and his goons, were some of the recurring themes of Chowdhury's films. Chowdhury's contribution was not only restricted to making super hit films one after the other, but he also brought new talent to the industry. He was solely responsible for establishing his assistants as independent directors, such as Bablu Samaddar, Haranath Chakraborty, Subhas Sen, Amal Roy Ghatak and Dulal Dey (who are commonly referred as 'team Anjan Chowdhury' in the industry).

It is also important to mention here the other film-makers who complicated the singular popularity of Chowdury. While on the one hand, Chowdhury received serious criticism from the bhadralok class for his films being excessively melodramatic and centered around the crises of domesticity, on the other hand, family melodramas and musicals like *Dadar Kirti* (*The Adventures of Big Brother*) in 1980, *Bhalobasha Bhalobasha* (*Love Love*) in 1985, *Poroshmoni* (*Philosopher's Stone*) in 1988, etc., by Tarun Majumdar were well-received by *bhadralok* audiences. Promod Chakraborty's *Teen Murti* in 1984 was a roaring success at the box office. There were also films like *Rajeshwari* by Salil Dutta in 1984, *Joy Porajoy* (*Victory and Defeat*) by Chandan Mukherjee in 1983 and *Parabat Priya* by Dipranjan Bose in 1984, which were not received well in the city cinema halls, but did extremely well in the suburbs and in cinema halls around West Bengal. However, by the mid-1990s, Majumdar began to lose his mettle by being excessively repetitive with his themes and not being able to adapt to the transitioning film culture and newer audiences.

By the mid-1980s, the two prominent directors who followed the the tradition of Tarun Majumdar were probably Prabhat Roy and Biresh Chattopadhyay, who consistently made films that were commercially successful and socially relevant. Roy and Chattopadhyay were also responsible for popularising new stars like Victor Banerjee, Ranjit Mullick, and for casting quite a few Bengali and non-Bengali actors from the Bombay film industry in their films. Biresh Chattopadhyay's *Ekanto Apan* (*Solely Mine*) in 1987, starring Victor Banerjee and Aparna Sen, released at Minar-Bijoli-Chobighar became a box-office success. Chattopadhyay's *Kori Diye Kinlam* (*Bought with a Penny*) in 1989 was also a moderately successful film, and was received well by the critics; the film starred Moushumi Chatterjee, Arjun Chakraborty, Utpal Dutt, Tapas Pal, Aparna Sen and Madhabi Mukherjee. In the very same year, his other film, *Tufan* (*Storm*), was a colossal hit.[31]

By the early-1990s, in Tollygunge, Prabhat Roy was often referred to as the expert film-maker who could walk a tight rope between cinema for commerce and cinema of social relevance. Roy came from the stage and had acted in more than 40 plays in Barrackpore, near Calcutta. He had initially migrated to Mumbai to make films, and had started by assisting Shakti Shamanta in directing his first two Hindi films, *Zindagani* (*Everyday Life*) produced by actor Rakhee in 1984, followed by *Hum Intezaar Karenge* (*I Shall Wait*) produced by Neelima Paul in 1989. Both the films were commercially unsuccessful, after which he debuted in the Tollygunge film industry with *Pratidan* (*Return*) in 1983, starring Victor Banerjee, Naseeruddin Shah, Sharmila Tagore and Ranjit Mullick. The story dealt with the reform of a villian. Roy's next massive box-office hit was *Pratikar* (*Remedy*) in 1987, starring Chiranjeet, Victor Banerjee, Debashree Roy and Utpal Dutt. Films like *Prateek* in 1988, and *Agnitrishna* (*Thirst of Fire*) in 1989, *Swet Pathorer Thala* (A *Plate of White Marble*) in 1992, *Laathi* (*The Stick*) in 1996, *Sedin Choitramash* (*The Days and Months of Chaitra*) in 1997, *Shudhu Ekbar Bolo* (*Just Tell Me Once*) in 1999, *Shubho Drishti* (*The Auspicious Sight*) in 2005, and *Pitribhoomi* (*Paternal Land*) in 2007, are some of the films for which this period and Roy are remembered and credited. *Swet Pathorer Thala*, based on a novel by the popular Bengali writer, Bani Basu, bagged the National Award (Silver Lotus) for the best family film. The story revolves around the struggles of a young widow who sacrifices her emotional desires for the sake of a thankless Bengali middle-class family. On the other hand, *Laathi* was based on Roy's own story, with Victor Banerjee portraying an old man crusading against elder abuse within the family; this film, too, won a National Award. Roy, being an important director, was often asked to comment on the present state of the Tollygunge film industry, and very scrutinisingly, on the one hand, he expressed his anxieties around the overproduction syndrome, where there were more films in comparison to the number of theatres that screened Bengali cinema, and on the other hand, he was also hopeful about the increase in able technicians in the film industry.[32]

By the mid-1990s, the television industry's rising popularity and invasion also impacted the Tollygunge film industry. The increasing demand for quality content in television attracted several film directors of Tollygunge to produce programmes for television. The actors, directors and technicians from the film industry rapidly migrated to television, for regular work and better remmuneration. The *bhadralok* section of the audience also generously endorsed television programmes, as they were able to identify better with the content of television than the mainstream films that were proliferating in Bengal. This situation, resulting in drastic audience segmentation, enabled certain new directors to make films in the Tollygunge studios, categorically targeting the mofussil and rural demography, possibly reshuffling Bengali film culture. Therefore, the following section discusses the shifting scenario of the film industry, and also takes into account the film-makers who dominated the post-Anjan Chowdhury phase in Tollygunge.

The Post-Anjan Chowdhury Phase

Haranath Chakraborty and Bablu Samaddar, who started their careers as assistants to Anjan Chowdhury, later went on to become two of the most popular directors; they churned out the maximum number of blockbuster films at the box office. By the late-1990s, several films scripted and directed by Anjan Chowdhury failed one after the other at the box office, resulting in the gradual falling apart of the 'Anjan Chowdhury team'.

Ananya (*The Unique*) directed by Dulal Dey, and scripted by Chowdhury, in 1989, was a flop, although noted actress Aparna Sen played the lead; *Debata* (*The God*) directed by Abhijit Sen, and scripted by Chowdhury, in 1990, did not fare well. By this time, the 'crisis narrative' was at its peak. The industry was divided into the polarities of 'good cinema' and 'bad cinema'. The press celebrated directors like Goutam Ghose, Mrinal Sen, Utpalendu Chakraborty and Buddhadev Dasgupta, who experimented with the form and content of film-making, and sometimes critiqued the social and political system. The press harshly criticised Anjan Chowdhury's over-the-top melodramatic films, which were allegedly lowering the standards of Bengali cinema; very often, they were copied directly from cheap Hindi *masala* films and were inferior in comparison to *jatra* or films from Bangladesh.

These works engaged with the notion of 'crisis' that the middle-class intelligentsia had constructed.[33] This 'crisis' was not seen in any way in economic terms; rather, the primary concern was the decaying quality of Bengali cinema.[34] Thus, the 'crisis' in Bengali cinema was dominantly understood from a perspective of 'taste' overlooking other important factors or dynamics of the film industry.[35]

The year 1991 marked the economic liberalisation of India. This had tremendous impressions on the Bombay film industry that witnessed several changes, gradually impacting the regional film industries. The term 'Bollywood' was gradually gaining currency then, and the corporatisation of film production was introduced. UTV

Motion Pictures, Yash Raj Studios, Dharma Production, and a few others became fully corporatised film production and distribution houses. In 1998, the then Minister of Information and Broadcast, Sushma Swaraj, made an official declaration terming Bollywood a recognised industry. This event changed the way in which films were produced, distributed and exhibited. A large number of films could now be released in territories outside the Indian nation. The diaspora as a category not only became a potential revenue-earning source, but the content, look and the narratives of Bombay films also began to cater to the expectations, sensibilities and aesthetics of the diaspora market. Bollywood industry and its films witnessed production changes in terms of economic development, wider distribution, technological advancement, and neo-liberal aesthetics in film content and narrative, which foregrounded a tension between the tradition of the East versus the liberal values of the West.

Interestingly, the Bengali film industry was still struggling to find a place in the minds of people beyond a certain class and section of audience. Popular films that were dominated by film-makers like Swapan Saha and Haranath Chakraborty were perhaps largely disowned by the Bengali middle-class *bhadralok* audience. By the mid-1990s, a peculiar phenomenon began in the Tollygunge industry. Films like *Beder Meye Josna* (*Josna, the Daughter of the Snake Charmer*) by M. R. Panu in 1991, *Shami Keno Ashami* (*Why the Husband is a Criminal?*) by Monwar Khokon in 1997, and *Baba Keno Chakor* (*Why is the Father a Servant?*) by Swapan Saha in 1998 were allegedly mere filmed versions of *jatra*, often enacted by actors from Bangladesh. The popular cinema hall chains of Minar-Bijoli-Chobighar began to concentrate primarily on Hindi films, which led to a gradual shrinking of the audience for Bengali cinema.[36]

Deviating from the dominant mode of the literary narrative, these films borrowed their structure from the myth and folklore that are popular in the peripheries of Bengal. *Beder Meye Josna*, inspired by a popular *jatra pala* (Bengali folk theatre performances) narrative, initiated this trend that almost acquired a cult status. In fact, this film was a remake of a popular Bangladeshi film. In Bengali, '*bede*' denotes a gypsy community of snake charmers who earn their living by entertaining people, selling medicinal herbs and jugglery. This film narrated a love story between a girl from the '*bede*' community and a local prince. One day, when a local prince was bitten by a snake, Josna, a girl from the '*bede*' community, was called to cure him. The king requested Josna to cure his son, and in exchange, promised Josna that he would give her anything she wanted. Josna risked her life to cure the prince, and when the prince recovered, she fell in love with him. When the prince found out about Josna, he, too, fell in love with her. However, the king objected to this since she belonged to the '*bede*' community. But at the climax of the film, it was revealed that Josna actually belonged to an upper-caste family. The king finally agreed to get them married. Following *Beder Meye Josna*, Bengali cinema experienced a body of films that dealt with snake charmers, snake goddess, female figures that possessed special powers from the cult worshipping of snakes, etc.: for instance, films like *Bedenir Prem* (*The Love Story of a Snake Charmer Woman*) by Saha in 1992, *Nagin Kanya* (*Daughter of a Snake Woman*) by Saha in 1995, *Nach Nagini Nach Re* (*Dance O Snake Charmer Woman Dance!*) by Chowdhury in 1996, *Mansha Kanya* (*Manasha's Daughter*) by Sujit Guha in 1997, and others. And there were films like *Pratirodh* (*Resistance*) by Srinivas Charaborty in 1997, which narrated the love story of an honest police officer who fell for a girl, Lakhsmi, who was a survivor of snake-bite and possessed special powers.

As mentioned earlier, at this point of time, a large pool of talents from the film industry, comprising actors, directors, writers and technicians shifted to television,[37] as it had a larger appeal among the Bengali middle and upper classes. Television content was once again close to literature. It was also more lucrative in terms of economic returns. But most importantly, it gave work to large numbers of actors and technician in the industry. Suddenly, Tollygunge became an industry catering to television audiences. At the same time, a few directors like Swapan Saha, Haranath Chakraborty, Sujit Guha and Bablu Sammadar continued to make films for a certain class and section of the audience.

In a special series of articles and interviews published by *Anandalok* titled, 'Why this Crisis in Bengali Cinema?', eminent film-makers, actors, producers and writers expressed their concerns about the decline in Bengali cinema, and its distance and shift from literary tradition. Dinen Gupta said that Bengali cinema was in a miserable state. He added that most of the directors were uneducated;

no one believed in doing homework before going on the floors, and they mocked at a certain group of directors and actors. He further stated, that 'these days if you go and buy vegetables for some of the directors they will cast you in their films, and moreover where can we find talented actors, actresses and directors these days?'[38]

Chowdhury, who once made blockbuster hits, but had gradually limited his film-making career by the late 1990s, was asked what the reason for the decline of Bengali cinema was. Chowdhury felt that the Bengali cinema audience had drastically changed by this time. There was a large section of audience who would watch Bengali cinema on television and VCR in their homes. On the other hand, a major section of Bengali cinema audiences were formed of rickshaw pullers, fish mongers and vegetable hawkers. Films made by Chowdhury would cater to the tastes and preferences of the latter class of people, who in fact comprised the main audience base for Bengali cinema. Chowdhury further provided instances of a few 'good' films made by celebrated and noted directors of that time, like Tapan Sinha and Tarun Majumdar, none of which could attract significant audiences. He also referred to 'good films' such as *Abbajan* (*Daddy Dearest*), directed by him in 1994, and *Sandhyatara* (*Evening Star*), directed by Prabhat Roy in 1994, both of which failed at the box office. Chowdhury emphasised on the fact that films have to speak about the contemporary times and provide wholesome entertainment, and only then will the industry surive and overcome the crisis.[39]

Since corporatisation had not made its entry in the Tollygunge film industry yet, it is important to study directors who were making films during the mid-1990s and at the beginning of the new millennium. What kind of films were they making? What kind of success were they getting? The following section sheds light on two of the most significant directors of this period: Haranath Chakraborty and Swapan Saha.

Haranath Chakraborty

Haranath Chakraborty, who began his career as an assistant to Chowdhury, debuted as a director with *Mangal Deep* (*Auspicious Lamp*) in 1989, starring Ranjit Mullick and Sandhya Roy. The film had a treatment, plot line and direction that were very close to

Chowdhury's films. Gradually, Chakraborty carved an independent identity for himself. He concentrated on the action genre and made films like *Nabab* (*Emperor*) in 1991, *Sangharsha* (*Conflict*) in 1995, *Mahan* (*Noble*) in 1996, *Bidroho* (*Rebellion*) in 1997, and *Ranakshetra* (*Battlefield*) in 1998, among others. Chakraborty established himself as one of the most commercially successful directors in Tollygunge. He was the busiest director of the 1990s and the early-2000s. According to him, *Ranakshetra* brought in several changes to the industry. He shot the film on a much higher budget than was the prevalent practice. The action sequences were choreographed with greater technical finesse in car blast and chase sequences, involving expensive cars. He said that he had never shot a film on 16 mm, but always on 35 mm. With every film, he increased the budget and the number of prints to be released.[40] In 2000, Haranath made the highest budget film of Tollygunge, *Shasurbari Zindabaad* (*Hail the In-Law's House*). This film was shot in cinemascope, which was a first in Tollygunge. It also had a costume designer, a publicity designer, and a set built on a very high budget that could have made several films all together. The film had pre-release publicity, a music release, as well as digital posters. All of these were uncommon for mainstream Tollygunge film productions.

Shasurbari Zindabaad was a massive hit across cities, suburbs, small towns and villages. Chakraborty says that he never wished to take a gap of more than a few weeks between two films, for he believed that his crew should always be working, as this would generate revenue for the industry and its workers, which would in turn ensure the survival of the industry. This film was released with 50 prints, which was in fact also a first for a Bengali film. However, critics were merciless. They lashed at Chakraborty for making Bengali films look like cheap imitations of Hindi *masala* films and frame-to-frame copies of South Indian hits. But Chakraborty believes that these were precisely the factors that made his films popular and commercially successful. Rs 70 lakhs spent on *Shasurbari Zindabaad* was recovered in just about 50 days. This was unbelievable and absolutely a first for any Bengali film in the past three decades.[41]

The film drew a full house in more than 25 cinema halls all over Bengal. Rs 70 lakhs for a Bengali film was a huge risk in 2001. Until then, Tollygunge had been experiencing huge financial losses.

Most hall owners had sold off or leased out their property by 1999. A few studio owners were negotiating with promoters to sell off their studio premises. Although Swapan Saha's *Baba Keno Chakor* and M. R. Panu's *Beder Meye Josna* were hits, these did not bring about significant changes in the economics of the industry. This was a time when corporate values had gradually begun to enter the Calcutta market, the neoliberal life style was picking up at a slow pace, and the urban population of the metropolis, Calcutta, was shopping at Pantaloons; mainstream Bengali cinema was a distant concern at this point in time. Quite unexpectedly yet surprisingly, Pantaloons cashed in on the success of *Shasurbari Zindabaad* and came up with a slogan during the Bengali festival *Jamai Shoshti* (a festival where sons-in-law are treated by mothers- and fathers-in-law and are gifted new clothes). The slogan went thus: '*Eibar shosthi te jamai bolbeiyee shasurbari zindabaad*!' ('On this festival the son-in-law will definitely say that his in-laws' house rocks!'). This was possibly the first recognition of a mainstream film and the Bengali film industry by a corporate brand. *Shasurbari Zindabaad* was a trend-setter, and this was not merely for the hero and heroine of the film, Prosenjit Chatterjee and Rituparna Sengupta—who had worked together in eight films the previous year but had given only one hit, *Kulangaar* (*Prodigal Son*) by Sujit Guha in 2000—but also because the film ran for a record period of time, crossing more than eight weeks.[42]

The story bore a strong resemblance to the Hindi film, *Jamai Raja* (*Mighty Son-in-Law*) by A. Kodandarami Reddy in 1990, starring Anil Kapoor, Hema Malini and Madhuri Dixit. It also bore similarities with two other Hindi potboilers, namely *Raja Hindustani* (*Raja, the Indian*) by Dharmesh Darshan in 1996 and *Biwi Ho Toh Aisi* (*What a Wife to Have*) by J. K. Bihari in 1988. The story is about a deprived child (Prosenjit Chatterjee), who grows up to come back and avenge the wrong done to him. Anamika Saha is the stereotypical wretched and wicked mother-in-law who is forced to accept this son-in-law as a *ghar jamai* (a son-in-law who lives in his mother-in-law's house), followed by a constant battle of wits between the mother-in-law and son-in-law.[43]

Robin Agarwal, the producer of *Shasurbari Zindabaad*, lamented that the present breed of Bengali films was poor in story and originality, that the industry lacked good actors, directors and when a film like this one became a hit, it was merely a question of chance. Despite all of this, the film had some novel elements. The credits of the film did not follow the established practice of a scrolling down of names and titles, but instead, as members of the audience were entering the hall, looking for their seats and settling down, the film introduced each and every member of the 'family' directly to the audience. The first few songs of the film, unlike contemporary Bengali song sequences shot in Nicco Park or other local parks and lakes in and around Kolkata, were shot against the picturesque backdrop of Kalimpong in northern Bengal.[44]

While regretting the pathetic condition of single-screen theatres in Kolkata, actor Ranjit Mullick complimented the film-maker for holding the audience captive with a 'clean family comedy film'. Nonetheless, Haranath Chakraborty analyses the raving success of *Shasurbari Zindabaad* quite differently. He states that the film explores comedy, a genre rarely found in Bengali cinema of the time. The audience appreciated Prosenjit Chatterjee in a comic role and Rituparna Sengupta in a different persona from her previous films. Also, the film deviates from the usual plot line of most commercial films. Instead of being a melodramatic story about a cruel mother-in-law torturing the weepy daughter-in-law, *Shasurbari Zindabaad* manages to execute chauvinism of a kind that is comical where the son-in-law tames his mother-in-law.[45]

Pratibad (*Protest*) in 2001, which followed *Shasurbari Zindabaad*, was another blockbuster by Chakraborty. *Pratibad* is remembered and marked for its contribution in initiating the trend of remaking South Indian hits in Tollygunge. Film-makers still making films in the so-called 'Anjan Chowdhury' style were taken aback with the gimmicks, action and the element of thrill that the film was filled with. *Pratibad* moved a step ahead from using fake revolvers to the use of Sten guns and dynamite blasts to the whip-lashing of villains. Cannon blasts were recorded authentically; expensive cars were blown off; the hero flew to a height of 40 feet; and there was a rocket launcher that burnt off an entire gang of villains. Added to these elements, the film had spectacles like bike-jumping and other action-filled stunts that Bengali cinema had never witnessed before.[46]

The cinema hall Prachi announced that *Pratibad* was one of the highest grossers in their 52-year-long history of exhibiting Bengali films. With the success of *Shasurbari Zindabaad*, almost all cinema hall owners increased the rate of tickets in West Bengal. *Pratibad* was Anjan Chowdhury's story; he scripted it and wrote the dialogues. Chowdhury agrees that the story was nothing new, but the film had technical advancements and the use of gimmicks similar to those in Bollywood films. Haranath Chakraborty remarked that it was high time Tollygunge film-makers incorporated these techniques and aesthetic advancements. An audience now exposed to international cinema through cable television would watch Bengali films only if they get more than what they have been getting from Bengali films so far.[47] The period around early-2001–03 was a defining moment for Bengali cinema, when both the industry and the press woke up to the possibilities of a new resurgence in Tollygunge in terms of technicalities and visual aesthetics.[48]

The success of *Pratibad* in Kolkata cinema halls, which were once known for their tradition of screening 'Uttam–Suchitra' hits, proved that audience taste had possibly changed and people wanted Bengali mainstream films to be technically advanced and at par with Bollywood films.[49] Haranath Chakraborty stated that films would work only if they could feel the audience's pulse, also going on to say that 'pseudo-intellectualism' would fail in Bengal. He stressed that one could neither waste the producers' money, nor cheat the audience in the name of art films.[50] The success of *Pratibad* was repeated by the 2002 musical blockbuster, *Saathi* (*Companion*), which, too, was a remake of a Tamil film, *Thulladha Manamum Thullum* (*Hearts that Don't Jump, Will Jump*) by Ezhil in 1999.

It is not surprising here that even Chakraborty's mentor, Chowdhury, remarked in a similar manner when asked why his films repeatedly dealt with mofussil problems of everyday life, like fights and quarrels in a kerosene shop, or in a queue for filling water from a municipal corporation public water supply tap in a village. Without hesitating, Chowdhury said that those who still cook their food using kerosene oil everyday, and who have only one municipal tap providing drinking water in their area are the ones for whom he makes his films; they are his customers and he caters to them. He felt that he would not be able to deliver and would fail miserably if he forced himself to make films like Goutam Ghose, Aparna Sen or Rituparno Ghosh. He knew his formula and he could deliver his best through knowing his audience and his own style. He wanted to make profits and there was no other way to do it than the way he wrote or directed his films; his film-making style guranteed profit and made the producers earn higher returns.[51]

Swapan Saha

During this time, film production in Tollygunge was controlled more or less by fleeting producers, who were mostly non-Bengali businessmen from the real-estate industry, among others. Around this time, the director who worked with the maximum number of independent non-Bengali producers was Swapan Saha. At times, he made more than three films with a cumulative budget of Rs 50 lakhs he received from a businessman. By 2003, Saha had completed 50 feature films. For the first time in Tollygunge, an average of four films a year were being made by a single director. Regardless of the flak that his films received from the *bhadralok* audiences for films like *Baba Keno Chakor*, the 1998 film, *Simul Parul*, or the 1999 film, *Santan Jakhan Satru* (*When the Child is a Foe*), his films continued to be extremely popular in the suburbs and villages of West Bengal. A certain section of people would walk into cinema halls knowing that it was a Swapan Saha film that they were going to watch, claimed several film industry practitioners and film critics.

According to Saha, a small group of 'serious' film-makers with National Awards and film festival screenings abroad would often label his films as 'photographed *jatra*'. However, none of their films ever drew a full house continuously for two weeks, thereby landing the producer in a lurch. Saha reiterates with confidence that he was perhaps the only director on whom producers could bank without doubt in Tollygunge for almost a decade. Out of the 50 films of Swapan Saha that had released till 2003, 15 have been super hits, 15 were hits, while the rest had all recovered the costs. Saha began to be looked at with greater suspicion and shock because he could make three films at a time on paltry budgets, which no film-maker had ever dared to do before in the Tollygunge film industry. He completed most of his films within two months, sometimes even within a month. These were issues about which the press wrote profusely, and most often, with a mocking tone and a sense of ridicule. Even on television shows, when 'parallel cinema' film directors were questioned about the films of Saha, they repeatedly held him responsible for the degradation of Bengali cinema.[52]

Saha began his career in Dhaka by assisting director Alamgir Kumkum. He even acted in two Bangladeshi films, *Monimala* and *Moner Moto Bou* (*Beloved Wife*). He assisted Dhaka's popular director, Johir Raihan, from whom he learnt the technique of completing a film shoot in less than a month. Subsequently, he shot *Shothbhai* (*Stepbrother*) in 2000 in less than 10 days. The film was released within a month of its production and had a total budget of only Rs 9 lakhs. Trained in Bangladesh, Saha's films had a strong influence of the tradition of Bangladeshi films, with in-your-face high melodrama and double-meaning dialogues, with an imitation of rural and kitschy *jatra* aesthetics. Saha admits that this was his speciality, and that these were attributes that made his films popular in the mufossil areas and in rural Bengal. His super hits included *Sujan Sakhi* (*Sujan and Sakhi*), *Bhai Amar Bhai* (*Oh! My Brother*), *Jhinukmala*, *Adorer Bon* (*Dearest Sister*), *Tomake Chai* (*I Desire You*), *Maatir Manush* (*Rooted*), *Baba Keno Chakor* (*Why is the Father a Servant*), *Kamalar Bonobash* (*The Exile of Kamala*), *Praner Cheye Priyo* (*Dearest of Dear*), *Santan Jokhon Shatru* (*When the Child is a Foe*), *Guru Shishya* (*Master Disciple*), *Jabab Chai* (*Answer Us*), *Strir Morjada* (*The Wife's Honour*), *Kurukshetra* (*The Battleground*) and *Sneher Protidan* (*Gratitude*). His hits were *Bedenir Prem* (*Love of the Snake Charmer Woman*), *Maan-Shomman* (*Honour and Pride*), *Bishwas Obishwas* (*Trust and Distrust*), *Naginikanya* (*The Snake Woman*), *Sokhi Tumi Kar* (*Whose Beloved are You?*), *Nishpaap Ashami* (*The Innocent Convict*), *Bakulpriya*, *Mayer Dibbi* (*Swear on My Mother!*), *Sundori* (*Beautiful Woman*), *Swamir Adesh* (*Husband's Order*), *Ghorer Lokkhhi* (*Virtuous Woman*), *Swamir Ghor* (*Husband's House*), *Maanush Keno Beimaan* (*Traitor*), *Ei Ghor Ei Shongshar* (*Home and the Hearth*) and *Bhalobashi Tomake* (*Love You, Dear*).[53]

Interestingly, contemporary Tollygunge's biggest and most successful production house, SVF, started their film production venture with Saha's *Bhai Amar Bhai* in 1996. Saha was confident that the 1990s was a crucial period when directors like himself gave hundreds of people their bread and butter, mainly the workers and staff of the studios in Tollygunge. Earlier, he released his films with a maximum of 12–15 prints, and a maximum budget of Rs 20 lakhs per film. In our discussion with Swapan Saha during 2010–11, he observed that Tollygunge had grown by leaps and bounds and was perhaps at par with Bollywood. But he was not hopeful about the numerous independent one-time production houses mushrooming across the industry. Saha was confident that these fly-by-night producers would disappear in no time, and that only Eskay Videos and SVF would thrive, as they seriously understood the business of film-making. When asked why his films no longer worked (for instance, *RUN*, *Private Practice*, *Love Story of a Super Star*, and *Warrant* made during 2010–12 were all flops), he said they still work in the rural areas.[54]

The journalistic and academic discourses on 1980s–90s Bengali cinema present a bleak scenario of the Bengali film industry as suffering from multiple crises. Beyond cinema and cinematic practice, this is also a period when the elite class of Bengal was facing a crisis of their literary self and the specific term, '*aposankriti*'[55] ('bad culture'), came into parlance largely to indicate the emerging culture of a newly privileged urban class as well as the westernisation of the younger generation, who were allegedly distanced from their literary root of Bengali culture. Amidst this crisis of the Bengali literary self of the *bhadralok* class, film-makers like Chowdhury, Saha and others continued with the formulaic films. While being popular, these films earned widespread criticism from a part of the urban intelligentsia for their 'vulgarity' and the 'crudity' of their narrative model. Popular newspapers and magazines published letters of dissatisfied Bengali film audiences who saw them as a marker of the 'crisis narrative of Bengali cinema' discourse. These critical perspectives of the Bengali intelligentsia, and not necessarily of the industrial formulation or the production and distribution circuit, made this new popular cinema classified as 'B grade' cinema of the Bengali film history. The term 'B grade' here is not applicable in terms of its production logic or for that matter of legal discourse, but rather as a result of a section of the urban intelligentsia's discourse of culture, where they considered this cinema to be a complete misfit.[56]

Tollygunge Industry becomes Tollywood

Kolkata witnessed the advent of multiplex theatre for the first time in 2003 through an initiative by Inox Forum in Bhawanipur. This was also the locality where the famous single screen-theatre chain, Minar-Bijoli-Chobighar, existed, which epitomised a cultured *bhadralok* audience base. The Inox multiplex not only changed the entire experience of film-viewing, but it also created a space for the niche audience that was desperately in search of a legitimised space for a certain kind of cinema that had just begun to get popular. Rituparno Ghosh's *Chokher Bali* in 2003 was the first Bengali film that got screened at the Inox multiplex, and it created a storm critically as well as earned reasonably well at the box office. However, there were a few critics who were not kind to the film at all, probably because they were against a Bollywood star, Aishwarya Rai, being cast in a Tagore interpretation, with her voice dubbed by a Bengali actress. By then, Rituparno Ghosh's, films had won National Awards and were credited for 'bringing back' the middle-class Bengali audiences into the theatres with his films like *Unishe April* in 1994, *Dahan* (*Crossfire*) in 1997, *Bariwaali* (*The Landlady*) in 1999 and *Subho Mahurat* (*Auspicious Moment*) in 2003. Ghosh not only garnered critical acclaim, but was also considerably celebrated for his 'rich aesthetics' and 'literature-centric content'.[57]

Chokher Bali was produced by SVF, founded by Mahendra Soni and Shrikant Mohta, who, as mentioned earlier, had entered film production in 1996 with Swapan Saha's film *Bhai Amar Bhai.* The film did moderate business at the box office. SVF continued to produce Bengali films, and became highly successful and popular after producing Haranath Chakraborty's *Shasurbari Zindabaad* and *Pratibad.* In 2003, SVF produced *Chokher Bali,* which had a budget of more than Rs 1.5 crores, a record for the time. The film was declared a hit, even though it mostly ran in Kolkata and other metropolitan cities. The press, public and critics saw the success of *Chokher Bali* as a starting point that triggered major developments in the corporatisation of Tollygunge and in initiating aesthetic changes in film production. SVF also produced Rituparno Ghosh's first Hindi film, *Raincoat,* in 2005, starring Aishwarya Rai and Ajay Devgan.

Around this time, actor-singer-film-maker Anjan Dutt made his first Bengali film, *The Bong Connection*, in 2007, a film dealing with the present-day young urban Bengalis. The film saw a pan-India release and popularity among diaspora audiences. This film opened the floodgates for the industry to experiment with different genres, subjects and treatments. The film was crucial in changing screening regulations of Bengali films in multiplexes. Multiplexes earlier screened only selected Bengali films, ones that targeted the niche urban audience. With the overwhelming success of *The Bong Connection*, the rules changed. The Eastern India Motion Pictures Association (EIMPA) made it mandatory for all multiplexes to devote at least 40 per cent of their screen time to Bengali cinema. Actor, director and producer Arindam Sil was confident to share his assessment on the success of *The Bong Connection* with the media to the changing mindset in the youth and the narrowing gap between the rural and urban psyches of people in Bengal.[58]

Following these developments, the Bengali film industry went through diverse changes; newer groups of producers, and directors and film technicians entered the industry, all of whom gradually led to the corporatisation of film production, distribution and exhibition. At the same time, post-liberalisation, there was a boom in private television channels. Several Bengali private cable television channels were launched, such as *Etv Bangla*, *Zee Bangla*, *Star Ananda*, *Tara Bangla*, *Akash Bangla*, and so on, with a wide range of information and entertainment-based programmes related to the Bengali film industry. This was followed by the entry of Bengali FM radio stations like *Amar FM*, *Friends FM*, *Big FM*, *Red FM*, etc., which, unlike public service providers, did not stick only to *Rabindra Sangeet* (songs of Rabindranath Tagore) and film music from old Bengali classics. These radio stations provided a new range of programmes, involving newer talent from the contemporary Bengali film and entertainment industry, and they also aired songs and music from contemporary films.

The English and Bengali language press altered their perception and approach towards the Bengali film industry. Press discourse and discussions related to the post-1980s 'crisis narrative' and the decaying quality of Bengali cinema began to shift towards a more celebratory discourse regarding the overall improvement of the Bengali film and entertainment industry. Articles and stories on this revivalist phase of the Bengali film industry began to circulate through newspaper supplements like *Calcutta Times* of *The Times of India*, *HT City* of *Hindustan Times*, *t2* of *The Telegraph*, and Bengali magazines like *Anandalok, Unnish Kuri* and *Sananda*. All of these featured columns, articles and pages, with a focus on Tollywood. New stars, new directors, corporatisation, film exhibition, film budgets, visual and techno-aesthetics, music and fashion,[59] etc., were increasingly featured in press writings and discussions. This was followed by reports of various business and economic collaborations and ventures that Tollywood experienced.[60] The word 'Tollywood' had gained currency in the popular press and media discourses, leading to its acknowledgement in the public sphere. The industry was hopeful about this turn, mainly because of the logic of sheer economics, as more numbers of films, and more press and media coverage meant sustaining employment in the film industry for people working and controlling the industry, and facing the unequal threat of competition from Bombay films. Nevertheless, Tollywood was not exempted from criticism by the press for making copies of Southern hits and morphing Bollywood.[61] With fewer exceptions, young film-makers, reclaimed Bengali cinema with the success of unconventional films at the box office, alongside regular 'pot-boilers', encouraging a collective drive towards the production of diverse Bengali content, aggressive marketing, all-round publicity, and even worldwide release. For instance, singer-director Anjan Dutt's *Madly Bangali* (*Madly Bengali*) in 2009 tried to break stereotypes of the staid and conservative *bhadralok* Bengali who cannot party and adapt to the global lifestyle and develop a cosmopolitan attitude; it was about city youngsters trying to make a mark in the music industry. Another film by Anjan Dutt, *Chalo Let's Go* (*Come On, Let's Go*) in 2008 was a travelogue based on challenging human relationships belonging to a post-global urban metropolis. Both these films did average business at the box office but generated renewed interest in Bengali films among the urbane Bengalis. Director duo Abhijit Guha and Sudeshna Roy's romantic comedy, *Cross Connection* in 2008 ran for a record-breaking 10 weeks in central Kolkata and elsewhere. Actor-turned-producer Rituparna Sengupta experimented with unconventional film plots, star cast and higher budgets in films like *Alo* (*Light*) by Tarun Majumdar in 2003, and *Potadar Kirti* (*The Adventures of Potada*) by Jeet Dutta in 2010. There were changes both within and outside the Bengali film industry that ushered in a revamp. These are possibly the changes and developments that outline the journey of the Bengali film industry's identity from the Tollygunge industry into Tollywood.

However, Tollywood's financial condition during the mid-2000s was still dominated by an extremely high rate of interest for film financiers and production houses. This was tackled through the vertical revenue earning model consisting of theatre release, satellite rights, home video rights, music rights and overseas rights. This model was most successfully practised and adopted by SVF.

In 2010, the number of films released increased from 45 to 80, following which media reportage launched into a series of articles on the transitions and developments in Tollywood. Press writings celebrated the colossal success of Raj Chakraborty's *Chirodini Tumi Je Amar* (*You're Mine Eternally*) in 2007, and reported the film's revenue returns to be 15 times the budget (Rs 80 lakhs) of the film. Chakraborty's other films like *Challenge*, 2008 and *Prem Amar* (*My Love*), 2009, too, were reported to have earned unprecedented box-office returns.[62] Celebratory writings like these continued to appear in the English and Bengali press, altering the 'crisis narrative' discourse of Bengali cinema to a resurgence narrative of becoming a formal and organised, profit-earning industry, Tollywood. Much of these developments and formalisation of the Bengali film industry could be accredited to the production house, SVF. SVF's emergence into this scenario was crucial in introducing corporatised strategies into the film industry concomitant to their rising status as the most powerful and prolific production house in Tollywood. Within this context of the resurgence of Tollywood and SVF's increasing dominance over the industry, we critically investigate these changes and their repercussions in the following chapter.

Notes and References

1. Sharmistha Gooptu, 'Changing Contexts, New Texts', in Nalin Mehta, ed., *Television in India: Satellite, Politics and Cultural Change* (New York: Routledge, 2008).

2. '*Bangla Chayachhobir Aro Ekta Mondo Bochor Paar Holo. Taholeo Unnishhochurashi ke Sheybhabe Mondo Bochor Bola Jay Na Bodhoy*' ('Another Bad Year of Bengali Cinema has Passed. Even Then, Nineteen Eighty-Four Cannot be Called a Bay Year Perhaps'), *Anandabazar Patrika*, 8 January 1985.
3. See Moinak Biswas, 'The Couple and Their Spaces: *Harono Sur* as Melodrama Now', in Ravi S. Vasudevan, ed., *Making Meaning in Indian Cinema* (New Delhi: Oxford University Press, 2000), p. 122, for the broader genre of the 1950s and 1960s popular melodrama.

   > The era of "Uttam-Suchitra", the mid 1950s through the '60s, is commonly designated as the "golden period" of Bengali cinema, and has been written and reminisced about pervasively. During these years Bengali directors were able to produce a genre of film melodrama that became integral to a Bengali sense of self. Identification was rooted in the figures of an idealized female and an idealistic and ethical male, embodied respectively by Suchitra Sen and Uttam Kumar, and their romantic love became the stuff of intense emotional identification among Bengalis of the post-independence generation. The same prototypes were common in films of that era which did not actually feature Uttam Kumar and Suchitra Sen together, and it has been suggested that "Uttam-Suchitra ... be used as a sign".

   Sharmistha Gooptu, 'Bengal and a "National" Cinema: New Theatres Ltd', in Gooptu, ed., *Bengali Cinema: 'An Other Nation'* (New Delhi: Roli Books, 2010), pp. 71–72.
4. Ansu Sur, ed., Bengali Film Directory, Nandan, Kolkata, West Bengal Film Centre, pp. 185–89.
5. Parivartan News Bureau, '*Sab Hall e Bangla Chhobir Baddhhotamulok Prodorshon Shattiee ki Shambhab*?' ('Is It Possible to Screen Bengali Films Mandatorily in All Halls?'), *Parivartan* 19, 1981, pp. 41–44.
6. Ibid., 41.
7. Bhaskar Chowdhury, '*Uttam Kumar er Obhab Tallyganj Para Ekhono Bisesh Ter Paini*' ('Tollygunge Has Not as Yet Woken Up to the Loss of Uttam Kumar', *Parivartan*, 15 July 1981, p. 43.
8. Ibid.
9. See Ira Bhaskar, 'The Indian New Wave', in Moti Gokulsingh and Wimal Dissanayake, ed., *Handbook of Indian Cinemas* (London: Routledge, 2013).
10. Mira Reym Binford, 'The Two Cinemas of India', in John D. H. Downing, ed., *Film and Politics in the Third World* (New York: Praeger, 1987).
11. Ibid.
12. Aruna Vasudev. *The New Indian Cinema* (New Delhi: Macmillan, 1986).
13. In an essay titled, '*Sattar Dashaker Bangla Chhabi*' ('The Bengali Films of the Nineteen Seventies'), Someshwar Bhoumik observed the deterioration of Bengali cinema in the late-1970s with films like *Amanush* (*Inhuman*),

Ananda Ashram (*Abode of Joy*) or *Baba Taraknath* (*The Lord Shiva*), arguing that these films were devoid of the 'clean entertainment value' that was a characteristic of Bengali films in the 1950s and the 1960s. Somen Ghosh has tried to analyse this 'crisis'-ridden period of Bengali cinema, when, he observes 'totally unrealistic, lower standard film made its silver jubilee at the box office, it expressed our shameless nature in our cultural characterlessness'; Someshwar Bhowmik, 'Sattar Dashaker Bangla Chhabi', in Anil Acharya, ed., *Sattar Dashak* (*The Decade of Seventies*) (Kolkata: Anushtup Publication, 1981), p. 135 (our translation). See also Someshwar Bhowmik, *Bharatiya Chalchchitra: Ekti Arthanaitik Pratibedan* (*Indian Cinema: An Economic Report*) (Calcutta: Papyrus, 1996).

14. Partha Chatterjee, '*Bangla Cinema Shonkot o Shomadhan: Chhobi Dekhte Kothay Jabo*?' ('The Problem and Resolution of Bengali Cinema: Where do We Go to Watch Films?'), *Anandalok*, 22 December 1979, pp. 23–26.
15. Chowdhury, '*Uttam Kumar er Obhab*', p. 43.
16. In their writings on 1950s and 1960s mainstream Bengali cinema, authors like Rajat Roy and Kiranmoy Raha, and film journalists like Bipra Das, Ranjan Bandyopadhyay, etc., point out a significant difference between Bengali cinema and other regional cinemas of that period. According to them, unlike other mainstream cinemas, in Bengali mainstream cinematic practice (films featuring the hit pair Uttam–Suchitra), the mythological narrative and 'vulgar' song and dance took a backseat. This feature, according to them, made this cinema more mature and 'distinct', as compared to the other cinemas of that period. See also Spandan Bhattacharya, 'The Post Liberalization Bengali "Parallel" Cinema: Bhadralok Nostalgia, the Politics of Past-ness, and the Discourse of "Difference"', Unpublished MPhil Dissertation, The School of Arts and Aesthetics, Cinema Studies, Jawaharlal Nehru University, New Delhi, 2011.
17. Parivartan News Bureau, '*Sab Hall e Bangla Chhobir Baddhhotamulok Prodorshon*, p. 41.
18. Ibid., p. 41, 44.
19. Ibid., 43.
20. Ibid., 42, 43.
21. Ibid., 44.
22. Ibid.
23. Ibid.
24. Ibid., 43.
25. Ibid., 43, 44.
26. Tapas Pal, '*Sukhen Da Nijeyiee Ghoranaa*' ('Sukhen Da Himself is a School'), *Anandalok*, 12 April 2004, pp. 16, 17.
27. Dipankar Chakraborty, '*Bangla Chhabir Ticket o Blackey Bikri Hocchhe*' ('Bengali Movie Tickets are also being Sold in Black'), *Anandabazar Patrika*, 1985, p. 1.

28. Ibid.
29. In a special feature story titled, '*Dorshokdhannya Shera 30 Bangla Cinemar*' ('30 Great Bengali Films of Audience Choice'), *Anandalok*, 27 June 2003, a public poll was published, which listed the 30 all-time hits from Bengali cinema, among which two films of Anjan Chowdhury had a place, namely *Shatru* and *Gurudakhina* .
30. Chakraborty, '*Bangla Chhabir Ticket*', pp. 1–2.
31. See Spandan Bhattacharya, 'The Action Heroes of Bengali Cinema: Industrial, Technological and Aesthetic Determinants of Popular Film Culture, 1980s–1990s', *South Asian History and Culture*, vol. 8, no. 2 (2017), pp. 205–30.
32. Ibid.
33. Kiranmoy Raha, *Bangla Chalachchitra Kathakata o Anyanya Prabandho* (*Tales of Bengali Cinema and Other Essays*) (Calcutta: Ratna Publication, 2004). See also Rajat Roy, *Banglar Chalachitra Sanskriti* (*Bengali Film Culture*) (Calcutta: Sristi Publication, 2001),
34. The special series, *Anandalok Prothom Pratibedan—Bangla Chhobi: Sankat Keno*? (*Film Magazine Anandalok's Special Series—Bengali Films: Why this Crisis?*), *Anandalok*, 18 January 1995, 28 January 1995, continued until the next four editions, interviewing several directors, actors and writers, and asking them about the crisis in Bengali cinema and the decline of audiences of Bengali cinema. Bengali cinema, in its present state and form in every way, is in a terrible state of affairs, whereas once upon a time, this very Bengali cinema and industry was a pride of Bengal and the rest of the nation. But today, its existence and identity is on the verge of decline and disappearance, and it is of great fear and shame. *Anandalok* tries to ask several talents from the industry, including the likes of Madhabi Mukherjee, Soumitra Chaterjee, Goutam Ghose, Buddhadeb Dasgupta, Haradhan Bandopadhyay, Anjan Chowdhury, Sabitri Chattopadhyay and Supriya Devi, that what is it that ails the industry? What are the reasons? What could be the possible remedies?
35. Somen Ghosh, *Bangla Cinemar Paalabadal* (*The Changing Phases of Bengali Cinema*) (Calcutta: Shyamali Prakashani, 1990).
36. See Anugyan Nag and Spandan Bhattacharya, 'The Politics around "B-Grade" Cinema in Bengal: Re-viewing Popular Bengali Film Culture in the 1980s–1990s"', *Acta Orientalia Vilnensia*, vol. 12, no. 2 (2011), pp. 13–30.
37. *Anandalok* carried articles in the mid-1990s about how Tollygunge was now a hub of television production and not so much an industry that focused on making films. '*Tollugunge Ekhon TV Gunje*' ('Tollygunge is Now a TV Gunje'), *Anandolok*, 28 January 1995, p. 38. See also Kamalendu Sarkar, '*Chhoto Pordaye Bartamaan e Tollywood Tarokader Bheer*' ('The Small Screen is Crowded by Stars from Tollywood'), *Anandalok*, 20 September 1997, pp. 61–65, which expressed the opinion that the stars of Tollywood

were busier doing TV serials, that the studios of Tollygunge were all booked for TV serial shootings and daily soap operas, and moreover, it questioned the decline in the tradition of Bengali cinema and expressed concerns about its future.

38. *Anandalok Prothom Pratibedan—Bangla Chhobi: Sankat Keno*?
39. Gopa Sengupta, Amit Bikram Dutta and Reshmi Banerjee, '*Bishesh Protibedan—Alochonar Ashor Bangla Chobi: Sankat Keno*?' ('A Special Report—Discussion on Bengali Cinema: Why this Crisis?'), *Anandalok*, 14 February 1995, pp. 35–37.
40. Authors' interview with Haranath Chakraborty, 17 October 2010, Kolkata.
41. Roopa Bhattacharya, '*Bangla Chhobir Jonnya Oxygen Noy, Chai Alookaabli*' ('Bengali Cinema Doesn't Need Oxygen, it Needs a Spicey Mix'), *Anandalok*, 8 June 2001, pp. 30–32.
42. Ibid.
43. Ibid.
44. Ibid.
45. Ibid.
46. Kamalendu Sarkar, '*Anjan Chowdhuryr Shibir Chhere Haranath Chakraborty Ekhon Tollygunjer Trata. Bannijjyo Shofolei Porichalokeniye Likhechen*', ('Haranath Chakraborty has Left the Camp of Anjan Chowdhury and is the Saviour of Tollygunge: A Writing on the Commercial Success of the Director'), *Anandalok*, 14 May 2003, p. 49.
47. Ibid.
48. Ibid.
49. Balmiki Chattopadhyay, '*Shasurbari Zindabaad, Tar Poryei Pratibad Chhobi Hiter Chabikathi*' ('Shasurbari Zindabaad: Just After that the Key to the Film Pratibad Becoming a Hit'), *Anandalok*, 8 June 2001, pp. 59–61.
50. Sarkar, '*Anjan Chowdhuryr Shibir*', p. 49.
51. Chattopadhyay, '*Shasurbari Zindabaad, Tar Poryei Pratibad*'.
52. Rupak Saha, '*Swapan Keno Shofol*?' ('Why is Swapan Successful?'), *Anandalok*, 30 March 2003, pp. 30, 31.
53. Ibid.
54. Author's interview with Swapan Saha, 15 October 2011, Technicial Studios, Kolkata.
55. See Ruman Ganguly and Roshni Mukherjee, 'Tollywood has Room for All', *Calcutta Times*, 3 July 2011.
56. Nag and Bhattacharya, 'The Politics around "B-Grade" Cinema in Bengal.
57. Anugyan Nag, 'Locating Rituparno Ghosh in Tollywood', S. Dutta, K. Bakshi and R. K. Dasgupta, ed., *Rituparno Ghosh: Cinema, Gender and Art* (New York: Routledge, 2015).
58. Subhra Konar and Debasis Sircar, 'EIMPA Plans Tollywood Survival Kit', *The Times of India*, 3 January 2003.
59. Yash Chopra, in-charge of the entertainment wing of cinema attached to the FICCI, led a delegation on its behalf to the then West Bengal Chief

Minister, Buddhadev Bhattacharjee, for the revival of the bengali film industry. This proposal included the construction of a chain of multiplexes, state-of-the-art entertainment plazas, shopping malls and food rendezvous, which would assure 'a sustainable revenue generation scheme' for the overall entertainment industry in the state; Pradip Biswas, 'Yash Chopra for Revival of the Bengali Film Industry', *Screen*, 6 December 2002. Vijay Mallya's United Spirits Ltd (the largest IMFL firm in India) expressed interest in promoting Bengali films through cobranding its highest-selling whisky brand, Bagpiper, beginning his Tollywood venture with Rituparna Sengupta's debut production, *Patadar Kirti;* Udit Prasanna Mukherjee, 'Vijay Mallya's Brand to Promote Tollywood', *Times City*, *The Times of India*, 10 November 2009.

60. See Bureau Report, '*Poran Jai*.... A Copy, Says Court', *The Telegraph*, 11 August 2009.
61. Ibid.
62. See Ganguly and Mukherjee, 'Tollywood has Room for All'.

2

The Consolidation of Tollywood and the Logic of Corporatisation

A Case Study of Shree Venkatesh Films (SVF)

In 1991, the Indian government, under the then Prime Minister P. V. Narasimha Rao brought in economic liberalisation, and the Bombay film industry began to change its *modus operandi*. A few years later, in 1998, this was followed by the National Democratic Alliance (NDA) government, bestowing 'industry' status to Bollywood.[1] As a result, Bollywood went through several internal changes that had a lasting impact on the content, visual aesthetics, and the overall mechanisms of the industry.[2] It took more than a decade post-1998 for the Bengali film industry to imbibe some of these changes.

This chapter will question, analyse and explore the success of Shree Venkatesh Films (SVF) to elaborate upon the corporatised structuring it brought about, which significantly transformed the landscape of the Bengali film industry. SVF adopted the vertical integration model of business, which to a large extent strengthened their monopoly over the production-distribution-exhibition machineries. In order to demonstrate the SVF phenomenon, we have primarily relied on media reportage, press discourse, and our discussions and conversations with SVF proprietors and office bearers. Throughout this chapter, the statistics and monetary figures mentioned are based on press and publicity reports.

Corporatising Tollygunge: The SVF Phenomenon in Tollywood

The entry of SVF into Tollygunge was significant for reasons that have already been discussed in the previous chapter. A new class of audience had emerged after liberalisation, and the Bengali film industry was struggling to find acceptance among this upwardly mobile section of the audience. Films made by film-makers like Swapan Saha, as discussed in the previous chapter, began to lose their credence by the early-2000s. There were paradigmatic shifts in the taste discourse and the new film market configurations reshaping the post-2000 Bengali film scenario. Pivotal to this transition was SVF and their interventions.

SVF was founded by two young entrepreneurs, Shrikant Mohta and Mahendra Soni, in 1995. The duo had begun their careers together with film distribution in the early 1990s. They were primarily distributing mainstream Hindi films and a few from Hollywood. The very first film, *Bhai Amar Bhai*, produced by SVF in 1996, was a failure.[3] They produced three more films in subsequent years: *Sakhi Tumi Kar* (*Whose Beloved Are You*) in 1996, and *Mayar Bandhan* (*Emotional Ties*) in 1997, directed by Swapan Saha, and *Tumi Ele Tai* (*Because You Arrived*), by Prabhat Roy, in 1999. SVF's first phase of film production was unsuccessful and perhaps a learning experience for their future endeavours.

SVF then attempted their first film with Tapan Sinha, an icon of Bengali cinema and a nationally recognised film-maker. The film was *Ajab Gayer Ajab Kotha* (*The Strange Tale of a Strange Village*) in 1998. Although the film was critically acclaimed, it fared adversely at the box office. SVF was desperately looking for a blockbuster, which eventually Haranath Chakraborty provided with *Shasurbari Zindabaad* (2000).

In our discussion with Shrikant Mohta, he shared the humble amount of money SVF spent on publicity for *Shasurbari Zindabaad*, which pushed the film to become a box-office hit, nevertheless facing negative criticism from the media. There was no looking back for SVF after the success of *Shasurbari Zindabaad*. All films produced after *Shasurbari Zindabaad* were blockbusters—*Dada Thakur* (*Brother Lord*, 2001), *Pratibad* (*The Protest*, 2001), *Saathi* (*Companion*, 2002), directed by Haranath Chakraborty, and *Champion*, directed by Ravi Kinnagi in 2003. By 2005, most films that were coming out of the SVF stable were grossers, earning a minimum profit of 25–40 per cent on an average, over the total budget of these films. This sudden financial dynamism in the film and entertainment industry led to the asking of questions as to what made these films so successful, what formula they were using, and who their audience was (see Figure 2.1).

The Multiplex Invasion and SVF

In 2003, Calcutta built its first multiplex cinema in the heart of the city, the Inox Forum Mall at Elgin Road. Multiplex theatres helped to provide space for films that were different and catered to a niche audience.[4] Shrikant Mohta, foreseeing the merits of such developments, ventured into investing higher amounts for unconventional films. The year 2003 was a turning point in the journey of SVF, with two films directed by Rituparno Ghosh, *Chokher Bali* and *Raincoat*. Both the films had Aishwariya Rai as the female lead and bagged the National Awards. *Chokher Bali* was perhaps the first film in Tollywood to have a budget that was over a crore. *Chokher Bali*'s release at the Inox Forum Multiplex generated an overwhelming interest among the people for both the film and the experience of a plush theatre. It is imperative to mention here that both the films fared moderately at

Figure 2.1: YouTube Screen Grab of *Sathi*

Source: SVF.

the box office but possibly uplifted the status of SVF within the film industry. *Chokher Bali* was also released in the UK and the US with 30 prints, in addition to being screened at the Locarno and Toronto International Film Festivals, among others.[5]

The Conflicting Economics of Organisations and Institutional Initiatives

In 2002, the Federation of Indian Chambers of Commerce (FICCI) initiated the promotion of Bengali films in the national and international markets. The eighth Kolkata International Film Festival in 2003 witnessed an impressive turnout and a film market to attract national and international buyers of Bengali cinema, although this initiative went completely unattended. FICCI's proposal to build a state-of-the-art film city in Kolkata, too, was dismissed by the state government for the lack of adequate funds and infrastructure. EIMPA's then president Arijit Dutta identified certain key issues that needed immediate amendments, the important ones being reforming archaic film laws, addressing cable and video piracy, adequate subsidy for Bengali films, and the revamping of film studio infrastructures in Kolkata.[6]

Pritam Jalan, a leading producer and distributor in Tollywood, mentioned, 'We need corporatization and multiplexes to promote Bengali films.'[7] On the other hand, NFDC (National Film Development Corporation) set up *Dhwani* a sound-video-film studio.[8] Responding to a request from the then West Bengal Chief Minister, Buddhadev Bhattacharjee, the Sahara India group decided to set up a 400-acre film city on the eastern fringes of the metropolis in order to rejuvenate the moribund Bengali film industry and service film-makers from elsewhere in the country and abroad. The Sahara India project had already acquired 50 acres of land from the state government.[9]

Since the condition of the single-screen theatres was a major concern for both distributors and exhibitionists, Priya cinema was one of the first single-screen theatres to bring in change by modifying its interiors and making it more viewer-friendly. Priya was followed by Minar, Bijoli and Chobighar, which introduced air-conditioning, comfortable seating, and an improved sound system. Urban centres demanded quality Bengali films, and the non-resident Indian (NRI) Bengali audience was perhaps rekindling their interest in Bengali cinema after witnessing *Chokher Bali.*

Renowned production and distribution companies of the Bengali film industry like R. D. Bansal Films, Chhayabani Films, Aurora Film Corporation, Daga Films, Damani Films and others started becoming redundant due to the lack of sufficient profits and business. Even the financial incentives by the state government were brought to a halt for established directors like Buddhadev Dasgupta.[10] Directors like Sandip Ray and Goutam Ghose managed to strike a balance in terms of revenue and critical appreciation with *Bombaiyer Bombete* (*The Smugglers of Bombay*) (produced by ETV, Hyderabad) and *Abar Aranye* (*Again in the Forest*) in 2003 by reaching out to the global business market, through festivals and overseas releases.[11] Amidst such a scenario, SVF instigated a business model that would bridge the gaps between popular mainstream cinema and quality cinema of the likes of Rituparno Ghosh.

Bandhan, *Juddha* and *Subho Drishti*: Big Budgets, New Faces and the Box Office

With *Bandhan* (*Ties*) by Ravi Kinnagi in 2004, SVF targeted a wider audience base by raising the production budget of the film and launching the new star pair, Jeet and Koel Mullick, daughter of veteran actor Ranjit Mullick.

What possibly enthralled the audiences and gave them a freshness quotient were the Singapore locales, and song sequences shot in Hyderabad's Ramoji Film City and across the mountainous hillscapes of North Bengal.[12] *Bandhan* was one of the highest-grossing films of 2004.[13]

SVF set the promotion and the publicity machinery of *Juddha* by Ravi Kinnagi, in 2005, in motion much before its release.[14] This film's budget was raised up to Rs 2 crores, including print and publicity. It became the first commercial and popular film in Tollywood to have such a high budget. *Chokher Bali*, until then, was the only film by SVF that had crossed the Rs 1 crore budget in Tollywood. In an article titled, 'Big Clash Means Big Cash', in *The Telegraph* on 29 August 2005, Reshmi Sengupta details *Juddha*'s success, by analysing how 'it has taken the might of Mithun-Jeet, the sizzle of an item number and a sliver of style to deliver Tollywood's first big hit of the year'.[15]

Juddha was released at Mitra, Bharati and Prachi in Kolkata. In the first week, it ran to 90 per cent occupancy at Mitra, while Prachi and Bharati recorded 100 per cent collections. The film drew a full house for the first two weeks of its release and recorded an unprecedented initial revenue of Rs 1.2 crores in the first week itself. *Juddha* grossed more than Rs 2.5 crores in a span of four weeks. Other factors also contributed to its success. It was simultaneously released with 41 prints across the state. Earlier, Bengali films were released with a maximum of 25–30 prints. At the time of its release, the ticket rates had also been increased by more than 50 per cent, which added to the profits. For instance, the new rates at Bharati cinema hall were Rs 20 for rear seats and Rs 25 for balcony. As per Dipen Majumdar, owner of Mitra cinema, *Juddha* was the highest grosser of the past 3–4 years.

Juddha had an unprecedented box-office success, which was SVF's second attempt at an action film. With a formulaic and predictable plot of a super-cop (Mithun Chakraborty) fixing a local rowdy (Jeet) only to bond over friendship, Mithun's wife (Debashree Roy) is killed by a corrupt MLA, settling an old feud. The film also had a pacy remixed Bengali folk song, *Saadher Lau* (*Delicious Gourd*) performed by Gladrags supermodel contestant Konkona Bakshi, in an exiguous attire. *Juddha* was a typical entertainer for the masses.[16]

Family-oriented Bengali films, once the hallmark of middle-class audiences, had become a rare phenomenon ever since Haranath Chakraborty's action genre films became recurrent. In order to shift its focus back to family-oriented films, SVF co-partnered with Sooraj R. Barjatiya's Rajshri Productions, Bombay, to produce Prabhat Roy's family melodrama, *Subho Dristi* (*Auspicious Sight of Love*), in 2005. This film was a loose remake of the 1994 Rajshri blockbuster, *Hum Aapke Hai Kaun* (*Who Am I To You?*). Starring Jeet, Koel Mullick and Parambrata Chatterjee, the film explores the story of two families bonding together during a wedding. The storyline was similar to its Hindi counterpart, except for the twists and turns surrounding a few tragic events in the narrative.[17]

The narrative develops a twist after the interval. The husband is diagnosed with terminal cancer and the wife decides to fight what looks like an imminent death of her newly married husband. The story caters to two central moods within the film. The first half is replete with frothy, song-and-dance, marriage-preparation routines; the second half is about the two families plunged into tragedy. Taking a leaf from the mythical story of Savitri and Satyavan, the wife vows to bring her dying husband back to life through her divine prayers and fasting. She evokes the feudal value of subservience, of an ideal *pativrata* (dutiful) Savitri, who vows to fast unto death until her husband is cured completely.

For publicity and promotion, SVF came up with a unique idea, a red card unfolded in theatrical and television promos, inviting everybody to a wedding on 4 November 2005. It also gave a sneak peek into the nuptials, where the glowing faces of the bride and the groom were visible, who stood happily dressed in the best of attire. The jewellery used in the film was sponsored by Anjali Jewellers, while Sarbari Dutta and Sudeshna Roy did flashy and colourful costumes. It was for the first time that big names from the fashion and jewellery industry were getting linked to a mainstream commercial film.

As weddings have always fascinated Indian viewers and more so, Bengalis, the film reiterates this very same *Bangaliyaana* (Bengaliness). A love story against the backdrop of marriage, *Subho Dristi* was a feel-good Bengali film along the lines of big Bollywood hits like *Dilwale Dulhaniya Le Jayenge* (*The Big-Hearted Shall Take the Bride*) in 1995 and *Kuchh Kuchh Hota Hai* (*Something Happens*) in 1998. The sets were lavish, as they always are in Rajshri films, and were reminiscent of the interiors of the ongoing popular Hindi soap operas on Indian television. According to Shrikant Mohta, one of the most important factors that contributed to the film's look and success was its production design by Indranil Ghosh. The production design of the film alone had a budget of Rs 20 lakhs, which was a very high amount for a Bengali film. Lavish sets reflected the opulance and grandeur of a *zamindar* household.[18] *Subho Dristi* was released during the annual Kolkata International Film Festival, and yet managed to witness substantial footfall at the cinema halls in Kolkata.[19]

Mithun Chakraborty: Defying Plots, Assuring Hits

In 2006, SVF produced Haranath Chakraborty's film, *Refugee*, starring Prosenjit Chatterjee and South Indian actress Rambha. The film flopped and got bad press by critics in the print media. This was followed by another unsuccessful venture, *Kranti* (*The Revolution*) directed by Ringo, in 2006, although it starred popular actors like Jeet and Swastika Mukherjee. Following these failures, SVF went back to collaborating with film-maker Swapan Saha to make *MLA Fatakesto* in 2006, starring Mithun Chakraborty, Debasree Roy and Koel Mullick. The film went on to become very successful and one of the highest grossers (approximately Rs 4 crores) of all time. *MLA Fatakesto* has somewhat gained an iconic status for its overt rhetorical dialogues like 'I don't read the news, I make news', which were written by N. K. Salil.

The film takes off from the Anil Kapoor starrer 2001 film, *Nayak* (*Hero*). Mithun Chakraborty takes over the office of a Legislative Assembly member for seven days; each day is ear-marked for exposing corruption and rescuing the collapse in different sectors of public service; one day is marked for the medical services, another day for the legal machinery, and so on. The other dialogue in the film, *maarbo ekhaane, lash podbey shashaane* (I'll bash you here and the body will fall in the crematorium there) has become part of Bengali slang.

N. K. Salil mentioned in an interview that he would deliberately spice up the film's dialogues whenever he wrote for Mithun Chakraborty. The reason he gave for the choice of such hyperbolic dialogues for Mithun's films was because most of the time he played a messiah figure fighting against injustice, for the poor and downtrodden people.[20] The film was released when the 2006 State Legislative Assembly elections were round the corner. Posters of the film with larger-than-life size images of Mithun were generously splashed across the walls of Bengal.

MLA Fatakesto was a film about a goon-turned-politician who was also the savior of the poor and underprivileged sections of the society, and who goes on to teach a lesson to corrupt police officers, politicians and bureaucrats. Mithun's character in the film has a mentor, a Chief Minister, who showed striking physical similarity to the then

Chief Minister of West Bengal. Released with an unprecedented 61 prints across Bengal, *MLA Fatakesto* out-did *Juddha*, which was the highest grosser of 2005.[21] The hype generated by the film had much to do with its release timing and the Election Commission's directive that wiped off pre-poll graffiti from the walls. The poster publicity was accordingly designed. It helped generate a lot of curiosity and media interest around the film. At the end of the fourth week of its release, the film had touched the mark of Rs 2.5 crores against *Juddha*'s Rs 1.75 crores. Shrikant Mohta remarked, 'There was no love story in the film, yet people liked it.'

The film's lead star, Mithun Chakraborty, however, did not accord all the credit to the political angle in the film's plot for its resounding success. He attributed it to the punchy dialogues, sleeker camera work and crisp editing along with some entertaining song-and-dance sequences, the quintessential elements for a successful mainstream film.[22] Mithun Chakraborty had emerged as one of the most bankable stars in Tollywood after his mega hit with *MLA Fatakesto. Minister Fatakesto* had a bigger budget, slicker sets, smart fight sequences, and a shocking makeover of Mithun, who rapped an item number on a psychedelic set. In fact, the Mithun Chakaborty brand of cinema was possibly a virtual industry unto itself that fitted neatly into the larger Tollywood workshop that was famous for producing a more sober, and urban theme-driven *Anuranan* (*Resonance*) by Aniruddha Roy Chowdhury, in 2006, at one end, a sloppy and sentimental melodrama like *Aloye Phera* (*From Darkness to Light*) by Subhash Sen, in 2007 in the middle, and films starring Prosenjit and Jeet, at the other end. In *Minister Fatakesto*, there was little progression in the storyline from its prequel. However, the film had a good opening in the first week, but gradually, the revenues began to fall and after its run for more than two weeks, the film somehow managed to recover Rs 2 crores. It was evident that Tollywood probably needed more time to accept sequels to such films, corroborated Mahendra Soni of SVF. The film was released with 50 prints, and had a budget of Rs 2.5 crores.[23] N. K. Salil, who had written the script and dialogue for both films, commented that the character of Fatakesto failed to meet the audience's expectations in the sequel, and said: '… May be people expected something like Lage Raho Munna Bhai…. Minister begins, where MLA ends.'[24]

I Love You: The Entry of New Faces into Tollywood

The following year, in 2007, SVF introduced two new faces to Tollywood—Dev and Payel—in Ravi Kinnagi's film, *I Love You.* The film was inspired by the 2005 Telugu film, Prabhu Deva starrer *Nuvvostanante Nenoddantana* (*If You Wish to Come, Will I Refuse?*). It was a typical romantic love story bearing a striking resemblance with Hindi films like the 1989 film, *Maine Pyar Kiya* (*I Loved*), and the 1998 film, *Pyar Kiya to Darna Kya* (*What's to Fear if You Have Loved?*), among others.

The story of *I Love You* revolves around a farmer called Indra (Tapas Pal) and his younger sister Pooja (Payel). Being an elder brother, Indra is always protective of his sister and pampers her like a daughter. One day, Shantanu (Rajatava Dutta), who is a rich businessman and Indra's childhood friend, invites Pooja to his house for his daughter's wedding. At the wedding, she befriends Shantanu's London-returned son, Rahul (Dev). Rahul's father is strictly against his son marrying a village girl. However, Rahul manages to win over his father's heart. Since Indra is also suspicious of Rahul's love for his sister, he makes him go through several daunting tasks to test his unflinching loyalty towards his beloved.

Dev and Payel were projected and marketed as the new poster boy and girl of Tollywood.[25] Despite being repetitive and formulaic in its plot and narrative, *I Love You* became successful at the box-office. Media reviews acknowledged the appeal of the star couple and the music of the film.[26]

Sangeet Bangla: The Promotional Window of SVF

To ensure pre-release publicity and promotion for the films SVF produced and to mark their presence in the television domain, SVF launched the first 24-hour national Bangla film music channel, *Sangeet Bangla*, in partnership with Media Worldwide. *Sangeet Bangla* provided a unique platform to SVF to publicise its productions worldwide.[27] One of the most popular programmes of the channel was the show called *Tollywood Reporter. Sangeet Bangla* offered programmes and news stories related to SVF-produced film music, behind the shooting floors stories, star and celebrity chat shows and song catalogue shows.

The Entry of Digital Projection in West Bengal

In 2008, SVF ventured into a new area in distribution by pioneering the digital projection of Bengali films in exhibition houses. This initiative introduced a digital cinematic experience for audiences in West Bengal for the first time on a larger scale, catering to Category B and Category C towns as well. Digital cinema marks a revolutionary change in the way movies were distributed, delivered and projected in cinema halls, with high quality, high definition, and powerful and flexible digital projection systems. Digital prints can be distributed via physical media, such as external hard drives and/or satellite, instead of conventional 35 mm film reels. With the mission of digitising all the theatres in Eastern India, Qube Digital had successfully installed digital projection of films into theatres. This not only improved the quality of film projection, but also gave a lease of a fresh life to the almost dead, defunct and discarded cinema halls in Bengal. By 2011, Qube Digital had achieved 'digitisation' of over 200 cinema halls across West Bengal, making it one of the fastest rollouts of digital cinema anywhere in India. The set-up provided high quality video projection and saving exhibitor celluloid prints costing around Rs 50,000 per print.[28] Vishnu Mohta of SVF added, 'Technology involves a high-end computer server and a digital projector linked to a high-speed satellite Internet network. The set-up provides high quality video projection.'[29] SVF released *Love* and *Chirodini Tumi Je Aamar* in the Qube mode. Shrikant Mohta believed, 'In terms of picture quality and sound, these films could now be at par with Bollywood.'[30]

Competition Setting in Tollywood

With SVF's constant efforts to boost the standard of Bengali cinema along with its revenues, other independent producers woke up to the phenomenal success of films starring Mithun. Many other directors and producers hiked their budget to live up to the standards of SVF films in terms of lavish mounting, starcast, music and releases. *Tulkalam* was produced by Pijush Saha, an independent producer, on an estimated budget of Rs 3 crores. Director Anup Sengupta directed *Mahaguru* (*The Supreme Master*), starring Mithun, jointly produced by Sengupta, Nimai Panja and Piya Sengupta on a big budget of

Rs 1.25 crores, possibly to compete with SVF's high budget standards. *Satyameva Jayate* (*Truth shall Win*) by Milan Bhowmik in 2008, produced by Ashok Kumar Bed and Soma Bhowmik, was made on an estimated budget of Rs 1 crore plus. Swapan Saha also managed to raise the budget of his Mithun starrer *Tiger* in 2006 to Rs 1 crore and above from independent producer Nishpal Singh. Debutant director Raja Mukherjee's 2007 film, *Bidhaatar Lekha* (*Destiny*) starring Jeet and Hrishita Bhatt, was made with a budget of above Rs 2 crores, but the film managed to garner only about Rs 50 lakhs, competing with producer Pijush Saha's 2007 film, *Tulkalam*, starring Mithun. Ashok Dhanuka's 2007 film, *Bondhu* (*Friend*), starring Prosenjit and Swastika Mukherjee, with an approximate budget of Rs 2 crores, failed to generate profits at the box office.

Giving tough competition to SVF were Anjan Dutt's *The Bong Connection*, produced by Moxie Entertainment, made with a budget of less than Rs 1 crore, and Aniruddha Roy Chowdhury's *Anuranan*. *The Bong Connection* recovered its cost within three weeks of its release, possibly being appreciated by its targeted audience, the young urban Bengalis, who wanted to watch new-age Bengali cinema in multiplexes. *Anuranan* was also made with a budget of Rs 2 crores; shot partly in London, it managed to earn a profit of Rs 65 lakhs. The film was produced by DVD and VCD makers and distributors, Shemaroo. The Vice-President of Shemaroo explained that they had done extensive market research before venturing into Bengali cinema and had found out that *Anuranan* would do extremely well in the multiplexes and the overseas market.[31] By 2007, the Bengali film industry, Tollywood, began to adopt the inescapable strategies of marketing and raising production standards of the films. The release dates of films were slotted in a fashion that would ensure optimum return by having their minimum run at the box office.[32] The trend of producing big budget films that was started by SVF had become the norm for Tollywood.[33]

Regional Remakes

It was not unusual to see Bengali films made (mainly during mid-1980s to the mid-2000s) being inspired and copied consistently from successful popular Hindi and Telugu films. In 2008, SVF's second venture with Dev, the new hero whom they had launched in *I Love You*, was *Premer Kahini* (*The Story of Love*), directed by Ravi Kinnagi; the film seemed like a *Dilwale Dulhaniya Le Jayenge* revisited. The film's music went on to become a chartbuster, and was heavily promoted through SVF's television channel, *Sangeet Bangla*. Dev's career certainly got bolstered with this film. *Premer Kahini* was a love story between Akash and Barsha (Koel Mullick); the film tells the story of Akash's journey to win over Barsha's heart, as she is already engaged to Goutam (Jisshu Sengupta), and resisting their love is Barsha's tough colonel father (Ranjit Mullick). Akash tries to win over Barsha's strict father by going jogging with him everyday, unlike feeding pigeons as in *Dilwale Dulhaniya Le Jayenge*. Dev was perhaps able to do all the acts of the romantic hero, fitting ditto to the archetype of Sharukh Khan's lover-boy image, and impressed both Barsha and perhaps the audience, too. The film managed to include all the elements of a mainstream commercial entertainer from the SVF banner, that is, melodrama, fights and action, tragedy, comedy, and singing and dancing around picturesque locations. T. Naidu, the cinematographer, shot most of the film at Hyderabad and Shakleshpur in Karnataka, and Jeet Gangully's music for this became a popular album, with the title track topping the Tollywood charts.[34]

Revamping Tollywood and the Bollywood Connection

Despite the positive interventions that SVF films brought through their box-office success, the ground realities of the industry were complex. Tollywood had yet to unleash its full potential. The size of the prospective Bengali audience was estimated to be high, considering the fact that the Bengali-speaking population is the fifth-largest in the world. The Mckinsey Report, 2006, stated that the Bengali film industry, in terms of size, ranked very low within the framework of the $6-billion estimate revenue of the Indian film industry. Hindi films captured a 30 per cent market share, followed by releases in Tamil (20 per cent), Telugu (18 per cent), Malayalam (10 per cent) and Kannada (9 per cent), while other languages, including Bengali, made up the remaining 13 per cent.[35]

A special session was organised by the Bengal National Chamber of Commerce and Eastern India Motion Pictures Association to discuss the revival of Bengali cinema on 16 May 2007, where Goutam Ghose lamented that the Bengali film industry was far behind the growth rate, as compared to Bollywood and the Southern industries. The number of Bengali films released over a year was still limited to 38–40 around 2007–08, which could not generate more than Rs 50 crores in revenue a year, although the potential viewership was at least five times more than that of Telugu and Tamil viewers. The discussions of the session concluded that Bengali films needed to adopt state-of-the-art technology that would help reduce cost and improve quality. Out of the 550-odd cinema halls in West Bengal, only 52 theatres were properly digitised with upgraded projection facilities till 2007.[36] EIMPA Executive Committee member Shyamal Dutta mentioned that unless Bengali films were not shot and processed in Bengal, the film-making could never attain the status of an industry. Although Bengali films were released in West Bengal, they were mostly shot and processed (celluloid film) in the South. A professional and thorough plan with corporatised mechanisms was necessary to professionalise the Bengali film industry in order to enable it to pitch for better investments, bank loans and insurance safeguards.[37]

There were reports about Tollywood's attempt to adopt a radical new strategy to churn out Hindi films, or at least have actors and stars from Bollywood in Bengali films, perhaps to prevent the complete fading away of the industry. The number of films released per year was stagnant for almost 10 years, at 40 films per year. Joy B. Ganguly and Arindam Sil of Moxie Entertainment said that most contemporary Tollywood actors neither had any poster value nor any star value. Besides this, most actors sustained themselves with work in *jatra*. According to veteran film-maker Buddhadev Dasgupta, the situation of the Bengali film and television industry was dire in comparison to the Hindi film and television inudstry. He further added that the increasing pool of talents from the Hindi television industry carved a niche for themselves outside the recognition of the mainstream film industry. Dasgupta expressed concerns that good scripts in Bengal hardly got good actors to back them.[38]

Following the legacy of collaborations and partnerships with the Bombay film industry or Bollywood, assuring higher returns and revenues for the Bengali film industry, Tollywood had begun making Hindi and Bengali films with talent from Bollywood. The makeover in the industry was evident with the use of improved camera, sets, costumes, sound and choreography due to a considerable hike in budgets, possibly enabled to a large extent by the initiatives of SVF. Goutam Ghose's *Yatra* (*The Journey*), with a budget of Rs 4 crores, starring Rekha and Nana Patekar, produced by SPS Arts and Entertainment, and Moxie Entertainment's Hindi film, *BBD*, directed by Anjan Dutt, featuring Naseeruddin Shah, Kay Kay Menon, Jimmy Shergil, Sonali Kulkarni and Sandhya Mridul, accelerated the budget of overall Tollywood ventures: the average budget in 2007 was a minimum of Rs 1 crore, as compared to the earlier average of Rs 10–20 lakhs. Rituparno Ghosh's 2001 film, *Utsab* (*The Festival*) had a budget of Rs 20 lakhs, and Nabyendu Chatterjee's 1997 film, *Souda* (*The Deal*) was made with a modest budget of Rs 9 lakhs.[39] Locations in Bengali films transitioned to foreign locales like the US, London, Singapore, Bangkok and Dubai. Bengali films by this time began to looked trendier, sleeker, and encouraged audiences to return to the cinema theatres.

The Big Budget

An interesting case study titled, '4 More Such Tolly-Blockbusters Could be Made with Saawariya's Promo Budget'[40] in 2007 underlined the finances and budgets of the Tollywood film-making scenario. The average budget of a Tollywood film was still below the Rs 1 crore mark in 2007. For the smaller films or the less ambitious ones with newcomers, producers hesitated to shell out more than Rs 50–70 lakhs. For big fims, with a bigger star cast (for example, Mithun Chakraborty or Prosenjit Chatterjee), the budget would be raised to Rs 1.25–2 crores. Producer Nishpal Singh, whose Surinder Films made *Hero* and *Ghatak* with Jeet and Koel in 2006, emphasised the importance of stars in a film and how that determined the budget as a standard norm.[41]

About 20 per cent of the total budget was being allotted for artistes and 8–10 per cent for the director and technicians during the mid-2000s. The film shoot would use up 45–50 per cent of the budget, and the producer's budget came under serious strain if Tollywood decided to shoot at foreign locations. The more affordable and regular shooting locations were Hyderabad's Ramoji Film City, shopping malls in Kolkata, Aquatica (a water park in Kolkata), and the Satyajit Ray Film and Television Institute (SRFTI) campus in the suburbs of Kolkata. Around Rs 4–5 lakhs were set aside for post-production. Editing and dubbing accounted for Rs 1 lakh each, mixing Rs 40,000, background score Rs 75,000, optical work Rs 1 lakh, and special effects Rs 50,000. Often, the producer doubled as distributor, thus saving on distribution costs. Screening rates depended on the theatre. If the rent was Rs 1.4 lakhs a month for the Minar-Bijoli-Chobighar chain and Rs 1.7 lakhs a month for Prachi-Darpana-Bharati, it was Rs 4 lakhs per month at Priya.

Most producers worked on a fixed budget for the minimum visibility required, which was about 10 per cent of the total cost. Thus, the publicity cost could range from Rs 5–7 lakhs to Rs 20–40 lakhs for big-banner Tollywood films, which would however be miniscule, as compared to Bollywood. But the bigger the name, the smaller would be the publicity budget. Mahendra Soni of SVF mentioned that in case of a Mithun Chakraborty film like *Minister Fatakesto* (made with a budget of Rs 2.5 crores) they only had to spend Rs 25 lakhs for publicity. However, when SVF launched new faces in *I love You*, they spent Rs 40 lakhs out of the film's Rs 2 crore budget for the film's promotion and publicity. Soni believed that for romantic films, the music release was a big event, but for action films, it was primarily radio and TV promotions.[42]

The promotions of *The Bong Connection*, Anjan Dutt's Rs 2.25 crore box-office hit, were marked by out-of-the-box publicity planning. Soumya Ganguly of Moxie Entertainment expressed the fact that during the post-production of *The Bong Connection*, it was the music of the film that set the mood for the publicity, thereby resulting in innovative promotional strategies like live concerts at Barista and Cafe Coffee Day (CCD) outlets alongside holding of premieres in cities like New Delhi and Mumbai.[43] The channels of communication were also beginning to grow beyond the conventional mix of television-radio-billboard-poster-print advertisements. Dev and Payel of *I Love You*, for instance, hit suburban roads to interact closely with the target audience of their film. *The Bong Connection* road shows remained popular in college and university campuses in West Bengal, even after its release.

Rethinking Narratives: Recalibrating Content in Tollywood

Monaik Biswas, in his essay, 'Changing Scenes', focuses on a few films made during 2005–07 that drew from the 'spectacle' and 'sensation' of certain political street events that had implications directly and indirectly on popular public imagination, which possibly inspired directors like Swapan Saha, Haranath Chakraborty and Raj Chakraborty to make films that represented these political expressions.[44] Biswas looked at films like *MLA Fatakesto*, *Minister Fatakesto* and *Tiger* by Swapan Saha in 2007, Haranath Chakraborty's *Tulkalam*, and box-office super hit *Chirodini Tumi Je Amar*, produced by SVF. All these films drew generously from the contemporary political scenario of mass protests, media spectacle and sensation in their narratives, inspired by Nandigram, Singur, Lalgarh and the Rizwanur Rahman incident (see Figures 2.2 and 2.3).[45]

Biswas comments that these films make a consistent effort to break free from the *bhadralok* aesthetics of Bengali Cinema and popularise a kitschier, *bazaar* or street culture in their narratives and visual treatments, drawing from the then present political upsurges in the streets of Kolkata and elsewhere in Bengal.[46] Reshmi Sengupta's review of *Chirodini Tumi Je Amar* in *The Telegraph* on

Figure 2.2: Film Poster of *Chirodini Tumi Je Amar*

Source: SVF.

Figure 2.3: Production Still of *Chirodini Tumi Je Amar*

Source: SVF.

20 August 2008, was titled 'Love in the Time of Hate', thereby making a clear connection to the tragic love story of Rizwanur and Priyanka, although she analyses that the connection to the real life incident was limited to a rich girl marrying a poor guy, much against her family's wishes.[47] Similar in plot line to *Qyamat Se Qyamat Tak* by Mansoor Khan in 1988, and several other tragic teen love stories that have been seen on the Indian screen, *Chirodini Tumi Je Amar* (mainly 'inspired' from the Tamil film *Kaadhal* by Balaji Shaktivel in 2004) was Raj Chakraborty's directorial debut.[48] In an interview to the media, Raj Chakraborty candidly agreed that his film was loosely inspired from the Rizwanur–Priyanka case. However, it was more about teenage love and the mistakes that they would unknowingly make (see Figure 2.4).[49]

The film launched two newcomers, Rahul and Priyanka. The film is set in Siliguri, where Pallabi (Priyanka) meets motor mechanic Krishna (Rahul) on her way to school. They fall in love and elope to get married. Pallabi is the daughter of a rich businessman who has underworld connections. Krishna is a school drop-out living in a shanty. Their runaway marriage does not have Pallabi's family's

Figure 2.4: Publicity Still of *Chirodini Tumi Je Amar*

Source: SVF.

approval. The father and his goons set out on a chase to hunt down the pair and separate them. Krishna and Pallabi land up in Kolkata. They take shelter in a shabby old mess hostel full of bachelor boarders, with the help of Krishna's friend, Ali (Rudranil).

Raj Chakraborty demonstrates an eye for detail, and the realistic production design by Preetam Choudhury, along with the locations, costumes, the song sequences of the film picturised by Premendra Bikash Chaki, Jeet Ganguly's music direction topping the charts, and an item number performed by actor Dev, probably worked perfectly to create the film's immense popularity, which turned out to be one of the highest-grossing Bengali films in Tollywood since the 1990s. *Chirodini Tumi Je Amar* was produced with a budget of Rs 1 crore. The overall gross turnover was more than Rs 2.5 crores, and it was released with more than 40 prints. Shrikant Mohta of SVF signposts *Chirodini Tumi Je Amar* as the turning point in their career, and stressed on the impossibility of a repeat success and the kind of phenomenal success and popularity that *Chirodini* received and earned.[50]

The Pervading Influence of 'Foreign Locations' in Bengali Cinema

Inspired from Allu Arjun's *Bunny*, a 2005 Telugu film, Raj Chakraborty's second film with SVF was *Challenge*, an action-comedy starring Dev and newcomer Subhashree. The film was marked for its stylisation and attitude, and catapulted Dev's film career to new heights. *Challenge* managed to avoid some of the usual clichés of the romantic-action-genre films of Tollywood. *Challenge* is about an obsessive father who is the boss of local goons. His mission is to protect his daughter, Subhashree, from the male gaze. Dev and Subhashree meet and fall in love, from where the film takes a turn towards the hero's mission to win the heart of his girlfriend's father. Dev's look and characterisation in *Challenge* earned him immense popularity among the semi-urban and rural audience (see Figure 2.5).[51]

The film also roped in SVF's most trusted music director, Jeet Ganguly, who composed a hard-rock style kirtan, '*Bhajo Gourango* ...' ('Sing Praise to Gourango ...'), where Dev dances with foreign background dancers, shot in an up-scale Mumbai studio, stylised as a music video. The other songs were jazzy and grundgy.[52] *Challenge* was cinematographed by Mumbai-based Shomak Mukherjee, who used a super 35 mm camera and hi-tech Arriscope 435 camera for the song and action sequences, a first in Tollywood.[53] The film was extensively shot in Dubai, Australia and New Zealand, generating ample hype and curosity among the audience. The promotions were aggressive, ranging from pre-release publicity through photo shoots, actor–director interviews, and repeated song trailers in *Sangeet Bangla*. *Challenge* was exhibited in multiplexes and drew substantial footfall (see Figures 2.6 and 2.7).

The Bengali film industry picked up the trend of foreign locations begun by SVF, and the biggest competition was from SVF's toughest rival, Ashok Dhanuka of Dhanuka Brothers Pvt. Ltd (earlier known as Eskay Cideos). Dhanuka produced Tollywood's costilest film ever, titled *Bhalobasha Bhalobasha* (*Love Love*) in 2008, directed by Ravi Kinnagi, starring newcomers Hiron and Shrabanti. The film had a budget of more than Rs 3 crores, and was shot in Vienna and Salzburg in Austria. *Bhalobasha Bhalobasha* triggered a trend in Tollywood around that time to shoot films in exotic foreign

Figure 2.5: Film Poster of *Challenge*

Source: SVF.

locations; there were three films in 2008 that followed this trend.[54] The first one among these is *Mon Mane Na* (*The Heart Never Agrees*) by Ravi Kinnagi, in 2008, produced by Nishpal Singh, made with a budget of Rs 1.5 crores, with two song sequences shot in Singapore. The second one was *Shukno Lanka* (*Red Chillies*) directed by Gaurav Pande in 2010, and produced by Mumbai Mantra, the production wing of Mahendra and Mahindra. It was a Bengali film shot for the first time in Berlin, capturing the Berlin International Film Festival.

Figure 2.6: Production Still of *Challenge*

Source: SVF.

Figure 2.7: Production Still of *Challenge*

Source: SVF.

The budget was close to Rs 2.5 crores, and the Berlin shoot took 20 per cent of the total budget. The third one was *Lakshyabhed* (*Bull's Eye*), directed by Raj Mukherjee and produced by Pankaj Agarwal, starring Swastika Mukherjee, Rachana Banerjee and Tapas Pal, shot in Pattaya in Thailand, on a budget of Rs 65 lakhs. The three-day Pattaya shoot cost about Rs 5 lakhs.[55]

The English language print media, which was otherwise less cognisant of the developments in the Bengali film industry, by 2008, began to acknowledge the growth and improvement spearheaded most ambitiously by SVF earning them the status of being one of the strongest and most powerul production houses in Tollywood. The year 2008 witnessed the highest revenue output of Bengali films, with more than 30 films made within the budget range of Rs 50 lakhs to Rs 1 crore, most of which broke even within two months of the films being released, alongside their continued run at the theatres in suburbs. The factor that made the public and the press come to watch these movies was the publicity and marketing thrust that production houses invested during this time. *Bhalobasha Bhalobasha*, one of the most expensive Bengali films until 2008, had its own website to mainly target the urban audience, which cost around Rs 20,000 to launch, another first in Tollywood. Production houses like Nishpal Films (which later became Surinder films Pvt. Ltd), Moxie Entertainment, T. Sarkar, Mumbai Mantra and Screenplay Films in association with Shemaroo Videos, were investing in youth-centric films and were concentrating on the glamour quotient by making foreign locations a *de rigueur*.

Tollywood's New Stars

The SVF banner introduced a new crop of young star faces into the Tollywood industry. Dev, Jeet, Koel, Subhashree and Srabonti were part of the SVF brigade. In an article, Mahendra Soni of SVF mentions how Dev, their new-found favourite hero, was someone who embodied a mix of everything the Bengalis wanted in their favourite star/hero on screen; he was chocolatey, and yet, rough-and-tough, and had the boy-next-door look with an attitude of an 'angry young man'.[56]

Soni empahsised how the new generation was conscious about how the hero would represent the new youth and its consciousness.

He was hopeful that Jeet, who they launched in *Saathi* in 2002, would emerge as a hero and a star along with Dev. The other two newcomers in 2008 were Hiran (in *Bhalobasha Bhalobasha*) and Soham (in *Bajimaat*). When Prosenjit Chatterjee, Tapas Pal and Chiranjeet were the regular faces of Bengali cinema during the 1980s and 1990s, the urban, English-educated Bengali youth had a possible disconnect with Bengali popular cinema. With the emergence of stars like Jeet and Dev, the urban young people showed some interest in Bengali films, and were curious about these new faces. The article, 'Hero Hunt ... ' by Kushali Nag, in *The Telegraph*, quoted viewers' choice from young professionals in Kolkata, who over the past two to three years were intrigued with what was happening in Tollywood. Pinky Bhattacharya, 29, a computer teacher in a South Calcutta school preferred

> ... a mix of macho-chocolate-boy looks. Toned body and good height are very important, but if one meets the other requirements (like good at dancing) then the height is immaterial. Heroes should be able to dance well, the Tollywood heroes look appalling when they shake a leg in garish costumes on those tacky sets.[57]

She voted for Dev, who, according to her looked 'okay and promising'. Sonia Banerjee, a post-graduate student, at a university in Kolkata, wanted Tollywood heroes to turn out in style, both on and off screen, discarding their orange shirts and blue pants. A toned body was definitely desirable, although not necessary, besides being realistic in their acting, avoiding overacting, and going for less melodrama. She picked Jeet, for his good height and better looks off screen than on screen. Prosenjit Chatterjee, now a veteran, suggested that the new crop of heroes would have to hone their acting skills and maintain their physique, so as to be able to convince the urban audience that they were also part of their family. He urged them to understand the economic structure of the industry and how it worked, shoulder responsibility for both success and failure, and keep good relations with people in the industry.

Copy, Inspiration, or Plagiarism?

Another media discourse attacking the Tollywood industry, in general, and SVF, in particular, underlined the ruthless copying of commercially successful South Indian (mainly Tamil and Telugu) and Hindi films. Bappaditya Bandyopadhyay, in his 2009 film, *Houseful*, takes on this Tollywood phenomenon where his protagonist, Prosenjit Chatterjee (who has also worked in several unauthorised remakes of South Indian films) is a failed art film-maker, and his assistant constantly pressures him to succumb to the norm of the industry, where a frame-to-frame copy of a South Indian film is the only way to box-office success.

In 2009, SVF's film, *Poran Jai Joliya Re*, directed by Ravi Kinnagi, got into major legal trouble, when the 2007 film *Namastey London* (*Hello London!*)'s producer-director, Vipul Shah, filed a copyright violation case in the Calcutta High Court on 10 August 2009. The Calcutta High Court declared that the film was a 'frame-by-frame' copy of *Namastey London*.[58] Justice Nadira Patheriya held the producers, Mahendra Soni and Shrikant Mohta, along with director Ravi Kinnagi, responsible for infringement of the Copyright Act, and charged them with copying the sequences and costumes of *Namastey London*. Within hours of the stay order, Mohta and Soni, moved the High Court Division bench to challenge the legality of the trial court order. The film, however, had already been running for two weeks in more than 115 halls across Bengal, and had been declared a box-office hit. SVF invested a handsome amount to get the film polished at Mumbai-based Futurworks Media, which did the post-production for *Aladin* by Sujoy Ghosh, *Aa Dekhen Zara* (*Come Let's See*) by Jehangir Surti, and *8x10 Tasveer* (*8x10 Image*) by Nagesh Kukunoor, all 2009 films.

This case was later settled out of court with an amicable arrangement between Vipul Shah and the SVF producers. Mohta and Soni paid Rs 75 lakhs and an acknowledgement to the former film in the title sequence. This was a result of the Calcutta High Court order that the Bengali film be pulled off screens.[59] Most producers backed the accusation of being called 'copycats' with strong logic that in a revenue-starved industry like Tollywood, most remakes garnered good business, and it was necessary to consider the fact that Tollywood films released simultaneously with Bollywood, Hollywood and Bhojpuri films in Kolkata, which generated tough competition for the Bengali films and the substantial returns from the box office. Industry officials claimed that popular films were mostly purchased unofficially, because before the *Poran Jai Jolia Re* case, there was no report or conflict on copyright issues with producers from the South or from Bollywood. Film critic Samik Bandyopadhyay stressed upon the fact that Bengali films were trying to be different in terms of look and style, following Bollywood films. Their main audience resided in small towns and villages. The bulk viewers were still dominated by the lower-middle class from the mofussils, who identified more closely with the structure, characters and plot of the films remade from the South, as the latter, too, have a similar target audience.[60]

One of the primary reasons for Tollywood not aspiring to officially remake Hindi films has been the budget constraint. While a big budget Bengali film could be made within Rs 2.5 crores, most mainstream Hindi film budgets would cross Rs 50 crores. Hence, buying the official rights of a big budget Hindi film was difficult, and recovering the costs of a Bengali film made on an ambitious production scale was risky. On the subject, actor Tota Roy Choudhury, remarked that the remake rights of a commercially successful Hindi film was above Rs 20 lakhs, while the remake rights of a Tamil or Telugu film was under Rs 3 lakhs, which worked better for the Tollywood market, considering the average budget of Bengali films and the estimated recovery returns.[61] The politics of language is another reason for Tollywood not encouraging Hindi remakes, as most Hindi films did not get proper releases in the South. There was a novelty factor in remaking them. Telugu and Tamil films are hardly released in Bengal. Thus, there is an anonymity in remaking them in Bengali. Director Raj Chakrabarty felt that the novelty factor of remaking a Hindi film is much more in the South than it is in Bengal: 'The industry down South is big and so is Bollywood. But interesting enough, both industries are mutually exclusive. Hence, both the industries can afford to indulge in official remakes and make profits.'[62]

In a conversation, SVF's Shrikant Mohta insisted that their films not be merely referred to as copies of Telugu and Tamil films. Mohta believed that they were professional remakes, not mere copies; he added that the subject, characterisation and other elements of the films were changed and tweaked according to the demands of the Bengali audience and their sensibilities. He also added that *Poran Jai Joliya Re* was an exceptional case, and it will never happen again with SVF.[63]

Reshuffling Scripts: Adaptions, Homages and Tributes

The Bengali audience profile was changing from a homogenous whole to being split along the lines of class, mass and economic status. Realising the potential lying latent in the audience of multiplex theatres that had grown by leaps and bounds by the mid-2000s, the middle-of-the-road Bengali cinema now found a stable market alongside the brazen commercial films. SVF turned its attention to a new director, Srijit Mukherjee, who had a script ready as a 'tribute' to Satyajit Ray's masterpiece, *Nayak* (*The Hero*), a 1966 film that featured Uttam Kumar in the title role. SVF quickly fathomed the tremendous pre-publicity, marketing and publicity potential that this project would generate, and took on the script, with Prosenjit Chatterjee stepping in to replicate the top matinee idol in Tollywood. This was a kind of relocation of the hero in contemporary Bengali cinema. The pre-release, during-shooting, music launch, and other paraphernalia were so huge and mesmerising that *Autograph*, the film, released in 2004, ensured a very good run at the box office, although it did not have the mainstream ingredients of a typical commercial film, like the other productions of SVF at that time.

The story revolves around Arun Chatterjee (Prosenjit Chatterjee), the biggest star of Tollywood, who sets out to take up a challenge when his run-of-the-mill commercial films are not faring well. He is persuaded by a passionate debutant director, Subhabrato (Indraneil Sengupta), with his script '*Aajker Nayak*', an adaptation of Satyajit Ray's *Nayak*. It is a self-reflexive film (film-within-a-film), where Chatterjee plays the fictionalised superstar of Bengali cinema. The name of the character has rhetorical and symbolic implications, along with being Uttam Kumar's real name (see Figure 2.8).

Srijit manages to enrich the film with his directorial touches, and presents a story and a film that bear little resemblance to Ray's film. *Aajker Nayak*, the film-within-the-film, carries over and modernises a few physical realities, such as the hero travelling on a flight where a co-passenger gets introduced to him from Ray's *Nayak*. While *Nayak* described in detail the inner struggle of the star Arindam Mukherjee during a train journey to get the National Award, *Autograph* deals with the brutal reality of how the film-making process can unwittingly bring up ghosts from the past, making the

Figure 2.8: Production Still of *Autograph*

Source: SVF.

numero uno come face-to-face with his utter loneliness, his not-very-happy past, and his desperate search for love that eludes and escapes him even when he feels it is just within his grasp.

Arun Chatterjee, one discovers in the end, is more sinned against than sinning; it is a feature common to all the top stars of the film industry who the media floods with negative qualities that may not be real at all, says Arun. It would be interesting to find out how autobiographical Prosenjit discovered the film was for him, both as the biggest star of Bengali cinema as well as portraying a top star in a film being made within the film. How these emotional and professional overlaps affected him as well as his relationships within and without the industry are issues that perhaps got blended into the script of the film.

Music director Debajyoti Misra's ingenious musical score, complimented by the inspiring and hum-worthy lyrics composed by Sreejato, Srijit and Anupam Roy, became extremely popular with audiences and listeners. The number, '*Amaake Amaar Moto Thaakte Dao*' ('Let Me Be On My Own') that literally carries the spirit of loneliness at the core of all the three characters' lives in the film is notable, while '*Benche Thakar Gaan*' ('The Song of Life') is equally haunting, and was possibly another distinguishing point of departure from the film's original inspiration, *Nayak*, which was a song-less film. Shoumik Haldar's cinematography attempted to achieve a classic model of how a film should be cinematographed to support the film's ambience and story, and at the same time become an aesthetic statement in itself, with the characteristic signature of the author who manned the camera. The long shots, which were shot from far above Arun's car driving at great speed across a national highway, are dotted with a bunch of white pigeons captured flying in the opposite direction, one after another. Haldar's camera captures Arun in large close-ups most of the time, and it is a pleasant touch with reality when we find Prosenjit's wrinkles up front, highlighting his sense of loss through a thin veil of arrogance and complacence and melancholia.

Hence, *Autograph* possibly marks the beginning of fashionable, stylised, sleek and polished films from the SVF house. Prosenjit, in his character of the superstar, signifies his star value and power position, who, in the then contemporary context was one of the biggest stars of Tollywood (see Figure 2.9).

Figure 2.9: Production Still of *Autograph*

Source: SVF.

In February 2011, Cine Central Calcutta published *Autograph Chitranatya Ityadi* (*Autograph, Screenplay, Etc.*), a book edited by eminent film critic Nirmal Dhar. In his Preface, he mentions that he does not qualify the film to be a classic like Ray's *Pather Panchali* (*A Song of the Little Road*), 1955, or *Charulata* (*The Lonely Wife*), 1964, or Ghatak's *Ajantrik* (*The Pathetic Fallacy*), 1958, or *Meghe Dhaka Taara* (*The Cloud-Capped Star*), 1960, but he firmly believes that Srijit Mukherjee definitely has the potential of being a new-found auteur, and Tollywood's popular star/actor Prosenjit being re-discovered with an image that is larger than life. The book is a compilation of the screenplay, and many published reviews of the film in the print media, along with discussions in blogs, interviews of director and producers, actors, and other important crew members. Film critic Nirmal Dhar acknowledged that *Autograph*'s tremendous popularity could not be surpassed, and thus, a book like this was possibly required, in order to make a small contribution to the largely undocumented contemporary history of Bengali cinema.

The book also had the note from the producers, Shrikant Mohta and Mahendra Soni as well as from Madhu Mantena of Cinergy Pictures, with whom SVF had formed an association for the production and distribution of the film. The note gauges the film's position in Tollywood and what it had done for SVF:

> … were very impressed with the vision of the first time director Srijit Mukherjee. The entire film was very well conceived and presented …. The accolades and attention that our film has garnered both in the domestic and international market, makes us believe that good content presented well and honestly will surely touch the hearts of millions …

The film earned record box-office returns for the makers.[64] *Autograph* premiered at the Abu Dhabi International Film Festival, 2010, and the Mahindra Indo-American Arts Council (MIAAC) Film Festival, 2010, in New York. It was officially selected at the Glasgow International Film Festival, 2011.

SVF produced two films in 2010, Aparna Sen's *Iti Mrinalini* (*An Unfinished Letter*) and first time director Sanjay Nag's English film, *Memories in March,* starring Rituparno Ghosh. *Iti Mrinalini* was the director's first venture in association with a production house like SVF.

On the other hand, Aparna Sen saw herself as experimenting with the new genre of cinema that aimed at targeting both the masses and the classy audience. The film was on the life and times of a yesteryear mainstream Bengali cinema star-actress, a look back at her life. Sen played the older Mrinalini, while her daughter, actress Konkona Sen Sharma, portrayed the younger Mrinalini. *The Hollywood Reporter* gave a glorious tribute to *Iti Mrinalini*, calling it 'a deep dive into the lush melodrama of Douglas Sirk along with a dramatic examination of the transitory nature of romantic passions found in Max Ophüls all set in the world of the Bengali film industry'.[65] Mainak Bhowmik, in *The Telegraph*, reviewed *Iti Mrinalni* as:

> ... transcending its regional mould and present[ing] Bengalis as part of a bigger global existence. It breathes of a veteran who has the freshness of a debutante who gets immensely personal and goes all out to make that one good movie. This is a new-generation film which doesn't need a hip youngster to make it contemporary.[66]

The film *Memories in March* was scripted by Rituparno Ghosh, and it starred veteran actress Deepti Naval. A departure from the regular big budget commercial ventures of SVF, this film is an intimate story of a mother's coming to terms with her son's sexuality post his death, as an undefined bond develops with her son's same-sex partner, played by Rituparno Ghosh. Sangeeta Dutta's review of this film in *The Telegraph*, titled 'An Ode to Grief', on 4 April 2011, stated that 'it is an enduring personal drama and it is heartening to see mainstream producers Shrikant Mohta and Mahendra Soni of SVF back an art house film such as this'. The film fared moderately at the box office, but gained positive critical responses from the press and public, and it was also awarded the National Award in 2011 under the category of Best English Film.

Thus, cinematic practice adopted by SVF became compelling, as they brought in the model and apporach of 'difference' and 'diversification' to Tollywood. By the end of the 2000s, SVF's production portfolio begins to capture different markets of audiences, a dual approach of balancing classier content and mainstream blockbusters. This could be SVF's horizontal integration, which is, to diversify across diverse film genres.

Dui Prithibi and *Baishe Srabon*: Studies in Contrast

SVF's mega budget film, *Dui Prithibi* (a remake of the Telugu film, *Gamyam*, 2008, by Sharwanand Allari Naresh), directed by Raj Chakraborty in 2010, and starring Dev, Jeet, Koel Mullick and Barkha Bisht Sengupta, was an ambitious attempt of a road movie in Tollywood, drawing inspiration from films like *Motorcycle Diaries*. The film paired the two popular stars of Tollywood, Dev and Jeet. The road movie needed a large canvas and a lavish mounting. For the first time, a budget of Rs 5 crores was commissioned for a Bengali film. The film was shot extensively in Kolkata and in the rural belt of West Bengal, like Lalgarh and Gopiballavpur, which are Maoist-infested areas, as well as in places like Purulia, Bantala, etc. A few of the song sequences were filmed in Venice. It was the first Bengali film to be shot in Italy and the second mainstream Bengali film to be shot in Europe, after *Bhalobasha Bhalobasha*. While the main film was shot by cinematographer Somak Mukherjee, Sirsha Ray came on board for the Venice schedule. It was released in 209 theatres across West Bengal on a Thursday during the festival of *Durga Puja*. This was the first big, extensive release to be distributed across the state. It ran for five weeks in the city, after which it had to make space for another release, *Mon Je Kore Uru Uru*, although according to *The Telegraph*, the film managed to complete a six-week run in the city (see Figure 2.10).[67]

The film had its longest multiplex run of four weeks at Bioscope, Axis Mall, in Rajarhat, and Inox, Burdwan. *Dui Prithibi* completed an extraordinary run of 50 weeks in distant rural theatres, Basanti at Dantan, and Haraparbati at Jhatipahari. It is understood that the producers of SVF deliberately withdrew the film from the city for *Mon Je Kore Uru Uru* since they share familial and friendly relations with the producers of Surinder Films, Nishpal Singh being the cousin of Shrikant Mohta and Mahendra Soni; Surinder Films returned the favour to SVF by withdrawing *Mon Je Kore Uru Uru* from city halls within five weeks to make room for the next SVF offering, *Sedin Dekha Hoyechilo* (*We Met Someday*) by Sujit Mondal, in 2010 (see Figure 2.11).[68]

Dui Prithibi was a soaring grosser of 2010, according to a study conducted by FICCI and Deloitte.[69] The film had the highest-ever

Figure 2.10: Film Poster of *Dui Prithibi*

Source: SVF.

opening-week box-office collection for a Bengali film. It grossed approximately Rs 5 crores in the first week of its theatrical release, while the producers raked in almost Rs 2 crores. The film continued a steady run in the city until the third week. The rural collections, however, witnessed a fall from the second week itself. Ultimately, after the less-than-expected five week city-run, the producers earned an impressive Rs 6.5 crores, as reported in *The Gulf Times*.

Figure 2.11: Production Still of *Dui Prithibi*

Source: SVF.

Considering the budget and the massive cast and crew of the film, nothing less than a 'blockbuster' was expected. The overall collections would have been good enough to merit a 'super hit' status for any other film, but the film's high budget of Rs 5 crores proved to be a deterrent in this context. *Dui Prithibi* could not manage to become a 'super hit/blockbuster'; but the collections were good enough to adjudge the film to be a 'hit' and a reasonable success (see Figures 2.12 and 2.13).[70]

In 2011, SVF's 'Durga Puja' release was Srijit Mukherjee's second film, *Baishe Srabon* (*Twenty-Second Day of Shravan*), a musical thriller, starring Prosenjit Chatterjee, film director Goutam Ghose, Parambrata Chatterjee, Raima Sen and Abir Chatterjee. The film had its plot line based on the Bengali avant garde hungry generation literary movement of the 1960s. The story is based on two journalists and two police inspectors, who chase a psychopath serial-killer. The killer leaves behind couplets of famous poets from the hungry generation at the spot of every murder. Prosenjit, who plays a suspended police inspector, brings in the twist and turns in the story line with an unexpected ending. *Baishe Srabon* was reported to have broken all records at the box office, and received extremely

Figure 2.12: Production Still of *Dui Prithibi*

Source: SVF.

Figure 2.13: Production Still of *Dui Prithibi*

Source: SVF.

positive reviews from critics across all media.[71] The film, however, had an 'A' certificate from the Central Board of Film Certification (CBFC) for its use of Bengali expletives. *Baishe Srabon* was the official selection at the Dubai International Film Festival, 2011, and it ran for a record 105 days in Kolkata with a stupendous opening, making it one of the biggest grossers of the year.[72] SVF director, Mahendra Soni, reiterated that:

> The kind of attention our films such as *Autograph, Memories in March* and *Iti Mrinalini* have garnered across the globe strengthens our belief that good cinema will have its audience. The acceptability of our films at various film festivals is proof of the fact that Bengali cinema, as a medium, has no limited boundary. With more films such as Rituparno Ghosh's *Chitrangada*, Sandip Ray's *Royal Bengal Rashaya* from the SVF camp are gearing up to elevate the bar of quality cinema further.[73]

It is imperative to note here that by this time SVF had the largest share in the revenue earnings from film production and distribution in Tollywood. SVF simultaneously invested in owning maximum numbers of single-screen theatres across West Bengal. Through this vertical model of integrating production-distribution and exhibition, SVF emerged as a successful production house without any competent competitive in the Tollywood market. The production house was strategically able to monopolise the market share and control film business as a singular and most powerful entity in Tollywood. The following section unpacks some these concerns around monopolisation.

Critical Responses to Monopolisation

The above sections chart some of the major interventions made by SVF, along with the films produced by them that introduced novelties and other production and publicity innovations. While doing so, we also signpost some of the changes that Tollywood as an industry witnessed as SVF strengthened its business by concentrating on factors like separate publicity photo shoots, hosting grand pre-release parties, premiere shows, and television promotion with star appearances in specially organised programmes. Another innovation implemented by them was the digitisation of more than 50 cinema halls across West Bengal, which was then the fastest rollout of digital cinema anywhere in India. Their financing and marketing strategies were also a marked change from earlier practices. Hence, on the basis of our industrial survey and research, it has been possible for us to conclude that SVF, with their films, played a central role in spearheading this change, and has become emblematic of the positivist and over-celebratory discourse of the press that has emerged as the popular discourse around Tollywood in contemporary times. Most media reports about Tollywood in print, electronic and internet portals are united in concluding that there had indeed been a revival in the Bengali film industry, and much of the credit for this revival was bestowed upon SVF. However, parallel to this discourse is a critical response to SVF, which is contrary to the revival narrative of Tollywood industry.

In August 2007, *The Telegraph* projected a detailed report on Tollywood's changing look, titled 'Facelift'. This analysis showed seven ways in which Tollywood films, both commercial and offbeat, were changing for the better, bit by bit. Some of the factors discussed were: (a) cinematography, (b) visual treatment, (c) experimentation that young camera-persons were pursuing with improved and advanced technology, all of which were introduced in films produced under the SVF banner. Areas such as special effects, exotic foreign location shoots, experiemental and out-of-the-box stories and thematic backdrops, music and dance, wardrobe and fashion, and most importantly, promotion and publicity, were classified. The data revealed that the films that had implemented these innovations were under the SVF banner. However, the studies added that a good number of films made by other small, independent producers had also implemented these innovations with success.[74] According to Ratnottama Sengupta of *The Times of India*, class 'A' cinema was drawing the masses (for example, *Autograph*, *Baishe Srabon*), and the mainstream had acquired a classy character. Alongside big banner Bollywood film releases in Bengal, films like *Moner Manush* (*Person of the Heart*) by Goutam Ghose in 2010, *Gorosthaney Sabdhan* (*Beware in the Graveyard*) by Sandip Ray in 2010, *Arekti Premer Golpo* (*Just Another Love Story*) by Rituparno Ghosh and Kaushik Ganguly in 2010, *Autograph* and *Baishe Srabon*, ran for record numbers of days, drawing full house both in Kolkata and in the suburbs.

The confines of the middle-class home had become an obsolete site for film exhibition. Contempary Bengali cinema now captured the city with both its changing interiors and exteriors. The historical banner, New Theatres, revived itself and produced the National Award winning film *Aami Aadu: Sound of Love* (*I am Aadu: Sound of Love*) by Somnath Halder in 2011. Television channels like *Tara Muzic, Mohua Bangla, Rupashi Bangla* and *Rose Valley* entered into film production in order to earn a higher gross revenue profit, as they also owned the satellite rights of the film.[75] It was as if a fine balance was achieved by moving from content-oriented to form-oriented narratives. The techniques of digital technology promotions (Facebook promotion, Twitter, mobile ringtone downloads, website advertisements), the marketing of films abroad (through Databazaar Media), the uploading of films on YouTube, satellite sales, pre-release music launches, and publicity press photo shoots added to the revival factor of Tollywood's films and the industrial change. Star actor Prosenjit Chatterjee stated:

> We must do local cinema, at the same time national appeal cannot be lost sight of. L. V. Prasad, Gemini, they are lost for good but New Theatres has revived! That speaks of the strength of the filmmakers of Bengal. Still, I wonder, why didn't we make *Saptapadi* in Hindi? Why have we repeatedly missed the bus?[76]

He chalked out the statistics and figures by projecting that there were around 26 crore Bengalis in the world, of which if 20 crore shelled out Re 1 each, the battle would be won. Joint ventures, according to him, were not the solution; he added that Bengali films needed to be released in Bangladesh, Tripura, Assam, UK and the US. Prosenjit further mentioned with respect to mainstream films, that they form the crux of an industry that keeps the industry alive, and therefore, the mainstream always has to adhere to a 'state-of-the-art *jhaanchak-chake* (sleeker) films'. He added that during the lowest phase of Tollywood, he ensured that he did a cinemascope film (*Shasurbari Zindabaad*) because technological advancement is always an impetus for the industry.[77]

Bengali films have found loyal audiences in countries such as China, Italy, Abu Dhabi, UK and the US, where these films are being treated as representing life on high quality celluloid, only with the original language being Bengali. Incidentally, some of the more recent Bengali films—*Memories in March, Autograph* and *Iti Mrinalini*—which made it big on the international platform, came from Tollywood's most powerful production house, SVF. Director

Srijit Mukherji, whose film made it to prestigious international film festivals, vouched that Bengali cinema was gaining recognition globally; and SVF facilitated this largely with a team of professionals headed by Ravi Sharma.[78] The director of *Memories in March*, Sanjoy Nag, whose film was selected in the Pusan International Film Festival, Korea, and was also awarded the Best Screenplay Award at MIAAC, New York in 2010, corroborated the same viewpoint.

Running parallel to this over-celebratory and positivist discourse of the press were views expressing severely contradictory and critical viewpoints that were set against the revival narrative. According to Haranath Chakraborty, the marketing budget was too high in contemporary Tollywood industry, which could be afforded only by big production houses. Most big budget films were backed by powerful corporatised production houses that spend crores on publicity and promotion. This was rare and impossible for the majority of independent producers and small-scale production houses.[79] Director Raj Chakraborty's view was that it was not enough to harp on the present success of Tollywood, and sit back and enjoy the revenues; rather, it was more essential to have 'script doctors' who could monitor and supervise better quality scripts and ideas, so that the stereotype of mainstream cinema could be broken.[80]

Shekhar Das, the director of the 2011 film, *Necklace*, was of the opinion that the average producer and director of Tollywood would select subjects without any marketing strategy in mind. There has also been an absence of proper and responsible distributors. The state government has not been taking any initiative about promoting good cinema for over decades, while all other state governments have been pursuing this very seriously, especially in the South and the North-East. Besides, the proportions of films produced are still far higher than the number of theatres available in Bengal. Ringo, director of films like *Love, System* and *Risk*, remarked that the biggest problem in Tollywood is the acceptability of new-age Bengali cinema among the masses. They would only watch the offbeat or non-mainstream films on DVDs. They were not willing to spend money to go to theatres and watch these movies. Anjan Das, director of *Iti Srikanta* and *Bedeni*, was also very sceptical about the state of Tollywood, and he stated that the present scenario in Bengal was ideal only for the big producers; the smaller ones would not be able to survive, since one needed a hefty marketing budget for a film to reach out to the masses before it released in the theatres. This was not possible for the small producers, who wanted to make small-scale but content-driven films. Somnath Gupta expresses concerns over the then contemporary industrial scenario because being a regional industry, it increased the risk of films that aimed at experimenting with form and content. The biggest worry for these producers was where would their films get sold since getting audiences into theatres seemed increasingly dependent on publicity and promotional mechanisms and other aggressive media promotions.[81]

The scenario of the 1990s and the first decade of the 2000s points out that the emergence of SVF had a large part to play in the survival of a crisis-ridden industry and the establishing of a stable Bengali film market that was based on the presumption of a 'class' of audience. However, there was a clear operation of a 'vicious circle' and the logic of monopoly, especially in the Bengali mainstream area of film production. Director Bappaditya Bandyopadhyay gives us an account of how production houses like SVF completely 'controlled' the industrial scenario. He further mentioned that SVF is not only the leading production house of Tollywood, but also the owner of more than half the total number of cinema halls in West Bengal (roughly out of the 260-odd single-screen cinema halls, more than 140 of them are owned by SVF), and thus, it also controls distribution and exhibition. According to Bandyopadhyay, if SVF spends Rs 3 crores on a film, they secure its market by roughly aiming to earn Rs 20 lakhs back from each of its 140-odd halls. Some of the halls would perhaps earn this amount in two weeks, and some in six or seven weeks, and since they are the owners of those 140 halls, and in most of the cases the distributors, too, it is not possible for any other distributor to release their films in those halls. However, when this question was posed to Shrikant Mohta during an interview with him, he denied the fact, saying that SVF only had some 50 halls on lease (by 2011), and they cannot exercise that kind of control. This was what Bandyopadhyay called the 'vicious circle' and the monopoly over the Bengali film market and of the Bengali commercial cinema chain. Veteran film journalist, Aniruddha Dhar, mentioned this 'unholy nexus' in Bengali film production-distribution practice, and confirmed that in some cases, SVF, while permitting other hall owners to exhibit their films, made them agree on the basis that the hall had to run their films for at least four weeks, even if it was a flop in the first week.

SVF operates across various verticals within the media and entertainment space, including film production, film distribution, film exhibition, television content production, broadcasting, music label under the banner of SVF music, with film, non-film and music videos, and digital cinema projection and exhibition and OTT (Over-the-Top digital platform) content production and dissemination. In our conversations with director Swapan Saha, he, too, reiterated that SVF was dictating the terms of the industry, that they were setting the trends, and a lot of people were following it blindly without understanding the repercussions; hence, in the last 10 years (that is, from 2000 to 2011), many small production houses that wanted to follow in the footsteps of SVF have disappeared and shut down.[82] National award-winning actress Rituparna Sengupta has stated that although it cannot be denied that SVF has brought in several changes to the Tollywood industry that has professionalised the scenario, it has also exercised tremendous control over stars and actors, sometimes over directors, forming a camp, so that their team would only work with each other, thus destroying healthy competition and forcing smaller production houses to fade away. However, Sengupta was optimistic that with the success of films like *Icchhe* (*The Desire*) by Shiboprosad Mukherjee and Nandita Roy in 2011 and *Jio Kaka (Cheers, Uncle)* directed by Parambrata Chatterjee in 2011, both of which were presented by her, smaller films, with better content and independent producers, would time and again alarm the strongmen of the industry.[83]

Moinak Biswas and his colleague, Subhajit Chatterjee, engaging in an online chat, which was later published in *The Times of India*, Kolkata, discussed the lack of variety in the content of contemporary mainstream Bengali cinema in terms of the entire range, from deadpan humour to boisterous fun. Biswas, referring to the kind of films that were being released one after the other, said

> ... Contemporary Bengali films make you feel that there is no thickness of community in them. There are almost no believable social embodiment.... It has to do with the decline of the vernacular. A certain humour, even if it is physical comedy, becomes possible when there is

> a sizeable section of people sharing vernacular codes. It is difficult to imagine good humour in a situation where one doesn't read Bengali, or write much in it. There has to be a depletion of resources of not only verbal wit but of humorous idioms of relating us to the world.[84]

Hence, a large volume of discourse could be identified that emerged with the growth of SVF and the transformation of the Tollywood industry. As SVF gradually established itself as one of the most powerful corporatised production houses of Tollywood,[85] its control and monopoly politics was also being sensed by people across the board, and the monopoly was not limited to just film production-distribution and exhibition, but there was also a certain degree of homogeneity and uniformity in the content, theme and narrative of their mainstream films. The Bengali community, language, mannerisms, social milieu, class and the overall presentation of Bengaliness was far from what the people of Bengal were. Post economic liberalisation, there has been a blurring of lines within communities, regions and classes both in terms of cultural differences and economics, with the success and popularity of certain kinds of films from Tollywood. Moinak Biswas, in his article, 'Changing Scenes', questions whether the *bhadralok* circle exists in the same form anymore. At the same time, he also suggests the fading away of the stark difference between *bhadralok* elites and the non-*bhadralok* due to the centrality of television in middle and lower middle-class lives, as well as the Bengali language itself getting hybridised mostly by *bhadralok* urban citizens. Moreover, he argues that television has also picked up this hybridity in the form of language and cultural content. Biswas also draws a parallel with the changes that took place in the then opposition party leader Mamata Banerjee's party that was accused of being full of hooligans, but changed as more and more intellectuals joined her protests to fight for a change.[86]

Thus, this chapter is an analysis of how the films in Tollywood began to change gradually as the system of production and exhibition of films transformed. SVF, as a corporatised production house, developed into a powerful entity in the industry, and played a crucial role in bringing about key changes in content and visual aesthetics, marketing strategies, introduction of new actors and stars, and producing films with a range of diverse film-makers. However, with this process of change in the industry, there emerged two dominant paradigms and narratives: on the one hand, the revival of the glorious history of Bengali cinema, and on the other, the excessive control and monopoly that SVF was exercising over the industry. We have selected a range of films produced under the SVF banner, only to map the microcosmic changes that can be traced alongside the journey of the production house's formation and growth over a period of almost two decades. However, we have avoided the detailed textual analysis of films; rather, we have looked at novelty factors like technical prowess, aesthetic treatment, cinematography, marketing, promotion strategies, music, new stars and actors, and media reviews of the films that have been selected and discussed here.

As much of the materials for the research related to this chapter were press articles and newspaper reports, it is noteworthy to mention how a voluminous discourse, largely optimistic and positivist, got generated out of the English and Bengali press, which largely celebrated the state that the Tollywood industry was in starting from the mid-2000s. At the same time, the fact that all local and regional media most certainly require a local culture industry parallel to the socio-economic and political life, in order to produce content, views and critique, cannot be denied. Thus, Tollywood re-shaping and re-emerging as an entertainment and culture industry post-liberalisation is also possibly a result of the convergence in media and the paraphernalia that is generated in the public sphere. The media of print, television and radio have wholeheartedly allied with the Tollywood fraternity and have symbiotically formed a nexus that has overlapped and converged to become one, but yet have maintained their own distinct characteristics, which shall be explored in detail in a later chapter. However, in this changing scenario, a few film-makers who were dissatisfied with the mainstream cinematic practice during the 2000s, set out to regenerate the literary-ness of earlier Bengali cinema, and a few floating producers, the setting up of niche exhibitions, and press discourses supported these film-makers. In the post-1990 moment, these film-makers, we argue, were seen as part of the new 'parallel' cinema circuit by the press and the discourse around Bengali cinema within the *bhadralok* sphere. The following chapter details the emergence of this new 'parallel' cinema and the 'parallel-ness' in the post-1990 period.

Notes and References

1. Madhava Prasad, 'This Thing Called Bollywood', Unsettling Cinema, *Seminar*, May 2003.
2. See Tejaswini Ganti, 'What is Bollywood?', in *Bollywood: A Guidebook to Popular Hindi Cinema* (New York: Routledge, 2004), pp. 2–4. She remarks: '"Bollywood" has become a shorthand reference not only to a specific industry, but also to a specific style of filmmaking within the industry which is aggressively oriented toward box-office success and broad audience appeal.'
3. Authors' interview with SVF's Shrikant Mohta, 18 October 2011, Kolkata.
4. See Aparna Sharma, 'India's Experience with the Multiplex', *Seminar 525: Unsettling Cinema*, May 2003, pp. 42–46.
5. Authors' interview with Subhasish Ganguly, Regional Director, Eastern India INOX, 16 April 2012, Kolkata.
6. Subhra Sircar and Debasis Konar, 'EIMPA Plans Tollywood Survival Kit', *The Times of India*, 3 January 2003.
7. Ibid.
8. 'NFDC Unveils Hi-tech Video Studio', *Mid-Day*, 11 July 2003.
9. PTI, 'Sahara to Set Up Film City Near Kolkata', *The Economic Times*, 6 January 2004.
10. Authors' interview with SVF's Shrikant Mohta.
11. 'Cliched Images that Shun Realism', *The Financial Express*, 2 October 2006, available at http://www.financialexpress.com/news/clichd-images-that-shunrealism/179240/0, accessed 6 June 2012.
12. Arnab Bhattacharya, 'Old, Old Hat', *The Telegraph*, 24 December 2004.
13. Ibid.
14. Reshmi Sengupta, 'A Match for Screen', *The Telegraph*, 1 November 2005.
15. Reshmi Sengupta, 'Big Clash Means Big Cash', *The Telegraph*, 29 August 2005.
16. Ibid.
17. Madhuparna Das, 'Quick Takes—Opulent Inspiration', *The Telegraph*, 11 November 2005.
18. Sengupta, 'A Match for Screen'.
19. Ibid.
20. Kushali Nag, 'I Am a Workaholic', *The Telegraph*, 6 November 2008.
21. Ibid.
22. Staff Reporter, 'Filmi MLA Sweeps Stakes, CPM Style', *The Telegraph*, 12 May 2006.
23. Kushali Nag, 'Mithun vs Mithun', *The Telegraph*, 11 October 2007.
24. Ibid.
25. See Kushali Nag, '32 Weeks of Right Mix', *The Telegraph*, 31 August 2007, where she comments on the film, *I Love You*, 'On the one hand, there's the year's biggest grosser, *I Love You* (the film's producers claim it has touched the Rs 4 crore mark)'.

26. Arnab Bhattacharya, 'Quick Takes: Fails to Conquer—*I Love You*', *The Telegraph*, 26 January 2007.
27. See http://www.sangeetbangla.com/aboutus.asp, accessed on 17 May 2012.
28. SVF official website, available at https://svf.in/, accessed on 30 July 2019.
29. Staff Reporter, 'Digital Shows the Day', *The Telegraph*, 2 September 2008.
30. Authors' interview with SVF's Shrikant Mohta.
31. Ibid.
32. Ibid.
33. Ibid.
34. Ibid.
35. 'Poor Revenue Plagues Bengali Film Industry', *The Financial Express*, 17 May 2007, available at http://www.financialexpress.com/news/poorrevenue-plagues-bengali-film-industry/199461/3, accessed on 29 May 2012.
36. Ibid.
37. Ibid.
38. Vishnupriya Sengupta, 'Hindi-Bong Bhai Bhai', *The Telegraph*, 22 April 2007.
39. Ibid.
40. See http://www.telegraphindia.com/1071106/asp/entertainment/story_8517766.asp, accessed on 1 June 2012.
41. Kushali Nag, '4 More Such Tolly-Blockbusters Could be Made with Saawariya's Promo Budget', *The Telegraph*, 6 November 2007.
42. Ibid.
43. Ibid.
44. Moniak Biswas, 'Changing Scenes', in Monica Narula, Shuddhabrata Sengupta and Jeebesh Bagchi, ed., *Sarai Reader 08: Fear Scared on Screen*, pp. 201–02.
45. Kushali Nag, 'Spot Light', available at http://www.telegraphindia.com/1080809/jsp/entertainment/story_9666418.jsp, accessed on 16 August 2015.
46. Biswas, 'Changing Scenes'. Also see Hemchhaya De, 'Filming Ferment: Tollywood Has a New Buzzword—Political Films that Capture Bengal's State of Political Unrest in Recent Times', available at http://www.telegraphindia.com/1110515/jsp/7days/story_13983689.jsp, accessed on 20 April 2020.
47. Reshmi Sengupta's review, available at http://www.telegraphindia.com/1080820/jsp/entertainment/story_9713945.jsp, accessed on 1 July 2012.
48. See Shoma A. Chatterji's review, available at http://www.upperstall.com/films/2008/chirodini-tumi-je-amaar, accessed on 17 May 2012.
49. Kushali Nag, 'Reality Show—The Rizwanur–Priyanka Tale is Ready for the Big Screen, with Some Tolly Masala', *The Telegraph*, 29 July 2008.
50. Authors' interview with SVF's Shrikant Mohta.
51. Kushali Nag, 'Time for Action', *The Telegraph*, 21 October 2008.
52. Mohua Das, 'All About Attitude—Challenge Surprises with its Mix of Style and Substance', *The Telegraph*, 21 March 2009.
53. Ibid.

54. Ibid.
55. 'Europe Calling', *The Telegraph*, 9 April 2009.
56. Nag, 'Time for Action'.
57. Kushali Nag, 'Dream Pair: Hero Hunt: Tollywood is Desperately Seeking the Next Stars', *The Telegraph*, 2008.
58. Bureau Report, '*Poran Jai*.... A Copy, Says Court', *The Telegraph*, 11 August 2009.
59. Ibid.
60. Ahana Chaudhuri and Chandreyee Ghose, 'Copycat Chronicles', *The Telegraph*, 12 September 2010.
61. Priyanka Dasgupta, 'B-Town Unwanted', *The Times of India*, 8 May 2010.
62. Ibid.
63. Ibid.
64. Author's interview with Shrikant Mohta, October 2011, Kolkata.
65. Kirk Honeycutt, '*An Unfinished Letter* (*Iti Mrinalini*): Movie Review', *The Hollywood Reporter*. 18 April 2011, available at http://www.hollywood reporter.com/review/an-unfinished-letter-itimrinalini-179447, accessed on 11 June 2012.
66. Mainak Bhowmik, 'Of Memories and Men', *The Telegraph*, 1 August 2011.
67. 'Tollywood 2010', *t2*, *The Telegraph*, 30 Decemver 2010.
68. Arijit Bhattacharya and Kushali Nag, 'Battle for Box Office', *The Telegraph*, 4 April 2011.
69. Piyasree Dasgupta, 'Film Industry Wants Mamata to Focus Right in Revamp Shot', *The Indian Express*, 19 December 2011, available at http://www.indianexpress.com/news/film-industry-wants-mamata-tofocus-right-in-revamp-shot/889518/, accessed on 12 June 2012.
70. Kushali Nag and Priyanka Roy, 'Tolly Rides Festive Flavour to Beat Bolly—*Autograph* and *Dui Prithibi* Score Over *Akrosh* and *Knock Out* with Stars and Style', *The Telegraph*, 19 October 2010.
71. Priyanka Dasgupta, 'Tolly All the Way', *The Times of India*, 2011.
72. Ibid.
73. Sreemita Bhattacharya, 'Tollywood in a Festive Mood', *The Times of India*, 27 May 2011.
74. Mohua Das and Kushali Nag, 'Facelift—Tollywood's Changing Look', *The Telegraph*, 2009.
75. Ashoke Nag, 'The Revival of Bangla Film Industry', *The Economic Times*, 13 April 2011, available at http://articles.economictimes.indiatimes.com/2011-04-30/news/29490800_1_bengali-films-bengali-cinema-mukta-arts/2, accessed on 13 June 2012.
76. Ratnottama Sengupta, 'Bengali Cinema on a New High', *The Times of India*, 11 January 2011.
77. Ratnottama Sengupta, 'Bengali Cinema can be Legitimately Proud Again', *The Times of India*, 20 October 2010.
78. Sreemita Bhattacharya, 'Tollywood in a Festive Mood'.

79. Authors' interview with Haranath Chakraborty, 17 October 2011, Kolkata.
80. Sengupta, 'Bengali Cinema can be Legitimately Proud Again'.
81. Priyanka Dasgupta, 'What Ails Tollywood Now?', *The Times of India*, 6 May 2011.
82. Authors' interview with Swapan Saha, 15 October 2011, Kolkata.
83. Authors' interview with Rituparna Sengupta, 16 October 2011, Kolkata.
84. Subhajit Chatterjee and Moinak Biswas, 'Moinak, Subhajit's Take on Bengali Cinema', *The Times of India*, 21 December 2010.
85. See Kushali Nag, 'Power List: The People Who Matter the Most in the Studios of Tollygunje', 11 July 2008. In her article, SVF ranks second only after star actor Prosenjit. About SVF, she writes,

    > Having set out to make Tollywood more happening while keeping both mass and multiplex appeal in mind, brothers Mani and Srikant have pumped money into movies as diverse as *Minister Fatakesto* and *Chokher Bali*. Shree Venkatesh has also launched its sister concern V Digital to screen films digitally in as many as 100 theatres at a time—a popular practice in Bollywood, a first for Tollywood. It also has four music channels on TV: Sangeet Bangla, Music India, Music UK and Sangeet Bhojpuri.

86. Biswas, 'Changing Scenes', pp. 203–204.

3

Situating the 'New Parallel' Bengali Cinema

The Logic of Production, Politics of Nostalgia, and Rituparno Ghosh

In this chapter, we study the post-liberalisation Bengali 'parallel' cinema, mapping its economy of emergence, production routes, release chains, marketing structure, and some of the exhibition sites associated with it. Through these different components, this chapter constructs the narrative regarding a production process that consolidated into a set of films commonly referred to by the media and the industry as 'parallel' during this period. At the same time, our effort will be to explore how the idea of 'new parallel-ness' associated with a new body of films is a conscious construct of not just their aesthetic dimension or their ideology, but is also in-built in their regimes of production, circulation and institutional policy. It is essentially related to an imagination of a 'class' of audience distanced from and dissatisfied with the so-called 'mainstream' Bengali films of that period.

The chapter's concern is to explore how the discursive domain called 'parallel' went through change(s) in the dominant imagination of production and consumption practices, and how social and cultural institutions contributed in this film culture. The realm of this new 'parallel' cinema is an essential idea that needs discussion. The discourse of Bengali cinema has historically been categorised through the binary of art/parallel and commercial/mainstream. Hence, this chapter will demonstrate whether and how this binary unfolded differently in the above-mentioned period. It further explores how the idea of an existing *bhadralok* niche audience was somewhat central to this parallel cinema discourse and understanding, the shift in the existing agenda of educating mass audiences through screenings of 'good cinema', and the various factors that began to play an important role in the production, consumption and reception of this new Bengali 'parallel' cinematic practice.

Late Bengali film director Bappaditya Bandyopadhyay, in a conversation with one of the authors of this book, recollected his experience of coming into film-making in the late-1990s, when he adapted Ramapada Chowdhury's story, *Sampradan* (*Giving Away of the Bride*), aiming for a mainstream release in 1999. The film revolves around the story of a mother (Anashua Majumdar) who brings up her two daughters on her own, without their father's name, and the trouble she faces during her elder daughter's (Indrani Haldar) marriage ceremony. In a Hindu marriage, it is considered compulsory to name the bride's father while performing the ritual of *Kanya Sampradan* ('giving away' of the bride by her father to her would-be-husband). In the film, the mother desperately tries to argue that there is no inevitable need of the father's name in one's life. *Sampradan* was almost immediately declared a flop upon its release.[1] According to Bandyopadhyay, the reason behind the film's failure at the box office perhaps lay partially in the contemporary Bengali mainstream cinema audiences' discomfort with the non-conformist woman-centric narrative, with its critique of patriarchal, patrilineal social structures. More importantly, the failure can be ascribed to the fact that neither did the film get a proper release chain, nor was it adequately distributed.[2] It was released in three cinema halls, including just one in Kolkata (Aruna). Bandyopadhyay continued making Bengali films, with *Shilpantar* (*Colours of Hunger*) in 2002, *Kaal* (*Our Time*) in 2007, *Kantatar* (*Barbed Wire*) in 2005, and so on. Although his films rarely attained much commercial success, his films gave him creative satisfaction and recognition for carrying the legacy of 'good cinema' among a certain niche Bengali film audience.

The second story that we would like to share here is how Rituparno Ghosh's 'path-breaking'[3] 1996 Bengali film, *Unishe April* (*Nineteenth April*) was produced. This makes us look back at the mid-1990s. Ghosh, who came from an advertising background, made his film debut with *Hirer Angti* (*The Diamond Ring*) in 1994. This film was produced by the Children's Film Society of India, and was broadcast on Bengali regional television several times. It did not have a theatrical release, as it faced distribution obstacles. The idea for *Unishe April*, as Ghosh had remarked, grew within him much before *Hirer Angti* itself.[4] Since the lack of proper distribution and marketing affected the response to *Hirer Angti*, it made Ghosh determined to have a 'readymade market' for his next venture. He first thought of making *Unishe April* in Hindi, with Waheeda Rehman and Shabana Azmi playing the roles of mother and daughter, the two protagonists in the film. However, the idea did not work out because NFDC rejected the script. When this script was rejected by more than 17 sponsors including SVF,[5] Aparna Sen introduced Ghosh to her friend, Renu Roy, who pitched in to help; this in turn resulted in the formation of Spandan Films, which also dealt with the film's distribution.[6] Ghosh's script was finally filmed at Response (the advertising agency that Ghosh was associated with), Aparna Sen acted as one of the two protagonists in this film, the film went on to win two National Awards, was released in the Minar-Bijali-Chobighar chain[7] in Kolkata, and it went on to become a 'hit' (see Figure 3.1).[8]

These two examples from the post-liberalisation Bengali film industry reflect two different situations and experiences of two film-makers of that moment in Tollygunge. But there was a similarity in

Figure 3.1: DVD Screen Grab of *Unishe April*

Source: Angel Video.

their approach towards the concept of 'parallel' cinema and the idea of a niche *bhadralok* film audience, which would provide the base for a 'readymade market' for their films, and also initiate the process of going beyond both the then contemporary Bengali mainstream production circuit and the state-sponsored film-making practice. Bandyopadhyay, while making his first feature film, experienced the existence of a 'vicious circle'[9] in the mainstream Bengali cinema circuit, which made him opt out of this space. On the other hand, Ghosh's never-released *Hirer Angti* and NFDC's rejection made him think of going beyond the state production agencies and to complacently rely on an existing audience base for his second film. The idea of a parallel film audience in Bengal as well as in other parts of India has earlier been associated with 'cultured' and 'educated' niche audience in film society writings. However, a significant aspect in film society writings and their approach lies in their emphasis to 'promote' and 'educate' people's taste so that they can appreciate 'better films'. Even in the early-1980s, soon after coming to power, the Left Front government invested in a better film culture in West Bengal.[10] In the then government's initiatives of 'promoting' film culture, the film education of the masses, particularly of the youth, was their primary concern.

What made the post-1990 'new parallel' stream think of an already-existing 'educated' niche audience, instead of an audience to be educated by film screenings? Was it the state's 'departure' from film scenario that made the idea of developing film taste or educating film audiences obsolete in West Bengal? Or was it the alleged dwindling of film societies during the 1990s that caused a sharp decline in the idea of 'educating' audiences through films? Or was it the phenomenal success of certain kinds of films, aimed at a certain class, which disillusioned this idea of developing 'film taste'? There were several such questions that cropped up. Maybe it was the idea of an urban, educated middle-class base as the target audience that helped in the imagination of an already existing niche market. In following sections, while mapping the emergence of the 'new parallel' cinema of the 1990 moment, we have explored probable reasons through and beyond all these possibilities. Furthermore, we have narrativised the emergence and the journey of this 'new parallel' stream in the film industrial logistics (eventually shaping up as

Tollywood), the constructs of the market, taste, and film promotional and publicity discourse.

'Floating' Producers, Limited Release, and the Parallel Market of 'Better' Cinema

Sandip Sen, owner of the National Advertising Agency, was in fraternity with Bengali film-makers like Goutam Ghose, Anjan Das and others. Sandip Sen was conscious of the ongoing 'crisis' of Bengali cinema, when Subrata Sen approached him with a Bengali film script, which was based on the Hollywood film, *Crush*.[11] Initially, Subrata Sen's script did not impress or convince Sandip Sen. Subrata Sen, however, convinced him that there was a sizeable section of urban middle class population, especially the youth, who might be his potential audience, and made Sandip Sen agree to invest in the project. Subrata Sen identified his debut feature film, *Ek Je Achhe Kanya* (*There is a Girl*) in 2001, as the first 'urban youth film' in the Bengali film industry, targeted predominantly towards the urban audiences.[12] Both Sandip Sen and Subrata Sen confirmed that there was an existing control of the distribution and release of films in the Tollygunge industry by a leading production and distribution house. This made them opt for a limited release of their films in urban centres, which worked as a strategy for their film to reach its already targeted audience. Sandip stressed upon the distribution obstacle that was an existing part of releasing films in the cinema hall chains and the reluctance of hall owners in screening their films, citing possible reasons for not matching up to the general audience expectations of mainstream Bengali films of that time. However, both the producer and the director were certain that their film would appeal to the educated niche *bhadralok* audience of Kolkata's premier cinema halls. The film-maker Subrata Sen asserted that during the mid-1990s a few production houses undeniably had a role in constructing a niche parallel film market in West Bengal. Subrata Sen reiterated that finding producers for his films was not difficult because he would make films at stringent budgets and release his films with a minimum number of prints, assuring the producer a profitable return.[13]

According to Sandip Sen, a total of Rs 30 lakhs was spent to produce *Ek Je Achhe Kanya*. It managed to earn Rs 19 lakhs from sale of tickets and electronic media rights. It earned another Rs 7 lakhs from corporate house publicity.[14] Nevertheless, Sandip considered the film to be a 'hit' because the film reimagined a Bengali film market and urban audience base outside the existing conventions of a Bengali film market. There were other films, too, that were a part of this effort, like *Unishe April* and *Paromitar Ekdin* (*House of Memories*) in 2000 by Aparna Sen. When asked why Deep Films, the production house owned by Sandip Sen, stopped investing in Bengali films after *Ek Je Achhe Kanya*, Sen blamed it on the lack of a conducive industrial culture within Tollygunge. Renu Roy's response was similar regarding her production, *Unishe April*.[15] The film was made on a considerably low budget. Moreover, it was mostly shot indoors with a small cast and released with only eight prints. Although the film garnered critical appreciation in the press, and attained financial success at the box office, the production house did not have a significant tenure in the post-*Unishe April* period. Justifying this, Renu Roy underlined that Spandan Films was not formed with the sole intention of producing run-of-the-mill Bengali films. Roy never really understood the complicated nature of film production, and that *Unishe April* happened quite accidentally for her. It just so happened that her friends were part of the Tollygunge industry and she was convinced by Ghosh's talent and potential as a film-maker. After *Unishe April*'s success when Spandan Films invested in other projects like *Shatabdir Golpo* (*Stories of the Century*) by Raj Mukherjee, suffering significant losses, she became wary of film-making as a business and refrained from further investments in Tollygunge.[16]

The concept of a 'floating producer' chain in the post-1990s Bengali 'parallel' film circuit that senior film journalist Aniruddha Dhar discusses fits in with producers like Sandip Sen and Renu Roy.[17] Dhar further added that such 'floating producers' lacked professional experience and mainly got involved in certain kinds of film business due to their upward social class background and the 'requests of their friends' from the Tollygunge industry. The owner of Piyali distribution and Priya cinema hall chain, Arijit Dutta, calls their approach unprofessional and amateur.[18] However, significantly, their social position and their association with art house film-makers distinguished them (Sandip Sen and Renu Roy) from the producers of films made by Swapan Saha, for instance. Some of the producers were not only 'outsiders' with respect to the industry, but they also lived outside Bengal, and in some cases, even outside India. Producers like Sutapa Guha, a US resident, who co-produced Ghosh's 2000 film, *Utsab* (*The Festival*), Eldrige Rodrigue and his co-producer, Mumbai-based Kesto Mandal, who co-produced Abhijit Dasgupta's 2005 film, *Dwitiyo Basanto* (*Beyond Tomorrow*), have dissociated themselves entirely from the Bengali film industry. Film-makers like Buddhadeb Dasgupta or Goutam Ghose, who earlier had the NFDC or WBFDC as sponsors, in the post-liberalisation period, had to depend on television and Bombay film producers like Ramesh Gandhi, Chitrani Lahiri or Jhamu Sugandh for producing their films.

Someshwar Bhoumik, in his book, *Bharatiya Chalachchitra: Ekti Arthanaitik Pratibedan* (*Indian Cinema: An Economic Report*), discusses in detail how, in the 1980s, most of the state-sponsored films in West Bengal could not even reach the theatres.[19] He points out that the reasons behind this were the lack of any kind of market research, poor advertising strategy, and no concept of secondary and tertiary packages for films produced by the state government.[20] Not only state initiatives, but also the film society movement of the previous decade came under criticism, both from within and outside the film society movement. Goutam Ghose, Programme Coordinator of the Eisenstein Cine Club of Kolkata, who has been associated with this film club since its inception, points out some of the reasons.[21] First, when one after another, the socialist countries started becoming non-existent in world politics, the easy and affordable supply of international art house films from all over the world came to a grinding halt. Second, Ghose feels that the vote-based electoral politics of the Left Front government was partly responsible for making people less interested in film societies. Significantly around this time, the conflict between the Film Federation of India and the Cine Central, which resulted in the shifting of Film Federation's headoffice from Kolkata to Bombay, came as an attack on the city's film society culture. Third, and most importantly, Ghose asserts that film club organisers in this period gathered that a large part of their audience used to come for film society screenings for 'pornographic pleasures' of uncensored European films. When these interests could be easily accessed through the VCR/DVD market, it automatically led to a decline in film society audiences. Besides, Ghose reveals some other reasons: the explosion of satellite television, easy availability of pirated world cinema DVDs, and the growing callousness of the foreign consulates and embassies (foreign consulates and embassies were earlier proactively involved in film promotion and screenings of their country's films) generally contributed to the diminishing film society culture in 1990s, including in West Bengal.

The point here is that the post-liberalisation 'parallel' circuit in Bengali films, unlike previous decades, shows a significant departure, both in terms of state-sponsored film production logic and the association with film society movement. Instead of a state body and a film society circuit being the primary sponsor and site of circulation of parallel cinema, there were newer entities like 'floating producers', and TV production houses that became the primary endorsers of this 'new parallel' film circuit. The association of television producers with this 'new parallel' cinema resulted in certain developments in terms of film exhibition and expanding viewership. First of all, Rainbow Productions, post the success of their popular Bengali soap opera, *Janmabhumi* (*Motherland*) and daily news bulletin, *Khaas Khabor* (*Special News*), both telecast on *Doordarshan*, produced two of Goutam Ghose's films, *Dekha* (*Sight*) in 2001, and *Abar Aranye* (*Again in the Forest*) in 2003. Besides this, there were TV production houses like Surabhi Productions (producer of *Paromitar Ekdin*), and Rosevalley Telefilms (producer of *Jara Bristite Bhiijechhilo* [*Those Who Got Drenched in the Rain*]) that emerged as consistent endorsers of parallel films. If the growing presence and popularity of TV in middle-class households accounted for their absence from cinema theatres, television producers through their investment and support of parallel films encouraged the audience to go 'back to the theatres' to watch these films. Subsequently, the parallel circuit directors and producers acknowledged TV's presence and the importance of TV rights as additional revenue returns on the investments for these films. An expanding market of VCR/DVD also provided a sizeable part of the film profit.

With cable TV's success and ever-expanding popularity, with Bengali mega serials like *Ek Akasher Niche* (*Under One Sky*), which was telecast on the channel *Alpha Bangla*, later renamed as *Zee Bangla* or *Tithir Atithi* (*Tithi's Guest*), which was telecast on *ETV Bangla*, the Bengali media entertainment sector witnessed unprecedented popularity with a new genre of television programming known as telefilms. TV channels like *ETV Bangla* invested in the formation of this genre, with short- or average-length films made for the TV audience, directed by the likes of Kaushik Ganguly, Partho Sen, Anjan Dutt, and others. This genre proliferated other channels like *Akash Bangla*, *Alpha Bangla* and *Tara Bangla*, which began producing telefilms for late-evening slots on weekends.[22] The West Bengal Film Centre, Nandan, recognising this popularity of telefilms, started organising telefilm festivals from 2003 onwards, 'with tremendous response from the public who battled long queues and inclement weather to ensure "house full" board in most of the shows'.[23] In 2004, Nandan inaugurated this festival with Tapan Sinha's 1984 telefilm, *Admi Aur Aurat* (*Man and Woman*), followed by telefilms like *700 Square Feet* by Atanu Ghosh, *Chilekothar Sepaira* (*Comrades of the Attic*) by Jayashree Bhattacharya, *Chhaya Chhabi* (*Moving Shadows*) by Kaushik Ganguly, etc., all of them telecast between 2001 and 2004, which people had already seen and appreciated. Interestingly, the idea of a film like *Ek Mutho Chhabi* (*A Fistful of Tales*), produced by Bengali film actress Roopa Ganguly's Our Films Production, in 2003, took shape by observing the popularity of the first telefilms festival at Nandan.[24] It was made of six combined telefilms. Each of the six parts was directed by a different director, such as Arghyakamal Mitra, Anjan Dutt, Kaushik Ganguly, and others. TV provided a market for the post-1990s Bengali cinema's 'parallel' stream, with an imagination of viewership that was predominantly middle-class. Apart from TV, parallel cinema imagines an audience of VCR/DVD, and also of a Bengali diaspora. It is essential to mention here the world premiere of *Utsab* and its pre-production narrative and marketing strategies in the following section.

Tapan Biswas, veteran producer of Bengali films, who has been producing films since 1981, with Dinen Gupta and Tarun Majumdar films as part of his portfolio, met Rituparno Ghosh in 1999, and planned to organise a retrospective of his films at the North American Bengali Conference that was being held each year in the US.[25] They organised the screening of Ghosh's first two films, *Unishe April* and *Dahan*, which witnessed overwhelming attendance in the auditorium at the conference. After this success, on their way back to India, Ghosh narrated the story of *Utsab*, and Biswas planned to produce the film.[26]

Utsab was made and it premiered on 24 June 2000 at General Cinema in Los Angeles, and after that, at three other halls across the US, in San Francisco, Houston and New York. It earned $20,000 from these screenings.[27] Post-screening discussions and interactive sessions were organised with the film's cast and director for the people who bought the 'dinner coupon'. Enthused by *Utsab's* success among the Bengali diaspora in the US, Biswas planned to produce at least two Bengali films every year to be premiered in the US, and to give respective VHS (Video Home System) of the films shown on the basis of membership. He calculated that if they had 6,000 members across the US, paying $30 or $40 as membership fees, it would be a profitable business plan. However, none of the Bengali diaspora organisations showed any interest in such a business plan. Biswas realised that perhaps for the non-resident Bengali people, a single day or event celebrating Bengali film screening might be 'fun', but nothing beyond that.[28] After this 'pioneering attempt' by Biswas, a Florida-based organisation, Databazar Media Ventures (DMV), initiated a global distribution and marketing of Bengali films, which also included e-marketing. DMV, in its attempts to bring 'quality' Bengali films to the US and Canada, teamed up with several other well-known Bengali organisations like Tagore Society and Durga Bari in Houston, Texas, Prabasi in the Bay Area, the Greater Bengali Association of Atlanta, and the Bengali Association of South Florida. DMV, in its partnership with Dingora.com, started releasing Bengali films online for an international audience. A website called Vinnamat News Network published reviews of these Bengali films distributed through DMV, and provided the link of Dingora.com, where one could watch the film online. A review of the Bengali film, *Shukno Lanka* (*Red Chillies*) by Gaurav Pandey in 2010 on Vinnamat News Network showcases how interestingly these online sites connected with such web portals to promote and enable links for the streaming of Bengali films among the diaspora.

> ... For Databazar group one can watch a film online at Dingora.com in USA on the same day of its release in Kolkata .... this month there is another Bengali film releasing, a filmic adaptation of Tagore's story Laboratory. (Trailer link provided). The North American audience can watch Shukno Lanka from this Dingora Link.[29]

It is interesting to observe how the advertisement of a Bengali film appropriated the amateur tone of a regular film viewer and provided the related links. The overriding point then was not merely about profits generated from diaspora releases of Bengali films, nor was it crucial for DMV to experience failure in global marketing and distribution of films like those of Tapan Biswas. The cardinal issue was the possibilities of alternative circulation and dissemination of these 'parallel films' worldwide.

Sites of Exhibition: Urban Films Versus Rural Films

Producers, directors, journalists and our interlocuters confirmed that it was the 1990s that experienced a division in the film distribution policy in Bengal for the first time, in terms of the location of exhibition sites. In press and public sphere discussions, this is popularly called the binary of '*gramer chhobi/shaharer chhobi*' (the binary of films made for the rural masses/films made for the urban masses). To be more specific, on the one hand, films belonging to the Bengali 'mainstream' released at the majority of the exhibition sites, while on the other, Rituparno Ghosh or Anjan Das films started being associated with some specific exhibition halls and their niche demography. The distribution binary or division not only worked through the logic of the rural versus urban, but also as a class category within the metropolis of Kolkata. This binary, resulting in the exhibition of non-mainstream films, got associated with the concept of 'parallel' film culture.

This section focuses on these exhibition sites, exploring their biographical detailing and locational importance in the process of getting associated with the post-liberalisation 'parallel' film circuit. To start with, Nandan was the most significant of all, both in the way it assumed and constructed a distinct 'Nandan film crowd'. This location was established in 1985 as part of the state initiative taken 'to promote film culture' in West Bengal, and as its former CEO and the Editor of *Bengali Film Directory*, Ansu Sur, asserted, its goal was to create mature young-adult film-goers who would learn to appreciate 'good' films, not only through watching films there, but also by taking part in film appreciation courses, seminars, lectures and interactive sessions organised by Nandan.[30] Nandan's former CEO, Nilanjan Chattopadhyay, foregrounded that the place has a specific film crowd, who often decided to watch a film just because it was being screened at Nandan.[31] Thus, a film show at Nandan by the 1990s gained a symbolic value, both for the film itself and its audience. Chattopadhyay and Sur considered Nandan as an outstanding intervention into the existing Bengali single-screen theatre chain like Minar, Bijali, Chobighar or Rupabani, Aruna, Bharati, to name a few, and also as different from the multiplexes because it never had an aim to create a film market, but rather, singularly aimed at engaging in the showcasing of quality films.

Priya, another important name that regularly released 'parallel' Bengali films, projected its position as exclusively catering to a niche *bhadralok* audience. Both Sagnik Michael Sinha, the Sales Manager, and Arijit Dutta, the owner, believed Priya's posh south Kolkata location as providing the basis of its middle-class and upper middle-class film crowd, which lives in close-by places like Rashbehari, Gariahat, Golpark or Ballygunge.[32] When Sinha was asked how Priya maintains its difference from any other single-screen theatre of Kolkata, he shared two main strategies adopted to maintain the 'class' and 'quality' of Priya cinema's film crowd. According to him, when in the 1980s, Bengali films with 'crude stories' and 'vulgar dialogues' started hitting the big screen one after another, the 'educated' urban audience stopped watching them at cinema halls. In those times, Priya released only Hollywood films for the city-based urban, 'educated' film audience. It did not associate its name with those Bengali mainstream products. When films like *Ek Je Achhe Kanya* or *Shubho Mahurat* (*The Auspicious Hour*) by Rituparno Ghosh in 2002, were released, the Priya-film-crowd began expecting something 'different' from the usual mainstream run-of-the-mill films. Sinha explained through a classist logic that the intentionally higher rates of ticket pricing in Priya was to target a certain class of audience. Another important factor is that Priya is associated with the Piyali films distribution company, which earlier released many 'quality' Bengali films, including some of the Satyajit Ray classics. The interior of Priya, with its decorated lobby showcasing and highlighting Satyajit Ray classics, along with antique furniture from his film sets, projects this glorious history of Bengali cinema through regular film shows.

Star Theatre, on the other hand, had a distinct cultural history associated with great theatre personalities, such as Girish Ghosh, and theatre performances by renowned actors and film stars in the Bengali cultural milieu. An over 100-year-old heritage venue turned into a popular entertainment site of north Kolkata, where cultural events are held regularly, and Bengali 'parallel' films are a regular part of their programming since the early 2000s. These specific exhibition sites that distribute many quality Bengali films, through their association with the film society culture, 'quality film' distribution companies, their marketing strategy of higher ticket prices, or simply because of possessing a rich cultural history, quite evidently reinstated their 'difference' from the regular single-screen theatre chain that run average mainstream films. Along with Nandan, Priya and Star, some other exhibition sites outside Kolkata, like Lok Sanskriti Mancha, Burdwan, Deenbandhu Mancha, Siliguri etc., facilitated this network of 'new parallel' cinema circulation. One can also say that these urban exhibition sites, working within the discourse of 'taste' and quality of Bengali cinema, have become an important part of imagining the 'new parallel'; and thus they complete the circle of production–distribution and public sphere imaginations regarding the idea of the 'new parallel' in the post-liberalisation moment of Bengali cinema, subsequently Tollywood.

Narratives of Nostalgia in Post-Liberalisation Bengali 'Parallel' Cinema

> This puja in my grandma's house is more than 150 years old, my mom's grandpa used to celebrate with brilliant fireworks, grand feasts, and ornaments imported from Germany .... (heard that) these utensils were used in Satyajit Ray's film 'Devi', Ray visited this house one day. My mother was just a kid then ...
>
> Now just my grandma stays here, her four children come with their families every year at this time .... the five days festival starts tomorrow, Banshida is late as usual, still chatting with Bumba just like the opening scene in Ray's film 'Elephant God' ...[33]

These lines from *Utsab* engage with past events and nostalgic imaginations in different patterns of memorialising. Here, the video voice belongs to the character of this film, Joy (Ratul Shankar), who introduces his ancestral house during *Durga Puja* (the festival of Goddess Durga) celebrations. The narrative here, as well as in the entire film, is full of different histories and references of past events of this house and his memorialising. The story is not only a memory of his childhood and his past, but also the pasts and memories that he learnt from the older generation. The larger frame of past-ness goes beyond the character[34] and speaks of a general past. Past-ness is not only evoked through the memory narrative of *Utsab*, but also through the film form that memorialises a cinematic past of Bengal, with some references and stylisations. We do not consider this film to be an exceptional case to study, which brought and evoked certain cinematic pasts in this particular manner. But rather, we argue that this memorialisation through the film form is a general feature of the post-1990 Bengali 'parallel' cinema that needs discussion. Hence, the following section will try to explore how the form of the post-liberalisation Bengali 'parallel' cinema memorialises earlier Bengali cinematic practices.

One of the important features of post-liberalisation Bengali 'parallel' films, which generated the 'feel' and 'pleasure' of earlier Bengali cinema, was their use of the literary narrative. Rituparno Ghosh's *Hirer Angti* (based on a novel by Shirshendu Mukhopadhyay) or *Chokher Bali* (based on the novel by Rabindranath Tagore), Anjan Das's *Iti Srikanta* (based on the novel by Sharatchandra Chattopadhyay), or Pinaki Chowdhury's *Ballygunge Court* (based on the work by Bani Basu), and many such other films were inspired by or were adaptations of Bengali literary creations. A significant point that came up again and again in public sphere discussions of the 'crisis narrative' of the 1980s–90s was the distance of contemporary Bengali cinematic practice from Bengali literature. This point was considered one of the possible reasons behind Bengali cinema's alleged decline in quality. Kiranmoy Raha, while discussing Bengali cinema's history, stresses on earlier Bengali cinema's closeness to Bengali literature, which, according to him, resulted in Bengali cinema's 'difference' from other regional cinemas of India.[35] First, he observes Bengali cinema's inheritance of a 'rich literary tradition' and 'literary attachment' that caused Bengali filmic texts to rely less on mythological stories, as compared to films made in Hindi, Tamil or Telugu.[36] Second, according to him, this literary trait made Bengali cinema less dependent on songs-and-dance sequences. Other writings on Bengali cinema also emphasised the association of Bengali cinematic practice with the literary tradition of Bengal in the silent era, during the emergence of the talkies and in the decades of the 1950s and 1960s. Raha states that in the very first year of the talkies, only one of six films made was mythological.[37] Nirmalya Acharya, in a different essay, observes that in those initial years of the talkies, Bengali cinema showed more interest in 'social subjects' rather than mythological narratives, and 'in this quest, literature expectedly enough, proved to be cinema's most accessible cornucopia'.[38] Interestingly, during this time period, many renowned writers from the Bengali literary tradition emerged as script writers of films, and many of them became directors themselves. Premankur Atarthi, who was a writer, made the first new theatre talkie, *Dena Paona* (*Debt and Returns*), in 1931, which was based on Sharatchandra Chattopadhyay's story. On the one hand, a large number of films were based on Bengali stories and novels, and on the other hand, many of the Bengali novelists wrote scripts for Bengali films. In those early years, many of Sharatchandra and Rabindranath Tagore's novels and stories were made into films. Tagore himself was associated with the direction of New Theatre's production of *Natir Puja* (*The Dancing Girl's Worship*) in 1932. Later, well-known figures from Bengali literature, like Bibhutibhushan Bandyopadhyay, Tarashankar Bandyopadhya, Premendra Mitra and Sailajananda Mukherjee became quite prominent in the scenario of Bengali cinema, which included films like *Saptapadi* (*Seven Steps*) by Ajoy Kar in 1961, *Jhinder Bandi* (*Prisoners of Jhind*) by Tapan Sinha in 1961, *Palatak* (*Truant*) by Tarun Majumdar in 1963, and *Nimantran* (*Invitation*) by Tarun Majumdar in 1971.

This association of Bengali literature and cinema made a section of the cinema-going public from the middle class refer to and understand film as '*boi*' which is the Bengali word for 'book'. Acharya says that such people inferred that cinema was 'a mere variant of literature', and Raha observed that because of this preference of 'good' stories in Bengali films, producers increasingly hired established litterateurs as script writers for Bengali cinema. This practice, however, became somewhat rare in the 1980s and 1990s. Writer and journalist Ranjan Bandyopadhyay[39] observed that in the 1990s, with Aparna Sen and Rituparno Ghosh, literary cinema (that the Bengali middle-class viewer used to refer to as '*boi*') returned to Bengali cinematic practice, something that had declined in the previous two decades. It was not only the case of 'period' films like *Iti Srikanta* or *Chokher Bali* that brought up the idea of the glorious past of Bengal or Bengali literature via the 'greatness' of a Tagore or a Sharatchandra narrative. But also, the very identity of Bengali cinema based on Bengali literature, even if it was from a contemporary popular novel by Bani Basu or Suchitra Bhattacharya, essentially brought back the legacy of 'good' Bengali cinema (*Bhalo Bangla Boi ba Chhobi*). Anjan Das memorialised this earlier tradition of literary films in Bengal and expressed his disappointment about the way in which it vanished from Bengali cinematic practice.[40] He therefore consciously tried to bring back the pleasure of literariness through his films. It is interesting to observe that most of his films are literary adaptations.

Along with the 're-emergence' of certain cinematic practices, such as films based on literary creations, certain directorial works and directors became central to the cinematic memorialisation of post-1990 Bengali 'parallel' cinema. Rituparno Ghosh, from the beginning of his film-making career, followed Satyajit Ray's aesthetics in different aspects of his film-making. *Hirer Angti* narrated the story of what happened to a family when a person arrived unexpectedly during the *Durga Puja* preparations and claimed to be the sole legal heir of their house. The narrative uncovers some of the buried secrets and histories of this ancestral house. It is important to underline how Ghosh made changes in the original story to construct the idea of nostalgia from the legacy of literary Bengali cinema of the past. First, the novel by Shirshendu was set in the time of '*Baishakhi Purnima*' (the full moon night of the Gregorian calendar month of the Bengali new year), which was changed to the time of the autumn festival or *Durga Puja* in the film. Shifting the event to the latter, first served to provide some essence of Bengali culture and feelings of some earlier Bengali films that dealt with similar joint family structures and *Puja* celebrations. Second, it specifically reminded its audience of a particular film by Satyajit Ray, one of the *Feluda* series stories, *Joy Baba Felunath*[41] (*The Elephant God*), 1979. The mood of the *Durga Puja* holidays, scenes of the making of the Durga idol, and sequences of preparations of the *Puja* celebration inevitably reminded the viewer familiar with Ray's film of *Joy Baba Felunath*. The spaces or *mise-en-scene* that Ghosh created between the young boy and the unexpected guest were strikingly similar to that of Ray's *Feluda* and his younger cousin and assistant Topshe. Ghosh further incorporated the nostalgia associated with the *probashi Bangali* or the NRI Bengali coming home for the *Durga Puja* celebrations, since in the film the family's second son comes with his family from the US for the *Puja* celebrations, something that was not part of the original story by Shirshendu Mukherjee.

Following *Hirer Angti*, Ghosh, in many of his films, evoked the nostalgia of Ray's films. It reflected in the way he developed his dialogues, designed a scene, used the lighting scheme, and created the overall visual atmosphere. This style of Ghosh's film-making was a form of memorialising that provided its viewers the pleasure of remembering Ray and his films. He also occasionally commented on them, referring to the memory of Ray films, as he did at the beginning of *Utsab*. Within the film, Joy's memory of Ray's films (*Joy Baba Felunath* and *Devi*) evoked the memory of viewers as well, who are familiar with Ray's films. In Ghosh's 2005 film, *Antarmahal* (*Views of the Inner Chamber*), the image of Soha Ali Khan instantly reminds the viewer of Sharmila Tagore in Ray's *Devi*. Besides the thematic resemblance, the narrative of feudal decay and the practice of idolising the woman as was shown in *Devi*, *Antarmahal* visually evokes the memory of *Devi* in the way Soha's looks were designed and the camera angles and lighting schemes were used.

Ghosh's *Chokher Bali* also visually brought the cinematic memory of Ray's films, especially in visual registers of the memory of *Charulata* (*The Lonely Wife*), Ray's 1964 film. The manner in which it captured Aishwarya Rai's image with an opera glass brought back memories of the sequence of Madhabi Mukherjee with an opera glass in *Charulata*. Even in *Noukadubi* (*Boat Wreck*), Ghosh's 2011 film, a whole discourse on Bengali cinematic past is evoked in its place-ness or the use of locations of the Benaras *ghat* (shore) and its interiority, the literariness of the film narrative, and the way in which the images of Raima Sen as Hemnalini were captured, reminding the viewer of her grandmother, Suchitra Sen's image in the same role in the earlier version of the film. In the 2010 film, *Abohomaan* (*The Eternal*), the *mise-en-scene* of the study of Aniket, the film-maker, played by Dipankar Dey, is a reminder of Satyajit Ray's own study room. In this way, Ghosh's film worked to generate the 'feel' of Ray's films. Goutam Ghose, however, worked on the memorialisation of Ray at a different scale while making the sequel of Ray's 1970 film *Aranyer Dinratri* (*Days and Nights in the Forest*). Ghose's 2003 sequel, *Abar Aranye* (*In the Forest Again*) started with visuals of *Aranyer Dinratri*, and with a voice-over of Aparna (Sharmila Tagore), describing the Palamou trip of four young men in April 1969. She, then, introduces the present conditions of three of them, Asim, Sanjoy and Hari, and mentions the absence of Shekhar. It seems that the characters in this film belonged more to a previous film than this one. It essentially established itself as a memory of an earlier film. The entire film can be seen as a memorialisation of *Aranyer Dinratri*. Not only did it evoke the memory of Ray's film in its characterisation, their conversations during the trip to Palamou, and the sequences, but there were also visual quotations from *Aranyer Dinratri*. The film used a cross-cutting device (scenes inserted from *Aranyer Dinratri*) to evoke the memories of some sequences of Ray's film. For instance, when characters in the film were busy chitchatting at a tea shop, scenes from *Aranyer Dinratri* appeared, in which four of them were seen wandering through the forest. Similarly, three of them were seen walking in the present through the forest in the next shot. The film cross-cuts and alternates between present-ness and past-ness. It is also interesting when sequences of a memory game within the film memorialise the memory game sequence of *Aranyer Dinratri* by using a black-and-white colour scheme to evoke the past-ness, and quotes scenes from the memory game sequence of *Aranyer Dinratri*. In this game of name-dropping, Ray's name appears, making the characters memorialise the creator (Ray) of their screen characters.

Along with *Aranyer Dinratri*, Goutam Ghose's *Abar Aranye* evoked the memory of Ray's 1991 film, *Agantuk* (*The Stranger*). The way the film talked about the binary of nature and civilisation, urbanity and innocence, and created a figure like *Mastermoshai* (teacher), it reminded one of Manmohan (the name of Utpal Dutt's character) from *Agantuk*,[42] and the now famous sequence, where he speaks at length on the conflicts between nature versus civilisation. The reference of tribal people and tribal colony also connected the film to *Agantuk* and the thematic of idealised nature and the people who live in the lap of nature. In this manner, these film texts memorialise the earlier cinematic practice of Bengali cinema. It is also important to note that Rituparno Ghosh shot a film like *Dosar* (*Companion*), in 2006, in black-and-white, and essentially evoked the past-ness of black-and-white film aesthetics in its form. Another important aspect of the form that acted on this memorialising is use of aesthetic devices like flashback and the epistolary mode. Flashbacks and voice-over narrations of poetry were used extensively as cinematic devices in these films to bring the idea of the character's past or general past-ness. Sometimes, the past was evoked. For instance, in *Asukh* (*Malaise*), by Ghosh in 1999, the past-ness was evoked and executed through the voice-over narration of Tagore's poetry in the voice of Aparna Sen. In Aniruddha Roychowdhury's 2009 film, *Antaheen* (*The Endless Wait*), Sharmila Tagore's character is shown talking to an unidentified person on the telephone, who had mistakenly dialled her number, and after that, would call and talk to her for hours which evolved into a romantic relationship. This was in reference to the 1993 Mrinal Sen film, *Antareen* (*The Confined*), which had a similar plot line. In *Dosar,* the memory of a past love affair was evoked by the voice-over of a love poem that was shared by the adulterous lovers. The tone of soliloquy in films like *Dahan* (*Crossfire*) by Ghosh in 1998, as well as *Bariwali* (*Landlady*), *Chokher Bali* and *Shanjhbatir Roopkathara* (*Strokes and Silhouettes*) often expressed a certain kind of past-ness of events in one's life. The epistolary mode of expression evoked the past-ness, adding a characteristic aesthetic dimension. Aparna Sen's 2011 film, *The Japanese Wife*, narrated the story of Snehamoy and Miyagi, and how their relationship evolved through pen-friendship. The epistolary mode, used extensively in the film, provided a sense of nostalgia and a homage to an obsolete art of romantic expressions (see Figure 3.2).

Interestingly, the post-1990s Bengali 'parallel' film text focuses repeatedly on narratives concerned with memory and past-ness. A film like *Dekha* (*Vision*) by Goutam Ghose in 2001 has as its central protagonist an aged Bengali poet, Shashibhushan (played by Soumitra Chattopadhyay), and his troubled 'vision'. In the section that deals with the 'present' of the aged poet, Shashibhushan is seen in his surroundings: his old house, the people he knows, the places he belongs to; but his 'vision' is absent since he has become partially blind. On the other hand, the sections dealing with his 'past' are shot from the perspective of Shashibhushan in his childhood, youth

Figure 3.2: DVD Screen Grab of *Dahan*

Source: Channel B.

and middle age. Each of these shots are taken from his point of view, underlining his perspective and the way he 'sees'. This is done so that Shashibhushan is rendered 'invisible' since what is realised on the screen is his point of view both literally and metaphorically (foresight). The film keeps going back and forth, and Shashibhushan's vision of the past and the way he is 'viewed' in the present are merged in the film. Some other films of the 'parallel' circuit, like Buddhadeb Dasgupta's 1997 film, *Laal Darja* (*The Red Door*) or Aparna Sen's 1995 film, *Yugant* (*What the Sea Said*) or *Paromitar Ekdin* similarly deal with the intermingling of the past and the present (see Figures 3.3 and 3.4).

In the nostalgia narratives of these films, childhood, memory and lost innocence are recurrent themes. In films like *Bhalo Theko* (*Forever Yours*) by Gautam Halder in 2004 or *Asukh*, childhood memories haunt the present of their characters. *Bhalo Theko* is based on a day in the life of its protagonist, Anandi (played by Vidya Balan). The film returns to past incidents of her life. Her childhood memory of going to a village *mela* (fair), where she was lost and later found by her elder brother, has been referred to more than once in the film.

Figure 3.3: DVD Screen Grab of *Paromitar Ekdin*

Source: Channel B.

Figure 3.4: DVD Screen Grab of *Paromitar Ekdin*

Source: Channel B.

A close parallel is drawn to Anandi's 'present' life, where her politically active brother has been missing for some years and she has not been able to find him.

In these narratives of past and childhood memories, the 'present-absent' father–mother figure plays a significant role. In *Dekha*, Shashibhushan's absent mother remains central to the development of his remembrance and the way memory maps out his traumatic present throughout the film. In *Laal Darja*,[43] the mother figure's presence is felt in references to letters written to her son. In *Dekha*, she is more prominent, shown as singing in the protagonist's memory. In one of the sequences, she lyrically merges with three other women in the protagonist's life, while he journeys through dream, memory and fantasy. *Unishe April* also evokes the past through memories of its protagonists, Sarojini (Aparna Sen) and Mithu (Debashree Roy). The film uses the flashback device to establish Mithu's childhood and traumatic experience of her father's death as well as Sarojini's married life with her husband. Subhadra Chowdhury's 2004 film, *Prahar* (*Hours*), shows a revisiting of the absent father in its narrative of past events. Buddhadeb Dasgupta's 2008 film, *Kaalpurush* (*Memories in the Mist*), also made its protagonist embark on a surreal journey to meet his lost father.

Along similar lines, Anjan Das' 2002 film, *Shanjhbatir Roopkathara* (*Strokes and Silhouettes*), based on Joy Goswami's novel of the same name, deploys this device of pastness and memory overwhelmingly and in a cyclical form. The novel, too, begins and ends with the same words and lines, where the protagonist, Shanjhbati, introduces herself and her surroundings. It foregrounds the very nature of how memory operates within the psyche of the present for the protagonist of the novel and the film. The film constructs this idea of memory and memorialisation visually through the image of a swinging cradle and the protagonist's (Indrani Haldar) voice-over in a memorialising tone. To quote an excerpt from it:

> My name is Saanjhbati endearingly Tukun. Ma gave me that name as I was born at twilight time .... Pa used to see a light around me ...
>
> Ma never saw that glow. Ma was like a water vessel. Light passed through Ma like water. But if you ever look through water, deep down under ... you will see a greenish tinge below the surface .... dissolving into darkness.
>
> Light never goes through Pa; he is like a massive tree. Light falls on the leaves but it can never go through the trunk.[44]

Memorialising almost became something that leads to dreaming. And the voice-over, along with the deployment of the soliloquy throughout the film blurred the line between dreaming and memorialising. Towards the end, Shanjhbati, after a long gap, returned to her father. Her father said, 'So you have come out from under water .... under fathomless water .... Wipe your face! Let me see your face. Is it full of algae or sand?'[45] The reference to water reminded of her dead mother. After this sequence, when her father started sketching a portrait of Shanjhbati, it became a portrait of Shanjhbati's mother. In a way, therefore, she became the embodiment of the memory of her mother. It was Shanhbati's dream to make her father draw a portrait of her mother. Finally, when Shanjhbati achieved her dream, she was able to write something. She started with 'My name is Shanjhbati endearingly Tukun. Ma gave me that name as I was born at twilight time .... Pa used to see a light around me ...' Before this sequence, the dream-like image of the swinging cradle returned, and the dream fairy brought back her memory.[46] Thus, here, memorialising is a two-way journey, both from and towards the dream, central to which is the father figure.

Politics of Past-ness and the Self-Image of the *Bhadralok* Class

The post-liberalisation period in India is marked by new economic policies, newer job sectors, and the growth of consumer culture, all of which merged and resulted in the idea of a 'new' middle class. At the structural level, Leela Fernandes defines this class as a 'social group that operates as a proponent of economic liberalization'.[47] In her words:

> This middle class is not new in terms of its structural or social basis. In other words, its 'newness' does not refer to upwardly mobile segments of the population entering the middle class. Rather its newness refers to a process of production of a distinctively social and political identity that represents and lays claim to the benefits of liberalization.

She further goes on to argue:

> At a structural level this group largely encompasses English speaking urban, white collar segments of the middle class who are benefiting

> from new employment opportunity (particularly in private sector employment). However, the heart of construction of this social group rests on the assumption that other segments of the middle class and the upwardly mobile working class can potentially join in.[48]

If measured in terms of access to consumer goods, incomes and infrastructure, the Indian middle class grew exponentially during the period between 1995 and 2005. Henrike Donner believes that the definition of the new middle class is based on the ideal of middle-class professionals, such as 'white collar workers' in private companies, possessing education, skills and expertise.[49]

Along with the 'emergence' of this 'new' middle class and its socio-political construction in the Indian economy, the creation of the media image of this new class is relevant for our discussion below. According to Donner, Rangaswamy, Wei and Steevson, the media image of the 'newness' of this class rests on its embrace of the social practices of taste and commodity consumption, which market a new cultural standard and is associated with liberalisation and the opening of the Indian market to the global economy.[50] This new middle class of IT professionals and others working in multinational companies is a symbolic, dynamic construct in which consumption markers played an important role. In West Bengal, this idea of being and becoming a 'new' middle class affected the *bhadralok* belief system regarding this 'new' class taste, their cultural need and social position. The rise of this 'cosmopolitanism of the "English-speaking"' that was required for the 'economic laws of the job market' came as an attack on *bhadralok* culture and its belief systems on a large scale. As has been discussed earlier in Chapters 1 and 2, the *bhadralok* culture (specifically, the film culture related to 'taste') had already been marginalised with the emergence of a new popular culture in urban and other suburban localities of West Bengal. However, still in this case, the 'cultural attack' on the 'taste' discourse of the *bhadralok* class was generated from outside the public sphere (*bhadra*) and its well-defined domain of '*bhadrata*' ('gentility'). Furthermore, the 'attack' of the new consuming middle-class came from *within* the very same Bengali middle-class sphere. The following section focuses on the cinematic construct and representation of the 'self-image' of the *bhadralok* class in the post-1990 Bengali 'new parallel' cinema.

At the outset, it is important to point out how the politics of nostalgia works on self-image formation and the extent to which it constructs the *bhadra* protagonists in the 'new parallel' cinema. The politics of nostalgia works here through different registers. The personal loss and nostalgia narratives go beyond an individual 'crisis', a reference to a degeneration of the *bhadra* ethos and worldview. Through threatened and vulnerable characters, these films present a marginalised self-image of the *bhadralok* cultural identity. The concept of an 'ideal and homogeneous culture' that defined the Bengali *bhadralok* class is repeatedly evoked by these films. And it is not incidental that we see 'artistic' protagonists in film after film who are either artists by profession, or truly devoted to art practices. The politics of having 'artistic' protagonists and their struggle allows for a narrative drive to 'reclaim' a certain *bhadralok* identity and 'good taste' lost due to degradation and retrogression. In a film like *Hemanter Pakhi* (*Autumn Bird*) by Urmi Chakraborty in 2005, the protagonist Aditi's (Tanusree Shankar) sensitive self is located in her deep-rooted interest in Bengali literature and her own writing 'talent'. The conflict and opposition to her sensitive self that she faces within her family from her husband and two sons is a challenge to her emerging literary career. In passage after passage in Suchitra Bhattacharya's novel, on which the film is based, this binary of the sensitive, artistic 'self' of Aditi, and the insensitive, rude 'other' in Aditi's husband is described in detail. Later on, this conflict goes on between Aditi and her sons, both in the novel and the film. Here we would like to quote a dialogue sequence from the film, where these conflicting positions lead to a setback in the relationships:

> Papai: Mom, why do you think one should return here (India)? What is the use of coming back? Suppose I get a chance for research in a good place (abroad).
>
> Tatai: What Rubbish! Tell the truth; put it frankly that you will earn much more money over there and live lavishly. For me my country is better; anyhow I will earn more money here.
>
> Aditi: Your only aim in life is earning money .... fantastic! I think I'll write something about this subject. Our children are becoming selfish and leaving everything aside. What sort of upbringing?[51]

Following this sequence, Aditi's husband interrupts, supporting their sons 'bright career ambitions', and says that his sons will fulfil the dreams that he could not achieve. Aditi reacts, saying that then 'our nationality', 'our tradition' and 'culture' will no longer have any bearing on 'our children'. One can observe how, in this particular film, the *bhadralok* anxiety and sense of degeneration was narrated in terms of generational conflicts and clashes of ideology. The anxiety here did not come from the so-called lower classes outside the sphere of *bhadrata* but from the next generation, within the family.

Another film, *Ballygunge Court* by Pinaki Chowdhury in 2008, stresses and expands on this theme; it is located in a residential locality in Kolkata, where in a particular apartment only aged parents live since the next generation has immigrated abroad for better prospects. The father had attempted to stop his ambitious son when he had wanted to move. After the son moved, his mother passes away and the father, as an act of revenge, does not inform his son about his mother's demise. When the son returns, he realises his 'mistake' and finally starts living with his father in their Kolkata residence. These kinds of narratives of generational conflict and the isolation of the older generation, be it in physical terms in a film like *Ballygunge Court*, or emotionally, as in *Hemanter Pakhi*, reveals the anxiety within the *bhadralok* community and its 'inner crisis'. This crisis is caused by a threat that comes from within the *bhadralok* home, family and the 'inner' world of middle-class dreams. The threat of growing consumer culture in a post-liberalised country and the anxiety of 'losing' one's self and one's *bhadralok* identity result in anxiety stories of relationships. Whereas in films like *Hemanter Pakhi* or *Ballygunge Court*, the crisis narrative is clear enough in its origin and nature, in Rituparno Ghosh's *Asukh, Unishe April* and *Utsab*, or Anjan Das's *Shanjhbatir Rupkathara*, the tension is more subtle and riding on memory stories and the desire for a nostalgic return.

In emphasising the vulnerable, artistic, sensitive self and the traumatised previous generation, they try to present a critique of the growing consumer culture, liberalised economy, and the threat it poses to *bhadralok* middle-class life. However, the 'critique' is incomplete and somewhat superficial since it denies a further exploration of the crisis of middle-class life, thus falling short in their constructions of the ideal 'self' that takes refuge in memories and dreams, and remains unharmed by ambitious, careerist, and aspirational new middle-class lives. In Buddhadeb Dasgupta's *Kaalpurush*, the protagonist (Rahul Bose) is posited against his ambitious and insensitive wife. The wife goes to America to write a travelogue series on America, whereas the protagonist, from time to time, goes back to his childhood memory and his father. Instead of critically engaging with the developing neoliberal lifestyle and its challenges faced by the middle-class, the film merely ends up idealising the *bhadralok* sensibility that perhaps lost its merit within the ever-evolving middle-class society. And in this imagination and construction of the self-image of this class, a certain kind of past-ness became inherent. Past-ness here again does not refer to larger or broader socio-political narratives, but rather alludes to memory, reminiscences and nostalgia. The ideal middle-class self appears in these narratives as essentially disengaged from the present, if not detached from it. That is why it is the personal memory of good times that is required to establish this self-image, rather than a pressing issue of the contemporary.

Anindya Chattopadhyay, the lead singer of the popular Bengali band, *Chandrabindoo*, debuted as a film-maker with *Open Tee Bioscope* in 2015, and created multiple registers of past narratives and nostalgia of a generation that had spent its childhood and adolescence days in the 1980s–90s north Kolkata. The film recreated the memory of *Chandrabindoo* songs and their lyrics that spoke about adolescent romance, juvenile activities, and north Kolkata *para* (community/locality) culture, which was immensely popular in the 1990s. Moreover, the space of north Kolkata households, narrow by-lanes, club grounds, *ghats*, trams, linguistic intonations, which are very much part of contemporary Kolkata, emerged as a space of the past. The protagonist of the film, Phoara (Riddhi Sen), who was once a part of the *para* fabric, left the place and after his return to his home and neighborhood the place-ness of his adolescence days appeared through the trope of memory. The music, songs, and the background score added to the affective registers of 1980s and 1990s nostalgia. The film went on to become highly successful, both commercially and critically.

Therefore, the politics of nostalgia in these films works to generate a sense of loss, lamentation, and in turn results in an imagination of a common 'glorious' past that a particular class (*bhadralok*) owned.

The nostalgic mode operates in ritualising that lost common past by imagining the commonality that a class 'shares'. However, there are film examples like *Herbert* by Suman Mukhopadhyay in 2005 and *Ekti Tarar Khonje* by Avik Mukhopadhyay within the 'new parallel' cinema circuit, which offered an alternative take on this eulogised ideal *bhadralok* past and somewhat criticised the politics of pastness represented in a majority of the films of 'new parallel cinema'. Nevertheless, the 'new parallel' cinema of the 2000s is predominantly defined by the narrative of loss and degeneration of the *bhadralok* culture and identity.

The Poster Boy of Post-Liberalisation Bengali 'Parallel' Cinema: A Study of Rituparno Ghosh's Stardom

> If my films help the Bengali film industry, Tollygunge, in any way, I'll be extremely happy. I'm extremely flattered that I'm being compared with Satyajit Ray. But I feel I'm majorly overrated. I came into Bengali cinema at a time when intelligent urban films were going out of fashion. That's why I found a place quickly.[52]

This is not a section aimed at any kind of auteur study of the director, Rituparno Ghosh, or studying film texts in accordance with the 'creative mind' behind them that has a certain kind of authority over a body of films bearing the 'signature' of his creativity. Rather, we are interested here in how a 'star figure' is constructed beyond film language and aesthetics, and is determined and regulated by subsidiary media texts, and how interest is generated in popular discourse. Some auteur studies have been carried out, of Bengali film-makers like Ghosh, who belong to the circuit of 'art house' cinema of Bengal. One of the most important texts in this genre of writing is John W. Hood's study of Buddhadeb Dasgupta in his book, *The Essential Mystery: Major Filmmakers of Indian Art Cinema*, where Hood describes Dasgupta's 'artistic vision' and 'technical excellence'. He discusses in detail the unique features of Dasgupta's films, like 'creative emotion', 'profound sense of realism', his 'concern for the individual in isolation or alienation', and the 'extraordinary originality' of both style and substance.[53] Hood sees Dasgupta as a director 'seeing beyond the material exterior to the yearnings of the simplest human heart',[54] and parallel to this, also acknowledges Dasgupta's presence at international festival circuits. Another book on Dasgupta, *A Poet with a Camera: Buddhadeb Dasgupta: A Monograph*, edited by Ajay Kumar Das and published by Nandan, is composed of critical reviews published in *The Statesman, The Telegraph, The Times of India, Deep Focus, Cinema Wave* and *Amritabazar Patrika*, with comments by Satyajit Ray, Mrinal Sen, Derek Malcom and David Robinson.[55] These reviews and their compilations have tried to project him as a poet and film-maker of fine sensibility and having 'a signature style', with an international reputation.

Shoma A. Chatterji's study of another contemporary Bengali film-maker, Aparna Sen, while recognising the art cinema tradition in Bengal, situates Sen's work as a cinema of 'authentic woman-experience'.[56] At the same time, Chatterji argues that Sen belongs to a shared tradition:

> Along with Buddhadeb Dasgupta and Goutam Ghose, she belongs to the young Calcutta school. Together yet not quite together, they confidently tread the path of meaningful cinema as an aesthetic expression. A cinema already formed and created by predecessors Ray, Mrinal Sen and Ritwik Ghatak. Each of these three, Buddhadeb, Goutam and Aparna are distinctively different from each other.[57]

Chatterji traces how Sen, in all her films, 'pays serious attention to a whole range of feminist concerns',[58] and she tries to establish Sen as a film-maker who is in constant opposition to Indian popular cinema in portraying urban womanhood against the grain of conventional Indian femininity.[59] Similar studies have been carried out of Rituparno Ghosh and his films by Somdutta Mondal, depicting Ghosh as a 'women's film-maker' in Bengal.[60] Considering Ghosh to be 'a bridge between good Bangla cinema and the crowds',[61] Mandal emphasised his directorial talent as a specialist in 'human relationship', and especially, of the female mind.[62] However, Ghosh and his films were not always appreciated for their humanist concern and he was not always praised as women's film-maker; sometimes they were also seen as limiting and conformist. Pachu Roy, quite contrary to Mandal's approach, writes about Ghosh in a brief essay titled, 'Paribarik Chhobir Master: Rituparno Ghosh' ('The Master of Family Films: Rituparno Ghosh') in the special film issue of *Madhyam O Sangjog*, February 2002.

In his essay, Roy traces Ghosh's conformist attitude in his first five films (from *Unishe April* to *Bariwali*) and argues how in each of these films, Ghosh expresses his 'fear' of going against the establishment of middle-class social life.[63] Sumit Dey, in his unpublished MPhil dissertation, 'Defining the Rituparnoesque: Rituparno Ghosh and Auteurism, Sexuality and Stardom', coined the term 'Rituparnoesque' to connote various aspects of authorship, aesthetics, sensibilities, gender politics, and so on, both in his films and his public life as the distinctiveness and individualism of Rituparno Ghosh.[64]

Our concern is, however, different from that of Roy and Mandal, or the earlier 'Auteur studies' of other Bengali film-makers who were contemporary to Ghosh. This section maps the 'emergence' of Ghosh's centrality in post-liberalisation Bengali 'new parallel' cinema, and how this celebrity persona was constructed in subsidiary media discourses other than the film media in which he was directly involved. At the outset, it is important to mention three points around which Ghosh's star persona as an 'alternative' film-maker was built. First, Ghosh is seen and imagined in *bhadralok* discourse as a continuation of the 'good' Bengali film tradition, to be more appropriate, as carrying on the legacy of Ray. Second, Ghosh is seen and mapped in popular imagination as 'someone with a difference'. And third, Ghosh is a strategic director figure in the formative phase of Tollywood for initiating and introducing innovative casting, promotions and publicity, alongside entrepreneurial collaborations and finally enthusing his own image as representative of this new revamped face of the Bengali film industry, Tollywood.[65] These points are crucial to the media discourse around Ghosh in the Bengali public sphere. To begin with, the realist charge of Ghosh's films, which come from their resemblance to the *mise-en-scene* of Ray's films, are frequently acknowledged in the public sphere discussions around Ghosh. Quoted below is an excerpt from the website India Net Zone's introduction to Ghosh:

> Rituparno Ghosh, often hailed as the rightful heir of Satyajit Ray, is one of the most talented Indian directors .... (a) feature of Ghosh's films (is) his cultural influence. The influences of Rabindranath Tagore and Satyajit Ray are apparent in his films. After Ray he is one of the few filmmakers who can use the songs from Tagore delightfully in his films. The sensitivity, passion and intellect with which he makes his films are

> well rewarded by awards. Apart from the National Awards, the films of Rituparno Ghosh are quite popular in the national and international film festival.[66]

The imagined legacy of Ray and the 'glorious' film-making past of Bengal facilitated Ghosh to establish himself and his 'parallel-ness' in West Bengal's public sphere discourse. The 'influence' of different stylisation and narrativisation techniques of Ray is quite evident in Ghosh's works. His films consciously regenerate the effect of Ray films, in terms of their style of dialogues, subtlety of action and *mise-en-scene*, resonating with everyday Bengali middle-class reality.

Goutam Ghose, Buddhadeb Dasgupta and Utpalendu Chakraborty, who belonged to the next generation of film-makers after Ray (a generation Shoma A. Chatterji refers to as the 'young Calcutta school', and Aruna Vasudev sees as 'Bengal's Second Breath'),[67] were not considered to be able successors to Ray, in terms of their narrative patterning or plot development; instead, it was Rituparno Ghosh who was hailed as the worthy inheritor of Ray's legacy. Ghose, Dasgupta and Chakraborty began their film-making careers when Ray was making some of his last films. This was also the time when art house or parallel films were not getting significant theatrical releases and commercial returns. Rituparno Ghosh's *Unishe April* overcame this jinx by finding its audience and commercial success. India Net Zone's community of Rituparno Ghosh, with more than 2,000 members, praised Ghosh's focus on commercial success, along with his film-making talent. Speaking of him, they said:

> One of India's most acclaimed contemporary filmmakers. He has redefined so called arthouse cinema by successfully marrying art and commerce. His films have won record number of national awards—best film, best director, best actress. A prolific filmmaker with at least one film releasing every year since his second film *Unishe April* (the first to release) in early nineties. Has always kept in mind a film's commercial success and never stayed away from using mainstream stars to his advantage.[68]

Budhdhadeb Dasgupta agreed that neither the masses nor the niche audiences of Bengal form the primary audience base for his films, but it is rather the international festival circuit and foreign organisations who buy the rights for his films.[69] The case was similar for other film-makers of the 'young Calcutta school' that was contemporary to Dasgupta. Obstacles to distribution or the lack of popular appeal, whatever the reason may be, they failed to form a film crowd for their films. In this scenario, Ghosh emerged with a 'difference' in successfully forming an audience base for his films.[70] His films are popular among a crowd, and yet, they manage to be 'different' from the so-called Bengali popular films. In this situation in the post-liberalisation Bengali film scenario, Rituparno Ghosh emerged as an exceptional figure in terms of following a method both in film aesthetics and publicity, in which regard he regularly geared the promotional strategy in his films to target the *bhadralok* audience that would form the base of his films. In order to successfully form an audience base, unlike Dasgupta, Chakraborty or Goutam Ghose, he simultaneously focused on his 'self-image' and on subsidiary media that would influence his films' reception in myriad ways. Ghosh was associated with leading newspaper organisations like *Anandabazar Patrika*, wrote film reviews or other feature stories regularly, became the editor of the film magazine, *Anandalok*, and after he left *Anandabazar Patrika*, he joined *Sangbaad Pratidin* and became the editor of their Sunday supplement, *Robbar*.

His active presence in the media discourse can be elaborated with this following example. Bengali film actor Barun Chanda reviewed Ghosh's 2010 film, *Abohomaan*, in *The Telegraph*, within a week of the film's release. Although Chanda found the film to be technically brilliant, he thought that the 'parallel storylines' and subplots should have added up to something more than a whole, which did not happen in *Abohomaan*.[71] Chanda wrote: '… A series of beautiful, evocative scenes, arbitrarily placed together does not necessarily make a great movie …. I have a suggestion for Ritu …. Before Ritu makes his next film he should ask himself just one simple question. What's the film about? The rest would take care of itself.'[72]

Within five days of this review being published, Ghosh responded, criticising Chanda's approach in the review. Calling Chanda's approach as one stemming from a 'fragmented understanding', Ghosh wrote:

> My 14 films released so far (with three still pending) have clearly established me as a competent storyteller on celluloid, if not a filmmaker of any worthwhile standing. Experimenting with the narrative style is

> something I think I have earned and I am entitled to, with or without anyone's advice, blessings or suggestions.[73]

Here Ghosh himself wrote about influences and comparisons with 'master film-makers', from Harisadhan Dasgupta to Ray, from Ritwik Ghatak to Ingmar Bergman. On Chanda's accusation about why the theme of death appears repetitively in his films, Ghosh's defence was, 'Other directors have had their pet preoccupations too; for instance, Ritwik Ghatak with the Partition.' And then a bit cautiously, he added, 'I am not for one moment claiming comparison with the greats, merely saying that I don't see recurrent theme as a problem per se.'[74] Chanda, comparing Ray's work with that of Ghosh, had said Ghosh could observe Ray in how he kept his beautiful scenes brief. Ghosh reacted to that by saying that he indeed adored Ray for his brief beautiful scenes, but Bergman, another director whom he hugely adores, 'was much given to long dialogue-driven scenes which are the inspiration of *Abohomaan*'.[75]

Then *The Telegraph* opened the issue for the readers to reflect on this debate and published a number of letters that were a part of this discussion.[76] Film scholar Pradip Biswas, who was a member of the NFDC Script Committee, reacted by saying it would be 'stupid' to compare Ghosh with someone like Ray, and wrote that he wanted 'Rituparno to review his own films so that he can wallow in ecstasy', whereas Subhankar Bhattacharya asserted that he completely agreed with Ghosh's 'defence', and said that he considered 'constant comparisons to Satyajit Ray to be unfair and tiresome, when Rituparno has already established his credentials as a director may in itself be self-defeating'.[77]

The point to be noted here is how the question of quality is presupposed in a 'parallel' film-maker's work. It is not just the simple fact of whether or not one may consider Ghosh to be a competent successor to the Bengali 'art' cinema tradition of directors like Ray or Ghatak. Rather, the question is this very comparability of Ghosh with Bengali quality cinema. The press and other media discourse in Bengal have worked on this comparison, to a great extent, to constitute and influence a regime of reception. And this *Abohomaan* face-off possibly illustrates how the directors themselves 'influence' this regime generated around their work. One of the reasons this discourse had reached this extent was because Ghosh could successfully establish himself as a popular press or media person. Moreover, the phenomenal emergence of Rituparno Ghosh in Bengali cinema in the post-liberalisation period had its root(s) in how he had employed various media platforms to mount his own stardom, in order to propagate and nurture a *bhadralok* taste for the reception of his own films and proliferate a discussion and discourse around his films.[78] In the second example, in a controversy centring on Ghosh's 2006 film, *Dosar* (*The Companion*), Sanjay Mukhopadhyay, film scholar, accused Ghosh's film of unethically 'omitting the cultural inverted commas' to go for a complete plagiarism of Krzysztof Kieslowski's *Three Colours Blue* on the first page of the supplementary copy of *The Times of India* on 17 November 2006.[79] Mukhopadhyay considered Ghosh's film to be 'a misunderstood carbon copy of the Kieslowski masterpiece', which has been redesigned and repackaged to suit box-office demands for the middle-class Bengali audience. *Dosar*, based on a couple's troubled relationship after the husband's mistress dies in an accident, and the wife becomes aware of an adulterous affair that her husband was involved in, is according to Mukhopadhyay, a complete thematic plagiarism of Kieslowski's work. Along with Mukhopadhyay's piece as told to Priyanka Dasgupta, there were three other pieces that were published. There was a piece by a director on the condition of anonymity on how he found *Dosar* to be a copy of *Three Colours: Blue*, and especially how he found 'the accident scene in *Dosar* a complete copy'.[80] Another small article introduced the brief narrative structure of *Three Colours: Blue*, and the third section was a notice to say that Ghosh was unavailable for comments. The discussion on the plagiarism of *Dosar*, however, did not stop at this. On 18 November 2006, *Calcutta Times* published film-maker producer Mahesh Bhatt, and musician Anu Malik's take on the plagiarism issue; and the day after, *Calcutta Times* published a set of remarks in favour of and against the plagiarism charge, and named it 'Punch/Counter Punch'. The contemporary Bengali film-maker, Ashoke Viswanathan, located Ghosh's alleged act of plagiarism in a set of master directors' (of world cinema) inspired acts, a sign in their own way of having 'paid "tribute" to the greats by using similar motifs and techniques'.[81] Viswanathan included the films of Buddhadeb Dasgupta, Mrinal Sen and Ray to trace influences of

Andrei Tarkovsky, Ingmar Bergman, Jean-Luc Godard and Federico Fellini in their works.[82]

In a side note, Shubho Shekhar Bhattacharjee, CEO of Planman Motion Picture, which had produced *Dosar*, replied to the allegations of plagiarism. He said that the accusation was disturbing and added that if the accident scene is a copy, then Billy Wilder's *Avanti!*, 1972, should also be questioned, and in that case, it could also be said that every action film is plagiarised from John McTiernan's 1988 film, *Die Hard*. Mukhopadhyay, in a brief note quoting Bertolt Brecht, tried to explain that he could not be responsible for each person's ignorance.[83] The anonymous director added to *Dosar's* alleged plagiarism, listing one more film of Rituparno Ghosh, *Unishe April*, and mentioned that even the Wikipedia acknowledges that it was 'loosely based' on Bergman's *Autumn Sonata*.

This open-ended discussion on whether to call *Dosar* an act of plagiarism or see it as paying tribute to the masters points out how discussions regarding these 'new parallel' films often end up in a discourse about 'taste' that becomes the central determining factor. The question was not so much whether Ghosh was praised for whatever tribute he has given or criticised for his unethical plagiarism; rather, the question was how this allegation along with the overall concern of the press positioned him on a certain plane.

Ghosh's *Dosar* and this allegation of plagiarism in newspapers was more than just an allegation against a director. Starting with Mukhopadhyay's comparison of the film to other adaptations from Ray, namely Kieslowski, to the question of an 'international flavour', to Viswanathan's comparison of the influence of Fellini, Godard and Tarkovski on Mrinal Sen and other Bengali art house directors, and the discussion of the inspiration of Bergman in Ghosh's earlier works positioned *Dosar* and its director in some 'higher' order, worth a serious discussion. An average Bengali film could not possibly have this privilege to be commanding of such elaborate and serious concern.

This illustrates that the columnist Rituparno Ghosh or the editor Rituparno Ghosh contributed to establish a niche for his films, and develop a star persona called Rituparno Ghosh, beyond his Bengali film-maker identity. In order to elaborate on this, a section from a report by Promita Mukherjee has been quoted below:

> ... he'll also be at his social best sitting back on a couch and interviewing famous celebrities in a TV chat show Ghosh and Company. The film-maker loves to test his creative strength and venture into unfamiliar and unknown territory .... he's a maverick at heart and even in this era of celebrity blogging, prefers to put down his thoughts using pen and paper.

She further writes:

> 'It allows me to practice my handwriting,' he jokes .... That he's an avid reader is obvious the moment you enter his small and neatly decorated study which has pictures of Satyajit Ray and Akira Kurosawa besides a laminated still from his film, *Chokher Bali*. Books are stacked all over the place and are neatly arranged in ceiling-high bookcases. Though he is fond of non-fiction, everything from the classics to the latest bestsellers finds a place in his collection.[84]

Thus, Ghosh's press persona is responsible, to a great extent, in establishing his stardom in public sphere discourse. Ghosh's reviews of films like *Devdas* by Sanjay Leela Bhansali in 2002 or *Chalte Chalte* (*On the Way!*) by Aziz Mirza in 2006 express his process of observation, critical skill, preferences, and other such qualities. Or, for instance, referring to an article like '*Atiter Khnoje*' ('In Search of the Past') by him in *Anandabazar Patrika* on the Bengali cinema tradition, it is clearly evident that his belonging to the Bengali cinematic tradition is deeply connected to his memory, sensibilities and experience of being an integral part of this tradition.[85] Similarly, an article like 'Soumitra 70' by Ghosh in the *Anandabazar Patrika* supplement about veteran actor Soumitra Chattopadhyay expressed his admiration for 'Apu' (since Chattopadhay had played the iconic character of Apu in the second and third parts of Ray's *The Apu Trilogy*, titled *Apur Sansar* [*The World of Apu*] and *Aparajito* [*The Unvanquished*]) of Bengali cinema.[86] When he became the editor of *Anandalok*, he came closer to the regime of reception and circulation of cinema, which worked to his advantage in the sense that he became a 'regulator' of public sphere discourse of *filmi khabar* (film-related news) through the editing of the leading Bengali film magazine.[87] Also, when he became the editor of *Anandalok*, the 'look' of the magazine changed. The advertisement claimed '*Ulte Dekhun Palte Gachhe*' ('Have a Look, it has Changed'), and apart from '*filmi*' news and interviews of individuals related to the film industry, *Anandalok's* regular sections also changed and now included news from other public sphere concerns and discussions. Moreover, as an editor of the Sunday supplement of *Sanbaad Pratidin*, *Robbar*, he used press discourse even more innovatively and to his advantage. Prior to the 2009 release of his film, *Sab Charitro Kalponik* (*All Characters Fictional*), in an editorial of the *Robbar* supplement,[88] Ghosh revealed how poet Joy Goswami had agreed to give his poems exclusively for this film and had promised not to publish them anywhere else. These poems, exclusively written for and used by Ghosh in *Sab Charitro Kalponik*, were published subsequently in *Robbar*. It is important to understand how Ghosh tactfully used his media engagement for the promotion of his films. Moreover, as a media persona, he was always present in public sphere discourse until his sudden demise in May 2013.

Along with this press persona, Ghosh developed a strong TV presence at a time when 'satellite channels and global media networks were beginning to make a home in (Bengali) middle-class households'.[89] In this post-liberalisation period of the cable TV boom, he got involved with more than one Bengali regional TV channel. He was actively associated with *Tara Bangla* since its inception, a channel that premiered his film, *Utsab*, and on *ETV Bangla*, Rituparno Ghosh started anchoring a talk show called *Ebong Rituparno* (*And Rituparno*). These associations helped him establish his TV persona as an 'alternative' film-maker. They were also a strategic step by Ghosh to promote his films, which resulted in almost an entire genre called 'Rituparno Ghosh films', and also simultaneously cemented his stardom. No Bengali film-maker except Aparna Sen, to some extent, has functioned as a successful media person, neither from the mainstream nor from the art house tradition, as much as Ghosh has. Apart from the ones mentioned, he also appeared for TV interviews, joined in Bengali film discussion forums, directed a TV serial called *Bahanno Episode*) (*Fifty-two Episodes*) that was telecast on *DD Bangla*, and made telefilms like *Avinoy* (*Acting*) or *10 No. Maltibala Lane* for *Zee Bangla*. These creative endeavours have worked in his favour to highlight his educated, cultured *bhadralok* middle-class identity, and have helped the audiences in imagining a *bhadralok* film-maker.

His physical presence and voice additionally bolstered his persona as an 'alternative' film-maker. To quote Kaustav Bakshi,[90] who stated how an AIR interview of Ghosh could generate interest and create the image of a 'sensitive' film-maker:

> ... my enthusiasm for Unishe April was triggered off by an interview of Rituparno Ghosh that was aired on HMV-FM. Listening to Ghosh, I discovered I had never heard a man speak so sensitively, or, even for that matter, so informally in a public space. Ghosh's mild voice, his effeminate accents, punctuated remarkably the thoughts he shared. He was not like the other film-makers .... Rituparno's emotionally charged talk (not verging on the sentimental, mind you) almost seduced me into admiring him.[91]

If just an FM interview could generate this amount of curiosity regarding a new director and his film, the impact of a regular weekend show like *Ebong Rituparno*[92] that lasted for two to three years can be estimated. The idea of 'meeting a very different man' was being extended in each show, where Ghosh talked with guests from various fields, from senior film-maker Mrinal Sen to the former captain of the Indian cricket team, Saurav Ganguly, from then newcomer actress like Sudipta Chakraborty to the veteran theatre personality, Chapal Bhaduri. The show's format was not like typical celebrity interviews since the host was no less well known than the celebrity guest. Ghosh, the interviewer, talked about his likes and dislikes, preferences and memories, and reacted to what the guests said.[93] The show was famous for his informal interaction with his guests, the way he showed respect and care for someone like Mrinal Sen, and how he treated his juniors in the film industry with love and affection. Generally, the two-episode long conversation took the shape of a middle-class *adda* (a casual hangout popular in Bengali culture) in a kind of informal drawing room setting.

The other interesting dimension of this programme was its *mise-en-scene*; the arty décor, well-lit room, designer showpieces, and a book case with well-organised books, all of which taken together conveyed the impression of the primary *mise-en-scene* of a Ghosh film. The decorated drawing room filled up with conversation voices could easily remind the viewers of a scene from *Unishe April* or *Dahan*. Ghosh was also part of social media discussions and debates.

To quote an excerpt from social networking site discussion forums on his 'new look':

> I admire him because he is not a hypocrite.... he has enough guts to present himself the way he wants to .... and he really looks good in those junk jewelleries and designer attires .... he carries himself pretty well .... he has made his own signature by nullifying the so called male 'ism' .... I simply adore him .... I wish I could marry him .... I'm serious.[94]

Another user responded to this post in these words: '... (H)is present look is horrible, he behaves more feminine than even women do. As far as styling and make up is concerned, he should keep in mind that he is ageing and any and every experiment does not suit him anymore, rather makes him look bizarre.'[95]

His turban, leather jacket, loose pajamas and pearl choker were brought into this discussion later by other members, to suggest what suited their favorite film-maker and what did not, from their point of view. But the point is to take notice of how interest and conversations regarding Ghosh often spilled beyond the film texts he worked on. Along with his 'relationship films', a star persona was also born in the public sphere at the centre of the public imagination of post-1990s 'new parallel' cinema. It was unusual for Bengali cinema to generate that much interest regarding a film maker, even when he was not making that many films then, but was simply 'present' with his looks, style and charisma. In this aspect, Ghosh could perhaps be considered to be the single star director of Bengali cinema. Sean Redmond and Su Holmes see stars as 'housing' our dreams and fuelling our fantasies, and this holds true for Ghosh's stardom as well; 'they address and represent (often implicitly) some of the most important political issues of the day, and they can give us both ephemeral and lasting pleasure, even if, in the end, this is a pleasure built on artifice and the lie of the possible.'[96] For Aparna Sen, a similar interest could be observed in the public sphere, but her almost three-decades-long successful acting career has a different logic of popularity and stardom discourse.

The curious case of Ghosh's stardom lies in the intersecting axis of making a 'difference' and carrying a chord of past-ness and nostalgia. The assurance of the 'difference' and the superiority from the run-of-the-mill Bengali films gave post-1990s 'new parallel' cinema a much-valued position of appreciation within the *bhadra* public sphere. His physical presence in the media shaped the idea of a chatty, informal, sensitive film-maker of Bengali cinema, who was at the same time educated, suave and eloquent. However, there is another aspect of this star persona. On the one hand, with the emergence of newer media, an increasing number of Bengali TV channels, the press's increased focus on Tollywood 'news', and the accessibility of YouTube interviews, blogs and social networking sites, the persona of Rituparno Ghosh gained a wider popularity. On the other hand, the mimicry of Rituparno Ghosh's mannerisms and his style of speaking were served at TV shows, and even in some advertisements. Especially a popular standup comedy show called *Mirakkel*, on *Zee Bangla*, and some other programmes hosted by a well-known anchor of Bengali television, Mir, caricatured Ghosh's star persona and his mannerisms. This mimicry of Ghosh's 'effeminate' gestures and his distinctive style of speaking were not exclusively meant as tribute to or admiration for the director; instead, this mimicry underlined a deeply sexist and homophobic form of expression without considerable objections from the middle-class audiences. Thus, it reveals the inherent contradictions present in Ghosh's star discourse. The appeal of his stardom did not simply lie in the simplistic acceptance of the 'difference', but also in the plurality of their meaning-making in the public sphere.

Conclusion

In this chapter, we have discussed how different logics and discourse operate within the realm of Bengali 'new parallel' cinema. Our focus has been on different dimensions of this 'parallel-ness'; first, at the production-exhibition level, how it functioned within a *bhadralok* frame and perspective. Second, how film content and form memorialised the cinematic practice of earlier Bengali cinema in their literariness, references of Ray, and the use of other cinematic devices. Third, how Rituparno Ghosh's star persona functioned in the formation of the self-image of a class, along with its taste discourse. There are other areas such as TV telecasts, awards, recognitions and DVD features that also one could include in the constructs of post-liberalisation Bengali 'parallel' cinema. For instance, in DVD shops in Kolkata, separate racks and shelves were maintained for contemporary mainstream and 'parallel' Bengali films. The 2011 award show organised by *Star Jalsa* (a Bengali entertainment TV channel) reinstated this 'difference' by giving awards to mainstream and parallel Bengali films through categories like best film/best innovative film, best hero/best actor, etc.

With an increase in the average budget for a Bengali film and an increase in the number of films released per year by 2012, the media focused on the expanding market possibilities of Bengali films, which included multiplex releases and the proliferation of Over-the-Top (OTT) platforms for the production and global consumption of Bengali content. As discussed in the previous chapter, SVF, post-*Chokher Bali*, took interest in 'new parallel' cinema and produced films like *Autograph*, *Memories in March* or *Iti Mrinalini*, designed for the urban audience of Bengali films.

In this context, the involvement of the production house, SVF, and subsequently, other such corporate companies that were producing and endorsing 'new parallel' cinema, expanded the market and circulation of Bengali cinema, alongside asserting the identity of Tollywood as a respectable and revamped film industry. The following chapter illustrates the different media impulses and developments that propel the identity of Tollywood and Bengali cinema further.

Notes and References

1. In discussion and conversation with the authors, 3 November 2010, Kolkata.
2. In discussion and conversation with the authors, 6 October 2010, Kolkata.
3. Press writings praised the release of *Unishe April* as a remarkable intervention in the Bengali film scenario. One can see Swapan Mullik's review of the film in *The Statesman*, 24 May 1996. Shoma A. Chatterji, in her book *Cinema Shudhu Cinema Noy*, praised this film as a 'new' experience in the monotony of Bengali films.
4. Shoma A. Chatterji, available at http://www.upperstall.com/people/rituparno-ghosh, accessed on 22 July 2012.
5. Authors' interview with Renu Roy, 14 December 2010, Kolkata.
6. Shoma A. Chatterji. Op. cit.
7. This is a dominant single-screen cinema hall chain in Kolkata operating from three different parts of the city.
8. Shoma A. Chatterji. Op. cit.

9. Bappaditya Bandyopadhyay. Op. cit.
10. After coming to power, the Communist Party of India (Marxist) (CPI[M]) government showed a serious engagement in the development of Bengali cinema, the formation of the WBFDC, the setting up of the *Rupayan* colour lab, giving of loans for quality films by the new generation of Bengali film-makers, and establishing exhibition sites like Nandan and Deenabandhu Mancha.
11. Authors' interview with Sandip Sen, 1 December 2010, Kolkata.
12. Authors' interview with Subrata Sen, 2 October 2010, Kolkata.
13. For instance, he gave the example of his 2005 film, *Bibar*, which was released with only 18 prints and made a profit.
14. Authors' interview with Sandip Sen.
15. Authors' interview with Renu Roy.
16. Ibid.
17. Authors' interview with Aniruddha Dhar, Kolkata, December 2011.
18. Authors' interview with Arijit Dutta, 4 November 2010, Kolkata.
19. Someshwar Bhoumik, *Bharatiya Chalchchitra: Ekti Arthanaitik Pratibedan* (*Indian Cinema: An Economic Report*) (Calcutta: Papyrus, 1996).
20. Ibid.
21. Authors' interview with Goutam Ghose, 19 November 2010, Kolkata.
22. An *Ananadabazar Patrika* report claimed that in 2004, a professional business organisation planned on investing in 206 films to be telecast on *Akash Bangla*. From the very number, one could imagine the possibility of profit from investing in Bengali telefilms, and its higher TRP rating; 'Manojit Sarkar, "Tele Hawa"/"Tele Wind"', *Anandabazar Patrika*, 27 January 2004.
23. Roopa Ganguly, Brochure of Second Bangla Telefilm Festival, Nandan, 2004. Ganguly is a film actress and Secretary of the West Bengal Motion Picture's Artiste's forum.
24. Roopa Ganguly wrote in the brochure of second Bengali Telefilm Festival how six directors had been selected, whose telefilms were shown in international film festivals. These six directors, Ganguly as a producer and director of Nandan, and Ansu Sur had a discussion, and the theme of *Ek Mutho Chhabi* was fixed.
25. The North American Bengali Conference (NABC) is an annual conference held in North America to celebrate Bengali culture, where people take part in discussions, literary readings, movie screenings, and other types of performances dealing with Bengali culture. It started in the 1980s in New York, and later spread all over the US and Canada
26. Authors' interview with Tapan Biswas, 13 December 2010, Kolkata.
27. It is interesting to note that the plot of *Utsab*, of four sons and daughters coming to their home during the *puja* holidays, thematically resonates with the sentiments of the overseas *probashi* (non-resident Bengalis) Bengali audience.

28. Authors' interview with Tapan Biswas.
29. Dingora.com is a site where one can watch film online. It was founded by Pankaj Sikka, who is also the founder of the group blogging site, PassionForCinema.com.
30. Authors' interview with Ansu Sur, July 2010, Kolkata.
31. Authors' interview with Nilanjan Chattopadhyay, March 2010, Kolkata.
32. Authors' interview with Arijit Dutta and Sagnik Michael Sinha, November 2010, Kolkata.
33. Subtitle of Title Track Voice Over, *Utsab*, Shemaroo/Eagle Video, DVD, 2001.
34. *Utsab* is a film that is centred not on a protagonist, but rather, on a family. However, the narrative voice, in many cases, merges with the character, Joy. The beginning and the conclusion of this film are voiced by his video voice that he recorded during the *puja* holidays in his ancestral house.
35. Kiranmoy Raha, *Bengali Cinema* (Kolkata: Nandan, West Bengal Film Centre, 1991), p. 32.
36. Ibid.
37. Ibid.
38. Nirmalya Acharya, 'Seven Decades of Bengali Cinema', Nandan, Kolkata, 1990.
39. Authors' interview with Ranjan Bandyopadhyay
40. Anjan Das. Op. cit.
41. *Joy Baba Felunath* is a film by Satyajit Ray set in Benaras, where private detective Prodosh Mitter (who is famously called Feluda, a literary creation by Ray) went for the *puja* holidays, with his assistants Topshe and Lalmohan Ganguly (Jatayu), and solved the mystery of a missing Ganesha idol.
42. *Agantuk* is the last film by Satyajit Ray that dealt with the events followed by the long-lost Uncle Manomohan Mitra's sudden visit to his niece's house, and the film posed the question: what is civilisation?
43. Buddhadeb Dasgupta's 1997 film, *Laal Darja* (*The Red Door*) is about Nabin's troubled life, who is a dentist by profession and is disturbed for many reasons.
44. *Shanjhbatir Rupkathara*, DVD.
45. Ibid.
46. In the film, the Bengali word '*Roopkatha*' (literally meaning 'fairytale') was translated in the subtitle as 'dream fairy'.
47. Leela Fernandes, *India's New Middle Class: Democratic Politics in an Era of Economic Reform* (Minneapolis; London: University of Minnesota Press, 2006), p. xviii.
48. Ibid.
49. For a detailed account, see Henrike Donner, *Domestic Goddesses, Maternity, Globalization and Middle Class Identity in Contemporary India* (London: Ashgate Publishing, 2008), p. 54.

50. See Jonathon Donner, Nimmi Rangaswamy, Molly Wright Steevson and Carolyn Wei, '"Express Yourself" and "Stay Together": The Middle Class Indian Family', in James E. Katz, ed., *Handbook of Mobile Communication Studies* (Cambridge, Massachusetts: The MIT Press, 2008).
51. *Hemanter Pakhi*, DVD.
52. Somdutta Mandal, 'Rituparno Ghosh: The Women's Director of Bangla Cinema', in Jasbir Jain and Sudha Rai, ed., *Films and Feminism: Essays in Indian Cinema* (Jaipur; New Delhi: Rawat Publications, 2002), p. 36.
53. John W. Hood, *The Films of Buddhadeb Dasgupta* (New Delhi: Orient BlackSwan, 2005).
54. Ibid.
55. Ajay Kumar Das, ed., *A Poet with a Camera: Buddhadeb Dasgupta: A Monograph* (Calcutta: Nandan, 1994).
56. Shoma A. Chatterji, *Parama and Other Outsiders: The Cinema of Aparna Sen* (Calcutta: Parumita Publication, 2002), p. 26.
57. Ibid., p. 17.
58. Ibid., p. 15.
59. For instance, Chatterji discusses in detail how, in Sen's films, the 'woman-as-mother and woman-as-sexual-entity are not mutually antagonistic images, but simultaneously present within the same woman'; ibid., p. 23.
60. See Somdutta Mandal, 'Rituparno Ghosh'.
61. Ibid., p. 17.
62. Mandal says that 'the raison d'etre for Rituparno Ghosh's films remains "I understand women"'; ibid., p. 38.
63. See Pachu Roy, '*Paribarik Chhobir Master*: Rituparno Ghosh' ('The Master of Family Films: Rituparno Ghosh'), *Madhyam O Sangjog*, February 2002, pp. 31–33.
64. Sumit Dey, 'Defining the Rituparnoesque: Rituparno Ghosh and Auteurism, Sexuality and Stardom', Unpublished MPhil Dissertation, The School of Arts and Aesthetics, Cinema Studies, Jawarharlal Nehru University, 2012, p. 8. See also Dey, 'Ritu Da's Home was the World', *The Pioneer*, 31 May 2013.
65. Anugyan Nag, 'Locating Rituparno Ghosh in Tollywood', in Sangeeta Dutta, Kaustav Bakshi and Rohit K. Dasgupta, ed., *Rituparno Ghosh: Cinema, Gender and Art* (London: Routledge, 2016), pp. 63–82.
66. 'Introducing Rituparno Ghosh', India Net Zone, available at http://www.indianetzone.com/34/rituparno_ghosh_indian_movie_director.htm, accessed on 17 May 2012.
67. Aruna Vasudev, *The New Indian Cinema* (New Delhi: Macmillan, 1986), pp. 65–74.
68. 'Introducing Rituparno Ghosh'.
69. Buddhadeb Dasgupta, in a face-to-face conversation organised by the Eisenstein Cine Club, Kolkata, Gorky Sadan, 22 March 2011.

70. The point we refer to here is clarified by the EIMPA Secretary, Ashis Kr Banerjee, the owner of Priya cinema hall, Arijit Dutta, and also producers like Renu Roy or Tapan Biswas, who produced some of Ghosh's films.
71. Barun Chanda, 'Fragmented Eternity', *t2*, *The Telegraph*, 26 January 2010.
72. Ibid.
73. Rituparno Ghosh, 'Fragmented Understanding', *t2*, *The Telegraph*, 30 January 2010.
74. Ibid.
75. Here we should mention that this is a regular feature in *The Telegraph* in their Thursday supplement, titled 'We've Got Mail'. Before *Abohomaan*, *The Telegraph* feature on 4 August 2007 was about *Anuranan*'s 'success' by Kushali Nag, which invited readers' thoughts on what they thought of the two characters' 'undefined relationship' in this film; and in the 9 August supplement, a few letters were published from readers like Amit Banerjee or Chitra Bagchi, commenting on this particular topic.
76. *t2*, *The Telegraph*, 4 February, 2010.
77. Ibid.
78. Sumit Dey, '"Just Like a Film Star!": The Style of Being Rituparno Ghosh', in Sangeeta Dutta, Kaustav Bakshi and Rohit K. Dasgupta, ed., *Rituparno Ghosh: Cinema, Gender and Art* (London: Routledge, 2016), pp. 83–103.
79. Sanjay Mukhopadhyay, 'Rituparno Accused of Plagiarism', *Calcutta Times*, *The Times of India*, 27 November 2006.
80. Ibid.
81. Ashoke Viswanathan, 'Ray's Nayak was inspired by Bergman and Felini', *Calcutta Times*, *The Times of India*, 19 November 2006.
82. For instance, Viswanathan writes, 'At the risk of being criticized, I would say that there are elements of Bergman's *Wild Strawberries* and *Eight and a Half* by Felini in certain stretches of Satyajit Ray's *Nayak* … '; ibid.
83. He starts with what Brecht said, 'Let others speak of their shame. I speak of my own', and even refers to Kaavya Vishwanathan's alleged plagiarism act that was in news at that time; ibid.
84. Promita Mukherjee, 'The Master at Work', *The Telegraph*, 17 August 2008.
85. *Anandabazar Patrika* Supplement, 15 April 2000.
86. *Anandabazar Parika* Supplement, 24 January 2004, p. 1.
87. Here one can also observe how his films like *Titli* or *Shubha Mahurat* use the name, '*Anandalok*', in showing the cover or referring to it in order to generate the pleasure of stardom and gossip columns.
88. *Pratidin* Supplement, 13 January 2008.
89. Kaustav Bakshi is Assistant Professor, Department of English, Jadavpur University, Kolkata, and an enthusiast blogger who writes about film, literature and his surroundings to give voice to his thoughts that, in his words, 'swim against the mainstream'. See *Kaustav's Arden*, available at http://kaustavsarden.blogspot.com/search?updated-min=2008-01-01T00%3A00%3A0008%3A00&updated-max=2009-01-01T00%3A00%3A00-

08%3A00&max-results=18, accessed on 5 February 2012, now defunct. See also Kaustav Bakshi, Sangeeta Dutta and Rohit Dasgupta, ed., *Rituparno Ghosh: Cinema, Gender and Art* (London: Routledge, 2015).

90. Ibid.
91. Ibid.
92. It was telecast biweekly on Saturday and Sunday evenings on a regular basis.
93. For instance, in a particular episode when Aparna Sen was invited, Ghosh shared his own childhood memory of watching an Uttam Kumar–Aparna Sen film, *Jay Jayanti*, and how he had convinced his aunt to take him for this film.
94. Available at http://www.orkut.co.in/Main#CommMsgs?cmm=25825635&tid=2537633778527773292&na=4&nst=1&nid=25825635-2537633778527773292-5323666123176041414, accessed on 18 May 2011. Orkut is now defunct.
95. Ibid.
96. Sean Redmond and Su Holmes, *Stardom and Celebrity: A Reader* (Thousand Oaks, California: SAGE Publication, 2007), p. 11.

4

Media Convergence and the Discursive Proliferation and Consolidation of Tollywood*

Along with the economic liberalisation of India and negotiations with the neoliberal conditionality of economic development, the emergence and proliferation of satellite TV and the rise of surplus electronic media intensified the processes of a cultural and economic transition in Bengal, albeit more than a decade after the economic liberalisation in 1991. In the post-global world, communication becomes a foremost factor in the proliferation and dissemination of the media and culture industries, and a symbiotic relationship resulting from the convergence of media, propelling a complex phenomenon. The constant flow of people, images, information, ideas, technology and capital is consumed and perceived as a 'convergence' of beliefs, attitudes, values and images, involving different forms of media.

In order to describe this phenomenon, we have borrowed the idea of 'media contagion' from Amit S. Rai, who uses the Deleuzian concept of 'assemblage' as a model for understanding the complex constellation of technological, historical and physical processes that enabled Bollywood cinema to be representative of transforming situations of media reception and consumption in the environment of globalisation. According to him, media as a form of contagion endlessly mutates and spreads, connecting human bodies, organisational structures and energies, creating an inextricable bond between 'affect' and 'capital'.[1] In this context, it is interesting to

* Spandan Bhattacharya, 'Writing a Biography of Bengali Film Publicity: The Logic of Differentiation, and a Journey of Desire', *Journal of Bengali Studies*, vol. 1, no. 2 (2012), p. 87.

explore and analyse the media's role in the formation of Tollywood as an all-encompassing media and entertainment industry. In the post-liberalisation era, the business of media in Bengal experienced a firm capitalist intrusion, similar to Bollywood.

Anustup Basu's study of popular Indian cinema in the age of globalisation, new media and metropolitan Hindu fundamentalism, focuses on the period between 1991 and 2004, when popular Hindi cinema took a spectacular turn from the early-1990s to a more characteristic or signature 'Bollywood style' that evolved during post-liberalisation, with the growth of global ecology in India. There was a rise in the featuring of post-global tendencies and an 'informational geo-televisual aesthetic' in films of this period.[2] The Bengali film, *Dui Prithibi*, is relevant here in the same way as Basu's example of the Hindi film, *Haqeeqat* (*The Truth*) by Sandesh Kohli in 1995. It featured poor working-class protagonists, but romantic musical sequences transported them abruptly to Switzerland, with actors dressed in designer outfits. In *Dui Prithibi*, almost 15 years after the release of *Haqeeqat*, we see a similar situation, where a song sequence is shot in Venice for the first time in the history of Bengali cinema, in a plot otherwise centred on personal friendships, relationships and misunderstandings in the context of the troubled Maoist era of West Bengal.[3]

This chapter examines and maps this industrial landscape of the Bengali film industry, affected by the omnipresent and omnipotent media convergence of TV, radio, print and new media. It also looks into the content of new global alterations, newer circuits and complicated pathways, which require detailed comprehension to explore industrial frameworks and processes that have produced the discourse of Tollywood, through which a cultural identity is created and ascertained. The chapter further focuses on the rise of new stardom, and as to how stardom is created and circulated through media like TV, radio, print and new media. The inclusion of Tollywood celebrities, content, films, gossip, news, talk shows, interviews, and the regular promotion of films and stars in TV programmes like *Sangeet Bangla's Tollywood Reporter*, and FM radio stations, have popularised new stars and have also paved the way for the construction of Tollywood. Media convergence has altered the public perception and that of the press, about Tollygunge, the yesteryear film industry, remarkably into its new avatar, Tollywood. This is indeed a shift in attention from the focus on Bengali cinema (film text/narrative and auteurs/directors) to one that foregrounds the film industry—Tollywood.

The obvious question is—why film? More so, why the film industry? Interestingly, cinema lies at the heart of media convergence. As Hamid Naficy mentions: '… Cinema as an industry has evolved, adjusted, adapted, adopted, assimilated, and grown vertically and horizontally. It has taken over, has been taken over, privatized, nationalized, divested, diversified and converged in myriad of ways.'[4]

As a medium, the film has not only remained relevant, but has also proliferated widely and deeply by a process that Marshall McLuhan had identified decades ago. He said that old media had survived by becoming the content of newer media: 'The "content" of any medium is always another medium.'[5] Today, therefore, it is apt to talk about this under the rubric of convergence, or in the words of Bolter and Grusin, 'remediation'.[6] Or in the words of David Thorburn and Henry Jenkins, who point towards a conscious cyclical progression that may be seen as especially significant in the Indian context, 'Old media rarely die; their original functions are adapted and absorbed by newer media, and they themselves may mutate into new cultural niches and new purposes. The process of media transition is always a mix of tradition and innovation, always declaring for evolution, not revolution.'[7]

Post the 1980s and 1990s, when the 'crisis narrative' had engulfed the Tollygunge film industry, liberalisation initiated a slow but somewhat steady process of evolution and modification within the industry, which the SVF then particularly capitalised on and initiated major changes in cinematic aesthetics and the overall production, distribution and exhibition system. The past decade, however, has ushered in a new chapter in Bengali cinema. With a few renowned directors taking the lead, the mindset for experimentation has grown, resulting in an increase in the number of films made for urban audiences. Also, the notion that experimental/thought-provoking films are 'art', and thus, non-commercial has often been progressively disputed because of films that are content-rich, yet commercially viable.

Tollywood in the Media Landscape of West Bengal

In 2010, the Central Board of Film Certification (CBFC) certified 110 Bengali films, two-and-a-half times the increase from 42 films in 2006. This was probably possible due to an increase in the diversification of content in films, an element that has greater commercial viability.[8] The state of affairs in Tollywood during this time, that is, from the year 2010 onwards, was a healthy mix of experienced and upcoming film producers and directors who could retrieve the disinterested audiences of Bengali cinema considerably. Although SVF continued to enjoy a stronghold in Tollywood and went on to strengthen its position as one of the most powerful production houses, exercising excessive control and monopolisation across the various levels of film production, distribution and exhibition, both old and new film-makers collaborated with newer producers and production companies to make films that had taken the audience, the media and the industry by surprise for their innovativeness, technical knack and matured approach: for example, *Moner Manush* (*The Quest*) by Goutam Ghose in 2010, *The Japanese Wife* by Aparna Sen in 2010, *Laptop* by Kaushik Gaguly in 2012, *Bhooter Bhabishyat* (*Future of the Past*) by Anik Dutta in 2012, and *Phoring* (*Grasshopper*) by Indranil Roy Chowdhury in 2013.

In 2010, regional films constituted 82 per cent of the overall films certified by CBFC. Bengali films constituted 9 per cent of that total, almost doubling its contribution of 4 per cent in 2006. During 2010–11, the average production cost of a Bengali film varied between Rs 60 lakhs and Rs 2 crores, excluding print and publicity costs.[9]

The entry of TV and satellite into the media-scape of Bengal enabled a newer form of showcasing different genres of Bengali films and of earning revenue from this form of exhibition. Post-1991, the presence of private TV channels created a riveting relationship between TV and Bengali cinema. Significantly, the one individual who played a fundamental role in initiating the launch of Bengali satellite TV was actor/star Prosenjit Chatterjee. It was mainly through his efforts that Subhash Chandra Goel of *Zee TV* agreed to launch the first Bengali television channel, *Zee Bangla*. According to Kakoli Poddar in her piece, 'Bengal's One-man Industry', 'Prosenjit understood the potential of satellite television in the mid-nineties .... In 1994–95, he concentrated on building the new generation television industry and also acted in some television serials (*Mama Bhagney, Kagojer Bou*) himself.'[10]

Satellite TV functioned as a boost to the Bengali film industry since the mid-1990s after *Zee Bangla* was launched. Several Tollygunge industry actors, directors and technicians began a parallel career in TV serials. By 2007, at least eight (*ETV Bangla, Akash Bangla, Tara Muzik, Tara Bangla, Sangeet Bangla, Star Jalsha, Sony Aath* and *Ruposhi Bangla*) privately-owned Bengali language satellite TV channels were broadcasting into Bengali homes, and among these, almost all of them included film-based content in their programming. TV in West Bengal, which was largely dominated by Hindi General Entertainment Channels (GEC), saw itself expanding significantly in Bengali. The beginning of this resurgence can be traced back to the period when the Bengali GEC space saw interest from key national players, such as the Star and Zee groups. The consequent increase in competition as well as programming standards resulted in the growth of the entire Bengali TV space. As a result, during 2005–06, what was around 500–600 Gross Revenue Profits (GRPs) in the Bengali GEC space, began bordering at edging 1,200 GRP levels. With this, Bengali TV viewership witnessed a remarkable upsurge by the year 2012 with the launching of channels (*Zee Bangla Cinema* by Zee Group and *Star Jalsha Movies* by Star Group), with exclusive programming dedicated to Bengali films.

Television and Tollywood

Star Jalsha and *Sananda TV*, both Bengali entertainment channels of the media house, *Anandabazar Patrika*, were launched (in 2008 and 2011, respectively) foreseeing a share for themselves in the West Bengal GEC market. In March 2011, *Star* announced its plan to launch the Bengali entertainment channel, *Star Jalsha* in West Asia, with the Arab Digital Distribution (ADD) pay TV platform. This Bengali general entertainment channel was aimed at being exclusively available on the *pehla* bouquet that caters to the expatriate South Asian population in the United Arab Emirates (UAE). In September 2010, Globesat Entertainment (GEN-I), in the business of the distribution of ethnic television networks in North America and the UK, partnered with Media Content and Communications Services India (MCCS) to distribute *Star Ananda* (now renamed *ABP Ananda*), the 24-hour national Bengali news channel, in the US and Canada. It is important to note here that *ABP Ananda* had several time slots within its 24-hour broadcast format exclusively dedicated to content and programmes on Tollywood (for instance, *Holly-Bolly-Tolly*), and the channel also collaborated as media partner for numerous upcoming Tollywood productions, for instance, *Kailashe Kelengkari* (*A Trouble in Kailash*), *Antaheen*, *Bhooter Bhabishyat*, *Chaander Pahar*, *Meghe Dhaka Taara*, etc. The channel regularly featured panel discussions and chat shows with the cast and crew members of films before their release, and they also featured a post-release discussion and evaluation. In June 2011, Sony Entertainment Television Network (SETN) announced its intention to expand the reach of its Bengali movie channel, *Sony Aath*, in the international market. The channel, already launched in the US and Canada, was slated to reach the UK and Australia as well. *Sony Aath* specialised in the latest and classic Bengali movie screenings, telefilms and movie-related magazine shows.[11]

Revenue from the content segment is yet to develop to the level of other regional markets, the reason being that there were only a limited number of independent production houses developing Bengali content. A large portion of content for Bengali TV channels was acquired from production companies that exclusively produced content for television. Almost all the GEC channels have dedicated segments that showcase Bengali films—both contemporary and classics. Therefore, where on the one hand, television snatched the film industry's Kolkata market to a substantial extent, on the other, it was largely through satellite TV that mainstream Bengali cinema, its stars, directors, technicians and music made their entry back into middle-class homes. TV as a medium has provided the film industry with a steady presence in the public domain, and gradually established Tollywood's identity in the public and press discourse. Elaborating on the symbiotic relationship between the film and television industries, Padam P. Govindan and Bisakha Dutta state the following:

> Satellite channels offer the film industry an exponentially increased ability to promote and market their films through television previews, programming the features song and dance sequences, and the purchase of telecast rights to popular films. Television shows (as well as print

> media) in turn depend on the film world—its music, award ceremonies, and celebrity gossip—for programming and articles.[12]

Sangeet Bangla, the 24-hour music channel, part of the Media Worldwide bouquet owned by SVF, was launched on 14 April 2005. The channel largely promotes film songs from the SVF and Surrinder Film banners, along with non-film music, and a very popular weekly magazine show, *Tollywood Reporter*, where news, interviews and gossip from the industry are presented to viewers.[13] The other popular programme *Tollywood Topper*, which runs back-to-back Tollywood hits, popular songs, and a special feature, where anecdotes of shooting and behind-the-screen details are provided as running texts in Bengali to generate more interest about the stars, actors, locations, along with a youthful interest in the content and industrial news that is otherwise not reported in newspapers and TV programmes.

The rise in the non-fiction content in the TV sector also tapped into the Tollywood talent pool. Reality shows, which comprise a large section of the programmes on GEC channels, include hosts, weekly special guests and judges from the Tollywood fraternity. Reality shows have become a potential site for film promotion, where the cast and crew make a special appearance on the show before the release of a particular film in theatres. Bengali TV channels also telecast awards, both live and recorded, and the Bengali film industry's most prestigious award ceremony, which happens to be the oldest film award in Bengal, the Bengal Film Journalist Association (BFJA) award, was a gala event that celebrated and honoured the Bengali film and television fraternity. However, the award has not been taking place since 2007. A few popular awards ceremonies are the *Anandalok Awards*, one of the most prominent film events for Bengali cinema in India; the *Kalakar Awards*, recognised as one of the top-most awards ceremonies of the eastern region; the *Tellysamman Awards*, organised by *Sangbad Pratidin*, a Kolkata-based Bengali daily; and the *Zee Bangla Gourav Samman*, an award that is designed for the people and by the people. *Zee Bangla* honours the rich culture and traditions of the land, felicitating evergreen personalities from theatre, film, music, and its own television shows. Added to this list of Bengali award ceremonies has been the International Bangla Film Academy Awards (IBFA), pitted as Tollywood's answer to Bollywood's International

Indian Film Academy Awards (IIFA), which conferred awards in 19 categories on actors and technicians for their contributions to Bengali cinema in 2011. IBFA is an association that helps to support, develop and promote art forms of the moving image. The event was organised by Jet Setters, in association with Amazing Thailand, Ramada Plaza, a regional vernacular news channel and a vernacular music channel.[14]

TV's role in highlighting the new stars of Tollywood in the public sphere, and providing them with a constant and consistent platform of visibility, is relevant to an understanding of its role in establishing Tollywood's identity as a culture industry. The satellite medium has generated a discourse that foregrounded the presence of a local entertainment industry countering the hegemony of Bollywood.

John Ellis argues that the 'television fame' is a more immediate form of stardom that creates a 'personality' instantly, and gives one overnight stardom through repeated appearances on the television screen.[15] Since 2011, a whole new line of actors and talents have been appropriated by the press and the public sphere as Tollywood celebrities and stars. Mir, for example, who began his career in the media as a news reader, began hosting a very popular comedy show, *Mirakkel* in 2006. He has become one of the most popular anchors and stand-up comedians. Similarly, actors like Jisshu Sengupta, who acted in several serials, mega soaps and tele-films earlier, have now achieved star status both in films and on TV. Actors who only work in Tollywood films have also realised the potential of the TV medium. A lot of them now dabble between the two mediums.[16] Star actor Jeet, for instance, hosted the Bengali version of *Kaun Banega Crorepati: Koti Takar Baji (Who Wants to be a Millionaire? Bet of a Crore)*.[17] Tollywood's superstar, Prosenjit, after 35 years of his film career, hosted the game show, *Banglar Shera Poribar*, on *Zee Bangla*; this was his first venture into TV as an anchor.[18]

Another common practice of Bengali TV channels is to invite at least one or two Tollywood celebrities or actors for panel discussions and debates on issues outside the area of cinema and entertainment. During the 2011 West Bengal state assembly elections, when the Trinamool Congress (TMC) and the 34-year-old ruling Communist Party of India (Marxist) (CPI[M]) were contesting a historic election, all the 24-hour Bengali private news channels telecast programmes in the form of debates and panel discussions with Tollywood actors/stars like Aparna Sen, Debashree Roy, Tapas Pal, Satabdi Ray, Ranjit Mullick, Shaheb Chatterjee, Parambrata Chatterjee, Swastika Mukherjee, Hiron, Rituparno Ghosh, as well as TV actors like Badsha Moitra, Sudipta Chakraborty, etc. This provided a different dimension and added glamour to what might otherwise have been a dull and drab political debate. It also attracted greater viewership by means of drawing in more people who were interested in discussions with the celebrities. Subsequently, some of these Tollywood stars entered mainstream politics by 2013, including contesting state assembly and general elections for the TMC and the Bharatiya Janata Party (BJP).

Christine Geraghty argues that the categories through which stars are examined and understood need to be re-thought; she claims that in the present time, the representation of the 'famous' differently shapes 'how film stars make meaning in contemporary cinema and culture'. She identifies three meta-categories through which stars generate meaning: first, through 'star-as-celebrity', second 'star as-professional', and third, 'star-as-performer'. Tollywood stars, such as Dev, who has been projected by the industry and the media as a 'superstar', is simultaneously a celebrity, a professional and a performer, and so are his contemporaries like Koel Mullick, Hiron, Soham, Shrabonti, Jeet and Subhashree, who have become celebrities in the public domain, professional stars, and regular performers at TV shows, award ceremonies and public functions. The mofussil areas host 'Dev nights', and 'Jeet and Koel nights', where huge numbers of fans sway to chartbuster songs to which these stars perform. These shows are currently managed by event management companies and are heavily sponsored by corporate funding and advertising. The local media, cable channels and newspapers also report these events as generating an abundant volume of publicity and awareness about the Tollywood industry.

Cable and Satellite Channel Rights for Bengali Cinema: A Point of Mutual Support

Cable and Satellite (C&S) Rights have emerged as an important channel of revenue, allowing the Bengali TV to capitalise promptly on the rising popularity of Tollywood films. Bengali broadcasters benefit from the purchase of movies that result in high TRPs among audiences. Interestingly, Bengali films have been able to garner high TRPs among rural and semi-urban audiences, too. The number of Bengali channels (including *Doordarshan*) rose from around four to five in 2000 to around 14–15 Bengali channels.[19] With new Bengali GECs entering the TV market, the competition for quality content increased manifold.

A typical GEC channel needed at least six hours of fresh software everyday,[20] films being one of the key content sources that filled this need. Hence, films have become one of the prime routes for entertainment channels to draw audience attention and push TRPs up. As a result, broadcasters have contributed significantly to the revenues of the film industry through the purchase of satellite rights at substantial prices. This resulted in a mutually profitable cycle, where production houses could be more confident of recovering their costs that could have led to a rise in the number of Bengali films produced. C&S rites have been cited as one of the primary reasons for the growth in the size of the Tollywood industry post-2009. The contribution of cable and satellite distribution and exhibition to the industry in 2010 was estimated to have been about Rs 35 crores.[21] The existing trend of garnering revenue contribution from the C&S segment has continued to progress.

The Print Industry: Providing Maximum Visibility to Tollywood

The West Bengal print industry is pre-eminent in eastern India, with *Anandabazar Patrika* as the leading publishing house in this sector. Its leading Bengali newspaper, of the same name, is the fifth-largest vernacular daily in the country, with a readership of approximately 60 lakhs (2009–10). It is also one of the most widely-subscribed and read Bengali newspaper outside Bengal and India. The second-most widely read Bengali daily was *Bartaman* till 2011, with an average issue readership (AIR) of 30 lakhs, the popular English daily, *The Telegraph*, being the third most-widely read daily, with an AIR of approximately 10.4 lakhs.[22] In 2011, the print industry in

West Bengal was estimated to be Rs 900 crores. Bengali magazines and newspapers dominated the print industry, accounting for 60 per cent of the market share. As of 2011, the combined readership of the two Bengali dailies—*Anandabazar Patrika* and *Bartaman*—was more than five times the combined readership of the state's top two English dailies, *The Telegraph* and *The Times of India*, Kolkata, although these were the two most circulated English dailies in Bengal and were highly popular among young readers.[23]

The size of the English publishing market was estimated to grow at a CAGR of 9 per cent, to reach a value of Rs 500 crores by 2015. It is common knowledge that the major revenue stream for the print industry came from advertisements. Advertisers targeted youth-based magazines and the supplements of English and Bengali newspapers like *Calcutta Times*, *HT city*, *t2*, *Saptahik Bartaman*, *Patrika*, etc., to reach out to their potential consumers.

t2: A Case Study on Mutual Symbiosis

The Telegraph introduced a new lifestyle supplement, *t2*, in tabloid form from 2 February 2007, in an effort to connect with a wider reader base and popularise content on the Bengali film and entertainment industry, Tollywood, among English language readers. For the first time, this supplement had an entire page dedicated to Tollywood, with a page titled 'Tollywood' in bold. This page dealt extensively with content on Tollywood films, stars and stories from the overall entertainment industry, and their weekly focus stories like 'From the Floors' that featured highlights and updates from the shooting floors from ongoing film productions. It became very popular among its target readership with the launch issue. Weekly and fortnightly magazines, mainly from *Anandabazar Patrika*, publications like *Anandolok*, *Unnish Kuri*, *Sananda*, and Rose Valley Group's *Cinema Ebong* have been consistently popular, featuring regular content on Tollywood, and remained profitable media for the publicity and promotion of the Bengali entertainment industry at least until 2014.

With the launch of *t2*, the public relations officers who had started working with Tollywood production houses began to promote the films, interview the cast and crew of these films, and organise exclusive photo shoots with the main protagonists of the film for wider publicity and promotion. This trend then became an established norm and was practised by all leading dailies, both Bengali and English. Clearly then, there was an invisible nexus between the print and the Bengali film industry that symbiotically benefitted from each other. Tollywood has consistently been heavily dependent on the print industry for maximum visibility, publicity and promotion, and similarly, the print industry manages to get a constant supply of voluminous entertainment content and advertising revenue from Tollywood. It is of common knowledge that 'paid news' and sponsored features in newspapers have become a common phenomenon. Leading production houses and publicists of Tollywood have used this opportunity to push certain kinds of content-related features with regard to films and their stars. Dev, one of the top stars in Bengali cinema, is an example of this. Hailed by the media as the next generation superstar after Prosenjit, Dev occupied exclusive photo shoots, interviews, shooting updates, and even full-page coverages of his personal life featured in newspapers and magazines. A new format for this coverage was conceived, which was conversational and somewhat similar to the format of audio-visual chat shows. The director of a film, usually post-release, was made to brainstorm in an informal conversational manner with another contemporary director or actor to dissect the film, and its merits and demerits. This format gained popularity because of *t2*. When *Aparajita Tumi* (*You, Undefeated*), by Aniruddha Roy Chowdhury in 2012, completed four weeks in the theatres, a conversation was organised by *t2*, where three other directors, namely Kaushik Ganguly, Suman Mukhopadhyay and Suman Ghosh, discussed the film and aired their opinions, views and comments about the film, putting director Roy Chowdhury in the 'hot seat'.[24] The conversation also led to discussions on topics related to other Tollywood films of the period, and their content and relevance. This was later followed by another similar exercise, after the release of Kaushik Ganguly's 2012 film, *Laptop*; the film was 'decoded', where Ganguly and Anik Dutta, director of the 2012 film, *Bhooter Bhabishyat* (*Future of the Past*), engaged in a free-flowing and uninhibited discussion about each other's films.[25] Thus, it was noteworthy to see this phenomenon as a joint attempt by industry-insiders and the media to thrust the new films of Tollywood into the public domain. These efforts contributed to the alteration of perception and discourse around Tollywood films, and the simultaneous changes in the industry, further facilitating and reinforcing Tollywood's brand image and brand value.

Anandabazar Patrika and *t2* also initiated the practice of getting Tollywood films reviewed by celebrities, actors and directors, probably with the vested interest of gaining readership mileage and attempting to raise the industry's standard within the purview of the educated middle-class *bhadralok* audience. Such reviews also attracted letters to the editor, public opinions and views, which were later published in respective newspapers. It is perhaps difficult to say what such a trend does to the actual task of film criticism and reviewing, as it cannot be denied that when industry-insiders review a film, it cannot be unbiased; however, this form of reviewing gave rise to healthy competition within the industry and added to the novelty value of the brand Tollywood.

With the 'Page 3' format in newspapers gaining popularity nationally, the Bengali print industry, too, began to follow the newspaper formats of national dailies that prioritised Bollywood content, for instance, full-page coverage, with 'photo captions' of events, star/celebrity birthday bashes, wedding parties, film launch parties and award ceremonies, and premiere show parties from Tollywood. This was not only exclusive to *t2*, but became a common feature of other newspaper dailies like *The Times of India* supplement, *Calcutta Times*.

To be precise, the print media helps us identify certain 'texts and efforts' that reside outside the immediate production system of post-1990s Bengali cinema, and are yet inherently related to the film culture that has been described and discussed so far. After discussing the economy of emergence and 'strategies' of parallel-ness of post-1990s Bengali film culture in Chapter 3, the following section addresses issues like the construction of parallel-ness or 'difference' in defining a cinema of a particular kind and class through published materials proliferating around the emergence and solidification of Tollywood. Issues like an imagined past and efforts at 'reclaiming' it, and an escape in the romanticism of the past will be addressed here through the nature of publicity, the formation of public sphere discourse, and the question of stardom. This section also explores the overall discourse of this new parallel film culture, examining the nexus of Bengali press, established magazines, contemporary Bengali literature, television, etc., in the creation of the discourse of 'good taste'. Moreover, it explains how this film culture, in its discursive domain, constructs a strong support system for itself, maintaining its 'distance' from the 'crude' and 'commercial' mainstream model of films from the Tollygunge days of the film industry. The effort is not only to engage with the texts, but also to concentrate on the relational aspect of these different kinds of texts across the boundaries, and the horizontal and the vertical dimensions of that relationality.[26] The idea of class in this method of reading the logic of 'difference' in these subsidiary texts[27] and their intertextuality is borrowed from Pierre Bourdieu's reading of systems of self-definition and self-differentiation, and how the class is important in this system of imagination.[28]

What is interesting in this support system constructed by media and some cultural institutions is that it often included 'personal' engagement beyond institutional frameworks and market mechanisms.[29] Here it is also important to mention how the film directors of this 'new parallel' cinema, in their active association with the Bengali press and media houses, 'influenced' the regime of reception constructed around this film culture, reinforcing the identity of Tollywood. Bengali television channels like *ETV Bangla* or *Tara Bangla*, in their afternoon or late-evening slots, regularly showed these 'new parallel' films, and some of the films were shown on these channels as 'world TV premiere' even before their theatrical releases.[30] Besides this, a number of TV shows consistently engaged in debates and discussions regarding the infamous history of the crisis narrative of Bengali cinema or the Tollygunge industry, and how the scenario was significantly altered by the emergence of the 'new parallel' film culture, alongside the maturity of the film industry as Tollywood. And the 'parallel' cinema directors or actors as talk show hosts or anchors regenerated this discourse.[31] The physical presence of the director as a talk show host is a crucial point that has been discussed in detail in Chapter 3 while analysing the 'phenomenal' emergence of

Rituparno Ghosh as a star director of post-1990s *bhadralok* or 'new parallel' cinema. These popular talk shows, internet discussion forums, blogs (like *Kaustav's Arden, Sen's Spot, Cinemascope, Alternative Movies*, etc.), Facebook pages and other web-based platforms, in their serious engagement with and discussion of 'quality' Bengali films, have appreciably contributed to the discourse. An entertainment news-based website like *Calcuttatube.com*, a site like *Vinnamat News Network*, or a live community Bengali radio station like *Washington Bangla Radio* that serves a global Bengali audience are all important names in this regard, as their active participation is important for forming the recent taste discourse within the transitioning discourse of the Tollygunge industry into its new avatar, Tollywood. This *bhadralok* 'taste discourse' confirms to what French sociologist and philosopher Pierre Bourdieau has called 'cognitive acquirement' of the 'cultural code', 'presupposing an act of cognition' through the logic of differentiation and legitimising and decoding that 'difference'.[32] The following sections aim at mapping out this act of 'differentiation' or performing 'difference' in publicity materials, promotional attempts, critical perspectives, and the discourse of stardom.

Publicising 'Difference'

Film director Subrata Sen spoke of how the urban audiences of Bengali cinema distanced themselves from of the titles of Bengali films of the 1980s, which, according to him, for years had continued using moral binaries like *Nyay Anyay* (*Virtue and Vice*), *Sadhu Shaytan* (*The Pure and the Evil*), etc., both 1981 films by Sukhen Das.[33] Thus, when he worked on films that had titles like *Ek Je Achhe Kanya (Once There was a Girl)*, *Swapner Feriwala* (*The Hawker of Dreams*), or *Nil Nirjaney*,[34] he consciously made a departure from such hackneyed film titles. As Kaustav Bakshi had mentioned in his blog, the very name, *Unishe April*, was an 'unusual title' that 'signalled a different film' for him and generated an interest even before he watched it. Along with the naming, the font, style and design of *Unishe April*'s poster attracted a crowd that was most likely reluctant to watch a mainstream Bengali film; it used the Bengali numericals, one and nine, and put images of Debashree Roy and Aparna Sen in two corners of the layout, indicating the distance between them via the use of the space in between. Newspaper advertisements, the unusual striking phrase like '*ma o meyer jatil samparko niye ek asadharon paribarik chhabi*' ('an extraordinary family film exploring relationship complexity between a mother and a daughter'), promised something other than what the usual family melodrama of a Swapan Saha or a Haranath Chakraborty film was providing at that time. Moreover, the 'realist' nature of the photographs of the two lead protagonists played by Aparna Sen and Debashree Roy in the *Unishe April* poster differentiated it from the kitschy family melodramas of that time.

Darkly lit spaces and characters' faces with restrained emotions tried to convey the 'difference' that parallel cinema had established with its middle-class audiences through the aesthetics of realism. Also, the poster highlighted the film's National Award recognition, especially Debashree Roy as an award-winning actress for this film. Another interesting publicity strategy deployed for this film was that before its release on 17 May 1996, an advertisement on 5 May attempted to arouse the curiosity of the audience by putting forth the question, 'Why is nineteenth April is a memorable day for Aparna and Debashree?' These interesting strategies promised a 'different' film in its newspaper advertisements that seemed to cater to an audience who may not have gone for other Bengali films like *Bhai Amar Bhai* by Swapan Saha in 1996 or *Nach Nagini Nach Re* by Anjan Choudhury in 1996.[35] Additional information that the newspaper advertisement of *Unishe April* provided was that the night show would be over by 10:30 pm. An interview with Uttam Kumar Basu, who was in charge of the publicity for *Unishe April*, on behalf of Cine Media, reveals that the show timing detail had been provided out of safety concerns, so that the middle-class *bhadralok* could go to the film theatre without worrying about transport.[36]

It is essential to note how this film imagined a class who might be bothered about their safety and availability of transport facilities in order to watch this film. In the following week, the *Unishe April* posters and newspaper advertisements added critics' statements from their reviews, which appeared in *Desh*, *Aajkaal*, *Bartamaan* and *Sonar Bangla*. Along with direct publicity, there were other features published in the newspaper columns that aimed at generating interest regarding this film. First, there were interviews of actress Debashree

Roy, who described her response after winning the National Award. This interview was not exclusively about her winning the National Award; instead, it revealed her longstanding career in the film industry mired with struggles, obstacles and unhealthy competition from her co-actors.[37] Moreover, the film magazine, *Anandalok*, had gossip columns, and the feature news of *Anandabazar Patrika* covered Debashree–Prosenjit's marriage break-up stories in detail, with full-page interviews.[38] The fact that Prosenjit and Debashree both acted in this film when their 14-year relationship was going through a break-off served to be an added interest in generating curiosity about their onscreen chemistry. In a similar vein, Rituparno Ghosh's *Titli*, in its publicity, brought up a comparison between Aparna Sen and Konkona Sen Sharma in different registers. The film magazine columns (for instance, of *Anandalok*) and the press entertainment news section during that period focused on the comparison between the two actresses, dealing with the question who is a better actress, who is more beautiful, and so on. Both *Titli* and Sen Sharma's first feature film, *Ek Je Achhe Kanya*, used a star discourse about Sen Sharma in their respective Konkona programmes. When Subrata Sen and Sandip Sen, the director and the producer of this film, respectively, planned *Ek Je Achhe Kanya* as the first Bengali 'urban youth film',[39] they felt it was necessary to establish Sen Sharma as the face of urban Bengali youth. The subsidiary discourse on her highlighted these above factors at the time when she debuted as the central protagonist of the film. Thus, *Anandabazar Patrika* and *Anandalok* columns highlighted her college life spent in Delhi as a St Stephen's College English Honours graduate, and her preference for English television serials on *Star World*.

A similar publicity strategy was adopted for Subrata Sen's next film, *Swapner Feriwala*, in which Nilanjana Bhoumik, the daughter of yesteryear Bengali film actress, Anjana Bhoumik, debuted. When Anjan Das's *Iti Srikanta* (*Yours Truly, Srikanta*) was released in 2004, the Bengali newspaper, *Pratidin*, publicised Soha Ali Khan's presence in this film, which was her debut Bengali film, in their *Mahanagar* supplement, on 4 June and 11 June 2004. The first highlighted her similarity with her mother, Sharmila Tagore, and the second tried to establish her presence and possibilities for the future, based on the columnist's conversations with Khan at

Tantra, a famous Kolkata night club.[40] Contrary to the flat, bright title fonts of the 'mainstream' model, these film posters used fonts of a 'different' style. In many cases, going against uniformly typed words, they consciously used fonts of an asymmetrical hand-writing style. Fonts of *Ek Je Ache Kanya*, *Titli*, *Utsab*, *Iti Srikanta*, *Shubho Mahurat* and Subrata Sen's 2004 film, *Hothat Nirar Janye* (*Suddenly for Nira*), were in this mode. Apart from that, the names of the films themselves were closer to the literary use of Bengali names than the names resembling popular *jatra* titles of the 'mainstream' model. There were instances when professional painters worked for publicity or font design of 'parallel' films. For instance, artist Anup Roy designed the letter type and overall style of the title for *Titli*, with the hand-written red-coloured word and an idle butterfly sitting on it visually, signifying the meaning of '*Titli*'.[41] On the other hand, films that were based on direct literary adaptations created a literary flavour in their fonts, such as posters of films like *Chokher Bali* or *Antarmahal* (*Inner Chambers*) by Rituparno Ghosh in 2005. Along with the font style, there was the strategic use of captions that helped differentiate these films from the mainstream model. In Subrata Sen's *Hothat Nirar Janye*, lines from Sunil Gangopadhyay's poetry were used for publicity. This film had a one-week delayed-release on the grounds of censorship concerning one scene, and this 'news' had already been beamed to the public to generate curiosity. When the publicity lines used a phrase like '*sharir jakhan maner kotha bole*' ('when the body speaks of the mind's words'), they tease an interest in the film effectively. Moreover, the publicity poster of the film used a very minimal style, unique in the Bengali film poster tradition: it just had a close up of Jaya Seal, who played the title role of Nira, against a white background, with Gangopadhyay's lines used above. Her face and that line with the 'A' in caps in a circle, connotative of its adult certification, was highlighted. The film is an adaptation of Gangopadhyay's short story, '*Rani O Abinash*' ('*Rani and Abinash*'), but it intentionally uses the name, Nira, in its title. Nira is an imagined muse that Gangopadhyay had written about in several poems. Thus, the figure had already been in *bhadralok* popular parlance and the cultural imagination for years. Sen, in this way, generated interest regarding his film by using a name from a *bhadralok* literary imagination that had a broad appeal.

Titli used two interesting captions: the first one, '*pahare premer galpo*' ('love story in the hillside'),[42] resembled the title of a travelogue; and the second one, '*Jibane kauke valobese hariyechhen? Titli dekhun*' ('Have you lost someone in your life whom you loved? *Titli* is a must watch')[43] seemed to evoke a personal resonance with the pleasure of memory and nostalgia, as discussed in the earlier chapter. Aparna Sen's 1995 film, *Yugant* (*What the Sea Said*), used '*premer galpo, ei prithibir galpo*' ('love story, the story of this world') in the *Anandabazar* advertisement, and later 'A film about Love and Change' in its advertisement in *The Telegraph*.[44] The poster of Goutam Ghose's *Abar Aranye* generated nostalgia in a different register; its caption read '*fire dekha aranya*' ('looking back the forest'), referring back to Satyajit Ray's film, *Aranyer Dinratri*, of which this film was a sequel. In the poster of Abhijit Dasgupta's *Dwitiyo Basanto*, the line used is, 'There are lots of secrets. In this life, nothing would be spoken of.'[45] Kausik Ganguly's lines on the poster of his 2004 film, *Waarish* (*Progeny*), is '*bhalobasha kakhano abaidha noi*' ('love is never illegitimate');[46] and the caption on the poster of Bratya Basu's 2005 film, *Teesta*, reads, '*amar kono shabda nei, shudhui naishabda …*' ('I don't have any words, only silence …').[47] These sentences, on the one hand, capture the theme of the film, and in a line, give an idea of what the film is all about; on the other hand, they establish their closeness to a certain kind of Bengali *bhadralok* rhetoric and culture, a kind of literariness of the *bhadra* cultural code. This is because a body of films rejecting the *bhadra* code and belief system used a different language pattern unauthorised and criticised by the 'better' cinema-going class that Subrata Sen, Rituparno Ghosh or Anjan Das, as also some other directors' films claimed was the 'lost' taste discourse in their publicity strategy, and in this reclaiming, developed a taste discourse attached to their films and their closeness to Bengali literary practice. It is important to note that the language they used resonates with a specific idea of Bengali cultured-ness that goes beyond the title and caption patterns, and when these films were shown on TV, the brief description of their plot line in press columns almost introduced them as novels published in *Desh* or *Anandabazar Durga Puja* issues.[48] Apart from the the popular press, even little magazines like *Kobita Pratimase* published special issues on films like *Jara Bristite Bhijechhilo* by Anjan Das in 2007 or *Sab Charitro Kalponik* by Rituparno Ghosh in 2009. An issue on *Jara Bristite Bhijechhilo* included an interview with Anjan Das and some other intellectuals of the literary field and brought about a discussion of the play by Joy Goswami, on which the film was based. In the *Sab Charitro Kalponik* issue, there were interviews of Joy Goswami, Rituparno Ghosh and others. Along with the special issue publication, *Kobita Pratimase* organised a yearly poetry workshop, and Rituparno Ghosh, while participating in this event, once spoke about cinema, poetry and his films.

Along with literary closeness and the mobilisation of materials relating to the star, the marketing logic of this *bhadralok* cinema resulted in giving shape to its broader appeal by subsidiary media and brand endorsements. Large-scale advertisements of *Chokher Bali* brought brand association to a new dimension hitherto hidden in Bengali cinema.[49] SVF, known as a big-budget producer of Bengali commercial films, began its association with 'quality' Bengali films with *Chokher Bali*.[50] This film also started a new pattern of film publicity in poster aesthetics and the logic of circulation. Sponsorship logic made the primary banners of this film advertisement look like brand endorsements of Anjali Jewellers. Primary posters, print advertisements and kiosks presented Aishwarya Rai dressed up in jewellery. The film poster focuses on Rai's stardom, and a caption, '*biyer saje Binodini*' ('*Binodini in bridal wear*') or '*Anjalir alankare aparupa Binodini*' ('*Beautiful Binodini in Anjali's ornaments*').[51] Most advertisements appeared on the second page of *Anandabazar Patrika* instead of the sixth or seventh pages where film publicity commonly appeared. In each of them, along with SVF, the name of Anjali Jewellers was printed in bold letters. Post-*Chokher Bali*, this jewellery brand, along with a few other brands, saw a new phase in their association with several Bengali films. Starting from Raja Sen's 2007 film, *Krishnakanter Will* (*The Will of Krishnakanta*), to Suman Mukhopadhyay's 2010 film, *Mahanagar@Kolkata* (*The Big City@Kolkata*) or Sandip Ray's *Kailashe Kelenkari*, this trend of placing jewellery houses' advertisements within the films became a trend, and jewellery brands used these films as a platform for brand endorsement. Aniruddha Roychowdhury, with his 2009 film, *Antaheen*, and his later production, *Ekti Tarar Khnoje*, extends this product placement strategy to a new scale, relating the film to numerous brands, starting from hair oil and skin clinics to investment plan banking, laptop brands, and even news TV channels. The use of the Peerless brand in *Ek Je Achhe Kanya* can also be mentioned in this regard. Moving one step further, a fruit juice company gave money to the producer of *Ek Je Achhe Kanya* only to serve its fruit juice free of cost during intervals of Priya shows to make its brand known.[52]

The use of subsidiary media is another significant intervention in press-based publicity of Bengali films. When *Titli* was initially planned as a big-budget film with a star cast like Aparna Sen, Mithun Chakraborty and Konkona Sen Sharma, Tapan Biswas thought of its publicity on a large scale and discussed it with Uttam Kumar Basu, and planned to shoot a 'Making of *Titli*', which was then telecast on *ETV Bangla* before the film's release.[53] Back then, this was part of the regular publicity of almost all big-banner Bengali films and channels like *Sangeet Bangla*, owned by SVF. They deployed this as an essential promotional strategy for their films, and even TV news channels like *Star Ananda* took part in this publicity mechanism. The telecasting of the 'Making of *Titli*' was the first attempt of this kind in the Bengali film publicity scenario. If the 'Making of *Titli*' started a new phase in the involvement of new media in film publicity, Anjan Das's *Shanjhbatir Roopkathara* extended it to a new scale altogether. Planman Motion Pictures beat earlier publicity strategies when its advertisements in newspapers described this film's release as 'heralding a new era in *Bangla* cinema'[54] since it had 'Hollywood giant Columbia Trister's first regional film distribution', and it had been 'shortlisted in the final seven movies this year for Oscar nomination from India'. Added to that in bold letters, the advertisement mentioned that it was selected for film festivals in London, Rome, the US and Canada (although the name of the festivals and the section in which it had been selected were not mentioned). The team organised a TV show on *Akash Bangla* before its release, the *Shanjhbatir Roopkathara* quiz, from 4–8 November, between 6:45 and 7:00 pm, and offered 'exciting prizes' for winners. The radio station, *93.5 Red FM*, also organised a *Shanjhbati* debate competition and offered prizes for the winner. The film also organised another competition called

'*Pujar Shanjhbati*' with a local organisation, Rajdanga Navyuday Sangh, and announced a prize money of Rs 11,000. The world of Titan produced the '*Shanjhbati* letter-writing contest'. Anyone could write and submit a letter at any Titan showroom in this contest, and the winner would win a watch worth Rs 70,000. The film publicity here described this film as a letter of *Shanjhbati* written to her father, and one willing to compete had to write a letter on this theme. The film producer also organised a book-reading evening as 'an exclusive evening of poetry, painting and music for the people of Kolkata',[55] sponsored by The Park, Kolkata. There were announcements promising a free family trip to Darjeeling if one purchased multiple tickets in advance, which were a part of a special 'lucky draw lottery'.

In this manner, the publicity of *Shanjhbatir Roopkathara* worked to promote interest in the film to new levels through lucky draws, an FM debate and a letter-writing competition involving media like radio and TV. Moreover, during this period, TV became a significant site to publicise and promote Bengali films. Later, this 'new parallel' cinema acknowledged the importance of TV, not only as a publicity medium, but also as a solid connection to the 'majority' of the audience. Rituparno Ghosh's 2008 film, *Khela* (*Game*), is an interesting case in point. The publicity caption for this film, before its release on kiosks and two-sheet and six-sheet banners, read '*baroparda r* "*Khela*"' ('"*Khela*" of the big screen'). *Khela*, directed by Ravi Ojha, was also a popular TV serial of *Zee Bangla* around that period. At the same time, the so-called mainstream Bengali film publicity since 2005 also became largely dependent on TV and TV-ness. Especially after the launching of *Sangeet Bangla* and film-based infotainment programmes on TV, with shows like *Film Star* on *Star Ananda*, TV became an essential medium for the circulation of film news. Music video aesthetics, which was quite evident in *Nil Nirjane*, both in its filming and its publicity that he had considered 'experimental', and to some extent, '*avant-garde*'[56] in that period, can now be found in any average *Sangeet Bangla* promo of a so-called mainstream film. Newer publicity media, such as film websites, social network communities and fan pages are not exclusive to 'marketing' the parallel-ness of a parallel film anymore. For instance, a social network community page like 'We Love Bengali films' is equally enthusiastic about giving information and personal reviews about a Haranath Chakraborty film and a Rituparno Ghosh film. In this context, the question of the new media public needs discussion.

For instance, when Haranath Chakraborty was questioned about the media's changed approach towards Bengali popular cinema, he stated that the press could not fool the audience as they have sufficient awareness. The electronic media cannot function according to the exclusive imagination of an ideal educated middle-class public as its consumer. It has to target or imagine a wider base. *Chokher Bali*'s jewellery house endorsement or the TV-ness of *Khela* publicity was no exception following that logic. On the one hand, it blurred the differentiating line between Bengali mainstream and parallel cinema and on the other hand, it raised questions about how we would formulate and relate this 'change' to the target audiences' imagination of parallel spectatorship.

Radio and FM: Tollywood's Aural Presence

Anandabazar Patrika, or the ABP group, owns an exclusive FM radio station called *91.9 Friends FM*; this station catered to a more mature audience, and gradually opened up to a wider audience base, playing a mix of Bengali and Hindi film and non-film music, both contemporary and retro. *Friends FM* regularly invites Tollywood talent and celebrities for talk shows, interviews and pre-release film promotions; the radio station also airs film and TV show promos. Other popular FM stations are *92.7 Big FM*, *93.5 Red FM*, *94.3 Radio One*, *98.3 Radio Mirchi*, *104.0 Fever FM* (owned by Hindustan Times Media and Entertainment), *106.2 Amar FM* and *107.8 Power FM*. Among these, *Radio Mirchi* has also become a very popular radio station, which exclusively dedicates shows to Tollywood, like *Kolkata Express* and *Dawsher Desh*; these two shows play a large number of contemporary Tollywood film music, with quizzes and games related to Tollywood celebrities, films and music. They also invite Tollywood celebrities and stars for chats, interviews and film promotion. It takes telephonic requests from fans who can talk directly to the stars, actors and celebrities present on the show. Another station, *Amar FM*, is the only 100 per cent Bengali FM radio station that describes itself as 'the radio station built for Kolkata by Kolkatans'. It plays music from the 1970s, 1980s, 1990s and contemporary films, ranging from popular film songs to non-film songs. The station also frequently holds contests, quizzes and interviews with Tollywood celebrities. It is important to mention here that over the last four to five years, popular films of Tollywood have had a revival in terms of their music. Compositions of Jeet Ganguly, Indradeep Dasgupta, Raja Narayan Deb and Debojyoti Misra have generated satisfactory levels of interest and curiosity for contemporary Tollywood music, especially among the youth. This has led to radio FM stations tapping into this genre and designing shows and content that can accommodate contemporary Bengali film music.[57] Moreover, content delivery in the new age of distribution has gone digital.

New Media: Tollywood's Tryst with Digital Technology and the Worldwide Web

If TV, radio and the print media individually act as vehicles for Tollywood to foreground itself in the press and public discourse, then the relatively new entrant in the media arena has to be the internet and the cyber world. The digital medium furthers possibilities of representation and image construction, and the reach of content and identities beyond regional/national boundaries.

The launch of film websites, although restricted to a limited number of films released every year, and individual websites, Facebook pages, Twitter handles and Instagram accounts of Tollywood celebrities and stars have added to the popularity and expanded the digital presence of Tollywood. With the rise of Over-the-Top (OTT) and application-based digital platforms for content production and dissemination, in 2016, Rajiv Mehra launched one of the first OTT platforms that provided content in Bengali and Hindi languages. The platform offered original web series, short films and music videos. SVF launched one of the most ambitious and exclusive Bengali OTT platform, Hoichoi, in 2017, which has a curated content, a mix of both acquired content and original productions. Some of their originals that went on to become popular are *Charitraheen*, *Hello* and *Dupur Thakurpo*.[58]

Fan Club Rituals and Fandom

Dev and Jeet, the two young-generation stars of Tollywood, each have huge fan followings, and their official fan web pages are meticulously maintained, followed and subscribed to by a large cross-section of the Bengali population from both urban and semi-urban regions.[59] A film release spurs their fans into action. Fan clubs organise *puja*s (offerings to God) and rituals in Jeet's name, praying for a hit at holy pilgrimage sites like Dakshineswar and Puri; Somnath Kar, who runs Jeet Fans Club in Kalighat in south Kolkata, proudly expressed this fact to the members of the club. The ritual at the theatre is as important. Jeet's cut-outs in every city hall are garlanded, 51 coconuts are broken to bring luck, and sweets are distributed among the audience. Moreover, confetti bombs burst. A fan club, says Babua Bhowmik, who organises live shows with actors, is of great help when the star goes to the districts for shows, for instance, to smaller towns in northern Bengal like Coochbehar and Malda; the star's fan club members give the team protection in the face of mob frenzy.

According to Jeet, a fan club also boosts the celebrity's ego, as no amount of success matches 'the roar of a crowd of 15000–20,000 people when they see an actor or star step out on stage'. Jeet often has fans waiting outside his New Alipore house. Sayantan Roy, a 21-year-old amateur web designer and a fan of Tollywood's 'newest heartthrob', Dev, has built the website, www.devthesuperstar.com. Earlier, he had created an Orkut and Facebook community, which proved to be very popular, with 8,180 members. He thus created this website and approached Dev for its launch. He actively manages the blog, with participation and followers even from Bangladesh. The site is the base for a fan club with paid membership. Identity cards, t-shirts and tickets for Dev films are sent to members. He also approached Dev with a request to start a blog on the site. A video portal plays Dev's bytes on occasions like Independence Day. Taking a cue from Roy, fans of other Tollywood stars have turned to the internet. Aritro Roy, a class 12 student of Bangur Boys School, created a website on Koel Mullick, www.tollyqueenkoel.com. He went to Koel Mullick's Golf Club Road house on 28 April, her birthday, to get her to launch the website. The website includes updated news on Mullick, collected from media reports. Tolly Queen Koel is now hosted on Facebook,

Twitter and Instagram, with an average following of 126,050, 5,420, 119,000, respectively. The interactive zones on these sites showcase the passion for such stars. Requests to the stars for their contact numbers are aplenty.

Producers have realised the potential of this new platform. Some have come forward to channelise this passion for helping their films. A contest specific to the above site ran on Mullick's 2012 film, *Prem by Chance.* Roy also received requests from Dev's producers to help promote films that do not feature Dev.[60] Recently, director Srijit Mukherjee personally called ardent film blogger Kaustav Bakshi to review his 2012 film, *Hemlock Society*, after he found out that Bakshi's blog had received the maximum number of 'hits' by readers when he had reviewed *Baishe Srabon*, Mukherjee's earlier film.[61]

Exploring Markets beyond Borders through Technological Strategies

The Bengali film industry has attempted to look beyond domestic theatricals and C&S rights to achieve its true potential in size and reach. The key objective is to target alternative and innovative distribution techniques, and cross over to overseas markets. However, given their existing budgets, Bengali films may not be able to replicate other regional film industries, such as Tamil and Telugu, which reach out to global markets on the strength of their international theatrical distribution platforms.

The Bengali film industry taps international markets through Bengali associations and clubs where the films have a provision for screening and audience appreciation. A few prominent directors and producers take their films to international film festivals and film markets for exhibitions and promotions. Films today are not just seen in theatres, but also on screens such as mobiles and iPads. Emerging platforms such as the Internet Protocol Television (IPTV), and furthermore, internet streaming services and OTT platforms continuously stream films to consumers worldwide. Such services are also accessible on several devices, apps and platforms.

All of these provide ample opportunity for Bengali films to reach out to these audiences through digital distribution platforms, and overcome marketing and distribution limitations. In September

2010, Databazaar Media Ventures, the US gateway for Bengali films, presented the producers of four Bengali movies, *Angshumaner Chhobi* (*Angshuman's Film*), *The Japanese Wife*, *Jodi Ekdin* (*If Someday*), and *Ekti Tarar Khonje*, with a release of their films in North America, and the producer's share added up to $20,000. Notably, this represented only about 30 days of revenue from the US market, thus indicating the potential for Bengali films in these markets.[62]

Washington Bangla Radio: Reaching Out to the Diaspora Market

An international avenue to exclusively promote Tollywood is the *Washington Bangla Radio*, a registered trademark and service of Washington Bangla Radio on the Internet (WBRi) Inc., incorporated in the state of Maryland, the US, an established and respected technology pioneer with a long list of ground-breaking internet firsts, including the first internet Bangla Radio, the first Bengali online music store, the first live concert internet broadcast from India, and so on.

WashingtonBanglaRadio.com is also a news website covering Bollywood, Hollywood and Indian regional films, with a particular emphasis on Bengali cinema. For over six years, the WBRi has been publishing exclusive interviews with famous singers and musicians, and also with film stars from Kolkata and around the world. The WBRi covers all established and upcoming Bengali artists, musicians and albums, and cinema releases with promos, trailers, stills and reviews. The goal of the WBRi is to promote Bengali music and films worldwide. Their Tollywood film news and reviews have been reported as being the most popular Bengali cinema blog accessed outside India; the WBRi also allowed the broadcasting of new albums live on the website. Bangla radio offered possibilities for global promotion, the selling of music as digital downloads from their exclusive online store, the promotion of movies among the global audience via exclusive movie news and announcement service; they could also be contacted if one wished to explore the electronic promotion and digital distribution of Bengali films in the US and Canada. The WBRi broadcasts under direct license from record companies, and is also the internet's first 100 per cent legal Bengali music streaming and MP3 download website.

Conclusion: On Mediations and Convergence

TV, print journalism, radio and the new media thus carry the 'four-pronged' imprint of a changing twenty-first century, affecting the cultures of everyday life, irrespective of areas in urban, suburban or rural India. Media, as Lawrence Grossberg argues, has penetrated into identity formations based on location, profession and various other factors. At the same time, the sense of unity among people, created by such powerful identities as were defined by religion, nationality, and work, have themselves been increasingly undermined by the powerful representations of difference that have come to define the media's cultural content, even as the media has come to shape social life. Ultimately, the media's ability to produce people's social identities, in terms of both a sense of unity and difference, may be their most powerful and important effect.[63] Convergence culture and various mediations have enabled the overhauling of the Bengali film industry, particularly since the beginning to the new millennium year, 2000, and its new avatar as Tollywood. We have mapped and accounted these mutations and symbiosis in order to draw parallels with other established media industry scenarios to understand and elucidate the similarities and differences that are typical to Tollywood. The sheer rise in the number of films produced in Tollywood, and the ability to fuse the two dominant practices of film-making (the popular/commercial with 'good' content and 'art') in a celebratory spirit, suggests the confluence of these categories of films produced, rather than the excessive discourse centred around film narratives, aesthetics, and their thematic components during the Tollygunge days of the industry. In other words, this signifies how what were earlier termed 'art' films are now infusing high-end technology on escalated budgets, stars and aggressive promotional strategies.

This chapter, therefore, has been an attempt to look at the evolving nature of Tollywood as a culture industry. It is perhaps evident that media convergence is at the crux of this consistent rise in the discourse about the Bengali film industry, Tollywood. The relationship between the TV industry and the film industry indicates the tight imbrications of Tollywood content and television rating points (TRPs). The growth of both industries is mutually dependent on each other. In the recent past, Tollywood celebrity marriages, birthdays, divorce controversies, personal affairs, and even sexual orientation have been reported by the press and covered on TV. Thus, images, stories, print visibility, publicity, self-promotion, and commodification of self-talent have been fractured and reduced to triviality, or sometimes, have been excessively hyped, thereby giving newer meanings to stardom and media. Tollywood's formation in this invasive world of image constructions could be a reverse cultural imperialism countering the excessive and dominant hegemony of Bollywood being synonymously recognised as an all-encompassing category for Indian cinema and for the overall entertainment industry. The visibility that the print medium has provided to Tollywood has also been crucial for its discursive presence and the diffusion of the imagination of Tollywood in the public domain. This presence of Tollywood within the print media space has repeatedly propelled the establishment of the film industry and its resurgence from the allegedly 'crisis-ridden period' during the 1980s and 1990s to a revamped avatar. However, popular press and the heavy influx of content and discourses on Tollywood have been mainly over-celebratory. There is possibly a lack of a serious critical framework that pushes this discourse beyond the celebration of Tollywood's identity and engages in analysing cardinal issues of labour, plagiarism, copyright, subversion of genres, and professionalising the bottlenecks and bureaucratic practices that interrupt the processes of film production, exhibition and distribution. Foregrounding of issues related to monopolisation by particular production houses, misleading or manipulative box office and trade reports, and film technicians' union matters have largely been absent from the media and press discourse. The slow but steady entry of a few individual producers and independent production companies has triggered the growth of healthy competition in the film industry, finally putting Tollywood on the cusp of transformation towards a dynamic regional film industry in India.

Notes and References

1. Amit S. Rai, *Untimely Bollywood: Globalization and India's New Media Assamblage* (Durham; London: Delhi University Press, 2009).
2. Anustup Basu, *Bollywood in the Age of New Media: The Geo-televisual Aesthetic* (Edinburgh: Edinburgh University Press, 2010).

3. Kushali Nag's interview of Raj Chakraborty, 'Point Blank', *The Telegraph*, 16 October 2010.
4. Hamid Naficy, 'From Accented Cinema to Multiplex Cinema', in Sabine Hake and Janet Staiger, ed., *Convergence Media History* (Oxon: Routledge, 2009), p. 3.
5. Marshall McLuhan, 'The Medium is the Message', in *Understanding Media: The Extensions of Man* (New York: Signet, 1964), p. 23.
6. J. D. Bolter and R. Grusin, 'Remediation: Understanding New Media', *Corporate Communications: An International Journal*, vol. 4, no. 4 (1999), pp. 208–09.
7. David Thorburn, Henry Jenkins and Brad Seawell, *Rethinking Media Change: The Aesthetics of Transition* (Cambridge, Massachusetts: The MIT Press, 2003).
8. 'Media and Entertainment Business Conclave—East (Kolkata)', A Symphony of Art Media & Entertainment in East India-Bengal, Deloitte, Kolkata, 22–24 December 2011.
9. Ibid.
10. Kakoli Poddar, 'Bengal's One-Man Industry', *Society*, November 2006, p. 140.
11. 'Media and Entertainment Business Conclave'.
12. Aswin Punathambekar and Anandam P. Kavoori, *Global Bollywood* (New Delhi: Oxford University Press, 2009).
13. Reshmi Sengupta, 'From Tagore to Tolly', *The Telegraph*, 30 April 2005.
14. Aparajita Gupta, 'Pattaya Gets a Taste of Tollywood Flavours', *The Times of India*, 4 July 2012.
15. John Ellis, *Seeing Things: Television in the Age of Uncertainity* (London: I. B. Tauris, 2000).
16. Actress Rituparna Sengupta has set up her production company called *Bhabna Aaj o Kaal* in around 2005, which has produced TV shows like *Dance Pe Chance Boudimoni* for *Rupashi Bangla*. Actor star Prosenjit Chatterjee's Ideas Creation produced the serial, *Gaaner Opare*, in collaboration with director Rituparno Ghosh, for *Star Jalsha*. Actor Jisshu Sengupta's Blue Water Pictures produced the chat show called *Ghosh and Company* for *Star Jalsha*.
17. Priyanka Dasgupta, 'Jeet in the Hot Seat', *The Times of India*, 31 August 2011.
18. PTI, 'Prosenjit Starts New Innings on Small Screen', *The Times of India*, 20 June 2012.
19. Ashoke Nag, 'Reliance Entertainment, Mukta Arts, Saregama, Mumbai Mantra, UTV and Eros Interested in Tollywood', *The Economic Times*, 17 September 2011.
20. Ashoke Nag, 'The Revival of Bangla Film Industry', *The Economic Times*, 30 April 2011.
21. 'Media and Entertainment Business Conclave'.

22. Indian Readership Survey Q2, Deloitte, Kolkata, 2011.
23. Ibid.
24. Mohua Das, 'Aniruddha in the Hotseat', *The Telegraph*, 14 February 2012.
25. Kushali Nag, 'Laptop Decoded', *The Telegraph*, 26 April 2012.
26. My methods of reading this relational aspect is deeply inspired by John Fiske's approach on intertextuality in his reading of television texts and discourses generated around them in his book, *Television Culture*; John Fiske, *Television Culture* (London: Routledge, 2011).
27. Here, by subsidiary texts, we mean the publicity and media texts that were generated, along with film texts, like posters, or other publicity materials, review columns of these films in newspapers, etc.
28. See Pierre Bourdieu, *The Field of Cultural Production: Essays on Art and Literature* (Columbia University Press, 1993).
29. For instance, the former CEO of Nandan, Nilanjan Chattopadhyay, wrote a story called *Dui Number Asami* (*The Second Criminal*), on which Shekhar Dash's film *Kaaler Rakhal* (*The Understudy*), is based. The former President of Eastern India Motion Pictures Association and the owner of the Priya Star Cinema hall chain, Arijit Dutta, appears in many of these films as a character actor.
30. For instance, *Tara Bangla* showed Rituparno Ghosh's *Utsab* on its inauguration day (28 April 2000), and later showed Buddhadeb Dasgupta's *Uttara* much before these films' theatrical release. Goutam Ghose's 2009 film, *Kaalbela* (*Calcutta My Love*), on the other hand, was initially made for *Doordarshan* as a mini-series to be shown serially; later, it was redesigned from the video format in Qube digital prints to release in cinema halls. A new Bengali channel, *Mohua Bangla*, recently announced that it would telecast a number of films made by Anjan Dutt, which they are planning to release later in theatres.
31. A popular talk show called *Ebong Rituparno* (hosted by Rituparno Ghosh) was telecast on *ETV Bangla*, followed by *Sange Indrani* (hosted by Indrani Halder) on *Tara Bangla*, *Aparna Online* (hosted by Aparna Sen) on *Kolkata TV*, and *Ghosh and Company* (hosted by Rituparno Ghosh) on *Star Jalsa*. A show called *Antaheen Adda* on *Rupasi Bangla* has even been named after the Bengali film, *Antaheen*, and is hosted by Kalyan Roy, one of the actors of this film.
32. See Pierre Bourdieau, *Distinction: A Social Critique of the Judgment of Taste* (London: Routledge, 1984), p. 3.
33. Authors' interview with Subrata Sen, 2 October 2010, Kolkata.
34. Translated as *There is a Girl*, *The Hawker of Dreams* and *Vacation Blues*, respectively.
35. These two films were widely advertised Bengali films around that time, and they were adjacently placed on cinema advertisement pages. *Unishe April* therefore had the challenge of how to look 'different' in its first appearance.

36. Authors' interview with Uttam Kumar Basu.
37. For instance, see the interview with Debashree Roy, '*Jhar Samlate Samlatei Bachhar ta Chole Gelo*' ('The Year Passed By Trying to Manage the Storm'), *Anandabazar Patrika*, 19 May 1996.
38. Especially the *Anandalok* issue of 29 June 1996, which covered this 'story' as its cover page story, with 'exclusive' photographs of them as well as interviews.
39. In my interview of the producer and the director of this film, both of them claimed *Ek Je Achhe Kanya* to be the 'first Bengali urban youth film'.
40. '*Sei Chokh, Sei Hasi, Shudhu Tol Chara Sharmila*' ('The Same Eyes, Same Smile, Sharmila Just without the Dimple') and 'Soha G', both by Ranjan Bandyopadhyay on 4 and 11 June, *Pratidin*, respectively.
41. Authors' interview with Uttam Kumar Basu.
42. *ABP* Advertisements, December 2001 (our translation).
43. Ibid.
44. *Anandabazar Patrika* and *The Telegraph*, December 1996 (our translation).
45. *Anandabazar Patrika*, August 2005 (our translation).
46. *Anandabazar Patrika*, March 2004 (our translation).
47. *Anandabazar Patrika*, September 2005 (our translation).
48. For instance, see how *Anandabazar Patrika* advertised Rituparno Ghosh's *Hirer Angti* on 1 November 2002, for its *Alpha Bangla* screening, or how *Utsab* was advertised for its 'world television premiere on *Tara TV* on 23 April 2000.
49. Tapan Biswas is a veteran film producer who has been associated with the Bengali film industry since 1981. He was the producer of Rituparno Ghosh films like *Titli* or *Utsab*, and the recent 2011 Kaushik Ganguly film, *Arekti Premer Galpo* (*Just Another Love Story*).
50. Authors' interview with Tapan Biswas, 13 December 2010, Kolkata.
51. *Chokher Bali* advertisement, *Anandabazar Patrika*, October 2003, p. 2.
52. Interview with Sandip Sen, 1 December 2010, Kolkata.
53. Authors' interview with Uttam Kumar Basu.
54. *Shanjhbatir Roopkathara* publicity advertisement, *Anandabazar Patrika*, November 2002.
55. Ibid.
56. Authors' interview with Subrata Sen, 2 October 2010.
57. Sushmita Biswas, 'Tolly Rockers', *The Telegraph*, 21 November 2010.
58. DQW Bureau, 'Hoichoi is Powered by International Digital Platform "ViewLift"', *The DQ Week*, 13 September 2017, available at https://www.dqweek.com/hoichoi-powered-by-international-digital-platform-viewlift/, accessed on 29 April 2021.
59. Dev the Superstar fan club, who is the founder of this page and website, explains elaborately as a quintessential fan the whole process of how he began this journey of developing, designing and promoting the fan page of Dev the super star. On the other hand, the two pages on star actor Jeet, available at

http://www.itimes.com/public/jeet.madnani and http://jeetfanclub.blogspot.in/, claim to be the official fan clubs of Jeet.

60. Sudeshna Banerjee, 'Fan-tastic', *The Telegraph*, Calcutta, 5 September 2010.
61. Authors' interview with Kaustav Bakshi.
62. The Producer's Note on the Databazaar Media Venture website states the following:

    > Databazar Media acted as an exclusive gateway for Indian content to North America, combining the latest in digital technologies with the best in traditional methods in a new, fusion distribution model (like theatrical screenings, DVD sales, IPTV channels and Web Streaming to PC and Mac) that maximised North American revenue.

    Producer's Note, Databazaar Media Venture Website, available at http://www.databazaarmedia.com/producer-corner.aspx (now defunct).
63. Lawrence Grossberg and Della Pollock, ed., *Cultural Studies*, vol. 12, no. 2 (London: Routledge, 1998), p. 206.

Conclusion

Tollywood Post-Resurgence

Post the celebratory resurgence narrative of the Bengali film industry post-2000, a new phase could be observed, wherein the stark distinction between the parallel and the popular was either constantly merging or fading away. In this context, Bengali cinema, post the demise of film-maker Rituparno Ghosh in April 2013, can be broadly understood by the works of certain film-makers like Kaushik Ganguly, Srijit Mukherjee, Mainak Bhaumik, Anik Dutta, Suman Ghosh, Shiboprosad Mukherjee and Nandita Roy (also known as Nandita–Shiboprosad), Raj Chakraborty, Q (or Qaushiq Mukherjee) and Pradipta Bhattarcharya.

The above set of film-makers have primarily been engaged in a certain number of films and have attempted diverse thematic contents. Post the success of *Arekti Premer Galpo* (*Just Another Love Story*) in 2010, which explores alternate sexualities and the documentation of *jatra*, and stage female impersonator actor Chapal Bhaduri, Kaushik Ganguly approached subjects that involved looking at the lives of foley artists in the 2013 film, *Shabdo* (*Sound*), and circus dwarf performers in *Chhotoder Chhobi* (*The Story About Small People*) in 2015. Srijit Mukherjee's 2013 film, *Jaatishwar* (*A Musical of Memories*), was modelled as a Bengali musical and was a contemporary take on the performer figure, *Antony Firingi* (*Hensman Anthony*), a Bengali language folk poet of Portuguese origin; it also referred to the popular Bengali film, *Antony Firingee*, by Sunil Banerjee in 1967, starring Uttam Kumar. His 2015 film, *Nirbaak* (*Speechless*), starring Sushmita Sen, dealt with subjects like the self-obsession of an older man, and the affective and emotional relationship with a dead body, casting a tree and a dog as essential characters. Mainak Bhaumik explored subjects like a lesbian relationship in his 2015 film, *Family Album*; the sensation around the nudity of a film star in his 2014 film, *Take One* was fuelled by the media sensation generated around the nude appearance of Bengali film actress Paoli Dam in Sri Lankan director Vimukthi Jayasundara's 2011 Bengali film, *Chhatrak* (*Mushrooms*). Raj Chakraborty's 2013 film, *Pralay* (*Disaster*), designed as a crime thriller, dealt with the real-life event of the murder of Barun Biswas, a social activist of West Bengal (see Figure 5.1).[1] Press columns and other media discourses show a serious interest in the richness of themes and the multiplicity of subjects. A new Bengali film cult has formed, first, with Q's 'path-breaking' 2010 film, *Gandu* (*Loser*), and then some of Q's later films. These films and film-related activities evoked a large fan following at some college and university campuses of Kolkata. They also generated regular discussions and debates on social media fan pages and other virtual community forums.

In this emerging attempt to blur the lines between popular and parallel cinema, director duo Nandita–Shiboprosad's success in Tollywood perhaps lies in their message-oriented films, mainly revolving around Bengali middle-class families and their everyday concerns. Their approach has been in bringing the middle-class family back to the theatres in its entirety. Their first feature film venture, *Icche*, followed by *Alik Sukh* (*Unreal Happiness*) in 2013,

Figure 5.1: DVD Screen Grab of *Jaatishwar*

Source: Reliance Entertainment.

Ramdhanu (*The Rainbow*) in 2014, *Bela Sheshe* (*In the Autumn of My Life*) in 2015, among others, deal with such familial themes. The above-mentioned films are neither produced by the big production cannons existing in Tollywood and not necessarily star-driven. *Icche*, presented by Rituparna Sengupta, a well-known star of Tollywood, found its way to the theatres post the celebratory resurgence narrative of the Bengali film industry. *Icche* is a simplistic narration of the complex relationship between an over-possessive and zealous mother and her only son. *Alik Sukh*, adapted from Suchitra Bhattacharya's novel, dealt with the ethical and moral dilemma of a doctor and his wife caught in a medical tragedy, for which the husband was held responsible. Subsequently, their next film, *Ramdhanu*, revolved around the recurrent and rampant issues faced by middle-class Bengali parents during the race of admitting their children in premier English medium schools of Kolkata.

The 2015 release, *Bela Sheshe* (*At the End of the Day*), entered into the lives of an elderly married couple and their family. The directors managed to deal with a scarce cinematic representation of the marital discord and the altering ideologies of an old couple, who subsequently strike a compromise and reach reconciliation. The film went on to become highly successful in terms of its box-office collections. These films find a sustainable audience appreciation and consistent viewership across the big towns and small towns of Bengal for their unabashedly conformist stand towards middle-class values and worldviews. Nevertheless, the end always results in a world where the middle-class ethos and institutions are kept intact. In the typical structure of popular melodramas, these almost formula-like films continue to dominate middle-class cinema in Bengal. Nandita–Shiboprosad have become the poster personalities for this kind of cinema in Tollywood. Big studios or corporate giants have rarely produced their films. However, they remain within the dominant structures of the mainstream industry in terms of their promotion, distribution and exhibition (see Figure 5.2).

As discussed in Chapter 3, the literary aesthetics, in more than one way, functioned as the politics and poetics of the post-1990 'new parallel' film culture, and aimed to address the question of 'taste' associated with this film practice, mapping it on the broader

Figure 5.2: DVD Screen Grab of *Ichche*

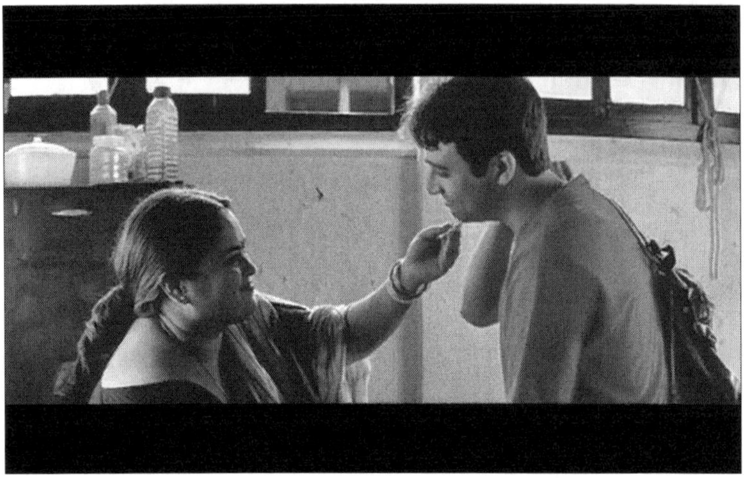

Source: Databazaar Media.

terrain of Bengal's film history. Thus, a binary was established in the popular press between the mainstream model, which was distanced from literary-ness, and the parallel, which was consciously generating literary pleasure. However, the discourse of literary-ness and the binary of popular and parallel have experienced some changes since 2012–13. Films like *Mishawr Rawhoshyoa* (*Mystery in Egypt*) by Srijit Mukherjee or *Chander Pahar* (*Mountains of the Moon*) by Kamaleshwar Mukherjee, both 2013 films, intervened into the idea of 'literary parallel-ness' of the industrial practice. The way in which these two films, or even *Raajkahini* (*The Tale of Kings*) by Srijit Mukherjee in 2015, have been publicised in the mainstream media prior to their release, as well as the pattern of their grand release, followed newer strategies or mechanisms in the literary film practice of Tollywood.

It would be relevant to read this change with reference to Kamaleshwar Mukherjee's films. He made his debut with *Uro Chithi* (*Unexpected Message*) in 2011, but his second film, *Meghe Dhaka Taara* (*The Cloud-Capped Star*) in 2013, which was produced by SVF, brought him to the forefront. It narrated the biography of noted film-maker, Ritwik Ghatak, and his struggling career. The release of this film was followed by appreciation from the press.

After *Meghe Dhaka Taara*, SVF produced Mukherjee's next film, an adaptation of Bibhutibhushan Bandyopadhyay's novel, *Chander Pahar*. Its publicity discourse in the press, rooted in the idea of the literary cinema, attained a new phase. The publicity of *Chander Pahar* started much before its theatrical release. The media played a significant role in advertising this film, leading to the creation of a hype among the audiences. Print media articles reported it to be one of the highest-budget Bengali films (reportedly made with a budget of nearly Rs 1.5 million).[2] The news and stories of *Chander Pahar* being shot at locations in Africa were regularly published. The fact that the film used computer-generated imagery (CGI) was also publicised. A website called '*Chander Pahar* Diaries' was launched during its shooting, bringing 'exclusive behind-the-scenes footages' from the shoot.[3] The website, in some of its videos, highlighted 'the immense risks, hardships and also the fun, frolic and new experiences' during the course of the shooting. It described the film as one epic adventure to look forward to, and instructed the viewers to get closer to the adventure by following its updates. In this way, the literary model of the parallel circuit designed for the niche *bhadralok* crowd was popularised as a mainstream cinema model. In addition to this, Dev, projected as the superstar of Tollywood, was roped into this literary adaptation to play the protagonist, Shankar, which was also a significant change in the literary-ness of the parallel film circuit.

A film-making style emerged within the realm of Bengali cinema, offering a possible critique of the literary cinema and the *bhadralok* cultural code of literary-ness. This critique can be studied both in terms of the technicalities of films and their narrative design. *Herbert*, by Suman Mukhopadhyay, based on the novel by Nabarun Bhattacharya, subverted the *bhadralok* belief system regarding the question of cultural superiority, literary taste, sensibility and other charismatic self-perceptions of this class. Anik Dutta's *Bhooter Bhabishyat* (*The Future of the Pasts*) in 2012 presented a unique mix of the literary mode and *masala* elements like song-and-dance sequences that was hitherto uncommon in Bengali literary film practice. Finally, with subsequent examples like *Kangal Malshat* (*War Cry of Beggars*) by Suman Mukhopadhyay and *Tasher Desh* (*The Land of Cards*) by Q, both 2013 films, Bengali literary cinema perhaps attained a new phase of subversion. These two films are literary adaptations of Nabarun Bhattacharya and Rabindranath Tagore's texts, respectively. The way they subverted the idea of refined taste, literary-ness, and art and aesthetics is noteworthy. Moreover, the change in distribution patterns, increased budgets, the intervention of new technology, and corporate investments have played a major role in changing the scenario of Bengali cinema in Tollywood. However, this does not mean that mainstream *masala* films have taken a backseat at the box office, or that the literary films are no longer treated as high quality content in the public sphere.

During this period, another film made its way quite interestingly into the Bengali film world—Pradipta Bhattacharya's 2013 film, *Bakita Byaktigoto* (*The Rest is Personal*). The film was produced on a modest budget by Tara Films, a film production unit of Tara Telefilms and the *Tara Bangla* TV network, and was later purchased by first-time producer Satrajit Sen of Tripod Films, who also distributed the film. The film breaks from the structured practices and norms of film-making conventions, primarily of the mainstream industry. The film was shot in a cinema verité style, dealing with a story about a fictional village, Mohini, where people find love and romance in abundance. Realism, being the overarching mode of this film, strongly questions concepts like reality, fiction, imagination, and the very idea of cinema itself. Bhattacharya's film found limited theatrical release in Kolkata and entered into a bureaucratic tussle with the West Bengal state-sponsored exhibition centre, Nandan.[4] According to the director, the film was an extension of his background and the way he saw life in reality. He felt that his film was a novel project that was outside the mainstream industry, and perhaps posed a strong threat to the nexus between the government and the existing industrial mechanisms, wherein the industry and the government mutually feed on each other for vested interests, materially and otherwise.

In order to counter this opposition and fight the exhibition and distribution deadlock, Bhattacharya went on an innovative exhibition strategy, almost single-handedly. He began showing the film privately. He promoted it by going door-to-door to gather people. In areas like Baharampur, Uluberia, Hoogli, Shantiniketan and Burdwan in West Bengal, he organised more than 100 private screenings by tying up with local cultural organisations, clubs and community theatres. The film received positive criticism and gained momentum in press and media discourse, ultimately bagging the 2015 National Award as a Special Mention in the Regional Cinema category. These private screenings continued, and the film-maker claimed that the number of screenings had crossed 500 by the year 2014. He asserts himself as an alternative film-maker who believes that it was the perfect time for an original experiment in the space of Bengali cinema, and even Tollywood. For him, it is high time that the film industry stops blaming the audience for their poor taste and takes up the challenge to come up with shocking, radical and original cinematic content.[5]

Another film, *Khasi Katha* (*A Goat Saga*), directed by Judhajit Sarkar in 2013, and produced by Star Fine Movies, a first-time venture for both the director and producer duo, dealt with a strange plot and subject. Set against the backdrop of a lower-middle-class, poor neighbourhood of Kolkata, commonly referred to as a Muslim ghetto, the film entered the magic realism mode through the conversations between a butcher and his goat. Neither did the film get a substantial release, nor did it recover its production cost from the box-office collections, although it managed to earn positive criticism from the critics. In a review, noted film critic Shoma A. Chatterji writes:

> … created a beautiful amalgam of form, content, narrative and music. For the first time in Bengali cinema, the audience is brought face-to-face with a real Muslim ghetto in Kolkata with its narrow gullies, the dirty leather factory, the unkempt boxing ring, the Eid or Muharram processions with festoons and music, the small telephone booth …[6]

Followed by this, *Asha Jaoar Majhe* (*Labour of Love*), a first feature film project by Aditya Vikram Sengupta, enjoyed tremendous visibility in international film festival circuits, besides winning more than 20 awards. The film revolves around the everyday life of an unnamed married couple working in Kolkata, after the global recession and the inflation boom in India. The film premiered at the Seventy-First Venice International Film Festival on 4 September 2014, where it won the best debut director award in the Venice Days Fedora category. Apart from being screened at several prestigious film festivals around the globe, the film has won the Indira Gandhi Awards for best debut film by a director and best audiographer at the Sixty-Second National Film Awards of India, 2015. The film was theatrically released limitedly on 26 June 2015 in Kolkata and in select metropolitan cities after being accepted for distribution by another Bengali film-maker, Suman Ghosh, as the presenter of the film.

The film stands out for its unusual treatment. It has no spoken dialogues, but a very richly textured and layered background sound design; with stunning visuals, the film manages to achieve a poetic quality. Complimented with visual and aural references from old world nostalgic characteristics of north Kolkata, it was a fresh and innovative attempt to make a film, and quite predictably, without the support of any leading film production unit of Tollywood. Noted film critic Aseem Chhabra elaborately writes:

> ... Life that Sengupta portrays in *Asha Jaoar Majhe* are the daily rituals of a man and a woman, perhaps a married couple at home and work, captured with fine details. But every move, every act, every detail adds to the hypnotic quality of the film .... It is like experiencing poetry and lyricism on screen.[7]

The film's screening at the Kolkata International Film Festival in 2014 was received with hearty appreciation from a section of film buffs and intellectuals. Post its theatrical release in 2015, the film remained majorly in press and public sphere discussions for its innovative and experimental content and treatment (see Figures 5.3 and 5.4).

In many ways, the emergence of Q as a film-maker and his film, *Gandu*, is a significant intervention in the scenario of Bengali cinema. First, the way in which *Gandu* was released online and the manner in which it was promoted on internet sites break the established conventions of film distribution and promotion in Bengali cinema. Second, starting from its very title (the word, *Gandu*, a slang that roughly translates as 'loser'), to its controversial scene with frontal nudity of both the male and female actors, and many instances of non-simulated sexual acts and usages of expletives, the film appeared to be 'path-breaking' in the traditional moral order of Bengali films. But apart from this, the significance of the film lies in the fact that it could establish itself and its director as a cult figure among its fans and followers. Q started his film-making career with the unreleased film, *Tepantarer Mathe* (*Beyond the Horizon*) and *Bish* (*Poison*) in

Figure 5.3: Screen Grab of *Asha Jaoar Majhe*

Source: Amazon Prime.

Figure 5.4: Screen Grab of *Asha Jaoar Majhe*

Source: Amazon Prime.

2009, which did not earn much appreciation and acknowledgement in the media. *Bish* was originally titled *3X*, but Q had to change it when the CBFC raised objections with the title. He completed his next venture, *Gandu*, which focused on the life of a boy called 'Gandu' (played by Anubrata Basu) who lives with his mother (Kamalika Banerjee) and aspires to be a rap performer. *Gandu*, primarily shot in the black-and-white mode, offers split screens, jump cuts, exciting soundscape, punk rock aesthetics, and a space design influenced by contemporary Southeast Asian cinemas.[8] A reviewer writes: '… He has no hope for the future, no prospects, and the constant pulsing, reckless tunes serve as a narrative device, driving the pace, plot, and film forward …. Thematically dense, dealing with identity, morality, sex, drugs, hope.'[9]

Gandu hangs out with his rickshaw-puller friend, who is incidentally called Rickshaw (Joyraj Bhattacharya) and is an ardent fan of Bruce Lee. Gandu and Rickshaw go on a road trip, and experience several events in various real and surreal spaces of the city. In the climax, Gandu wins a huge amount of money from a lottery jackpot and manages to record a demo of his rap songs, and he also has sexual encounters with a girl (played by Rituparna or 'Rii' Sen). The film merges the spaces of reality with Gandu and Rickshaw's fantasy, and out of this merger, a metaphysical space emerges, which has registers in everyday reality, myth, desire and sexual fantasies. Another website reviews *Gandu* in these words: '… The film, which seems designed to batter the Indian censor board with its liberal use of frontal male and female nudity, profanity and drug use, has gained a cult following …'[10]

After its online release, *Gandu* gained immense popularity from internet cinephiles and young film enthusiasts. The DVD of the film was released by Artsploitation later, which comes with a well-packaged, 12-page-long booklet, and an introduction from Q, followed by an essay by critic Travis Crawford. The essay elaborates how *Gandu* is distinct and different from 'what is traditionally considered "Bollywood"'.[11] A 33-minute documentary on the making of *Gandu* was also made available, which 'takes you behind the scenes of the film in almost every conceivable way'.[12] In this DVD, there are a series of archival footage and interviews where the director narrates how the story was improvised from a musical collaboration.[13]

A particular segment focuses on the heavy deployment of sexual content in the film. It deals with both the technicalities of filming and their thematic implications. After the film earned praises at several European and American film festivals, Q formed a rap band called *Gandu Circus* in February 2012. He joined as a vocalist in this rap band, with Neel Adhikari on the guitar and Jiver Singh on drums. Since then, *Gandu Circus* has been performing at several places within India and across the world, acting as a major player in the construction of Q as a cult figure and continuing the legacy of the film. The tracks composed and played by this band generally have accompanying visuals, which are produced by Q and are projected on a screen behind the musicians during the performances. *Gandu*'s pirated copy also went viral in the Kolkata streets post the media hype that the film had garnered. In this context, a newspaper report published in *The Times of India* mentioned: 'The online leak of *Gandu* has taken the piracy of the movie to a different level altogether .... The surprising bit is that though the other pirated Bengali movies are of films that have been released and censored, *Gandu* is yet to get released anywhere.'[14] Subhajit Chatterjee, Assistant Professor of Film Studies at Jadavpur University, was quoted in this article: '... Given the nature and circulation of Asian cinema .... that it is now being resituated in the local pirate market as a regional Bengali movie is disheartening but also objectively interesting.'[15] Q had commented elsewhere: 'This city (Kolkata) has always produced cutting edge commentary on society and the world. But somewhere along the way, we seem to have stopped in our tracks. We have stagnated, bound by our past, and a distinctly class value system.'[16]

Gandu literally broke the class value system and the memory of 'good Bengali cinema'. The film's traction was followed by *Tasher Desh* (*The Land of Cards*) in 2013, Q's adaption of Tagore's classic play of the same name, which was premiered at the Rome International Film Festival and had a regular theatrical release in India. The film attempted to redesign and reframe the Tagore text. Q's *Tasher Desh* literally and cinematically declared a war against the middle-class value system. Chatterjee noted that Tagore's *Tasher Desh* being adapted by Q, that too in the league of a camp musical, would perhaps create a new perspective for regional audiences and their negotiations with new forms and aesthetics of world cinema.[17]

What was more enthralling about *Tasher Desh* was that the stylisation of experimental film (the breaking of the *bhadra* taboo of sexualities, and adopting an alternative exhibition pattern through internet release, etc.) propagated by Q was followed by a few other film-makers, generating a certain amount of enthusiasm among young film buffs and film-makers in some of the colleges and universities of Kolkata. Amitabha Chakraborty's film, *Cosmic Sex* in 2014, which he claimed to be a sex spectacle, was released online. The film deals with the story of a young man, Kripa, who thinks he has murdered his father and is on the run from sex and violence, which leads him to encounter a woman, Sadhavi. She strangely resembles Kripa's dead mother. She gives him shelter and teaches him *Dehotatva* (a cult practice that deals with worshipping through the body), and the connection between sex and spirituality. Rii Sen played the role of Sadhavi and won the best actress award at Osian's Cinefan Festival. Putul Mahmood, the producer of this film, admits that she is not a conventional film producer, and the sole reason behind her producing *Cosmic Sex* was to ensure that such an unconventional film got made in the first place. Film-maker Amitabh Chakraborty stated that he was ready to embark on a battle with the Censor Board to exhibit a film like this, which would add to its initial promotion and publicity. According to the producer, Putul Mahmood, the image of Bengali cinema had drastically altered, and *Cosmic Sex* was 'very much in the popular mode.... which has great possibilities in the districts as well'. Mahmood laid emphasis on the fact that 'since Bengal is a one city state, you have to look at a commercial film or a mainstream film you have to have a film which can do well not only in Kolkata but in the districts as well'.[18]

In order to bring in innovative production and distribution impulses into Tollywood, films like *Noukadubi* (*Boat Wreck*) by Rituparno Ghosh in 2011, a bilingual venture backed by Bombay film-maker and producer Subhash Ghai's Mukta Arts, and films like *Tasher Desh*, have been co-produced by NFDC, along with several other national and international financiers and producers. In continuation of this trend, the 2015 release of *Open Tee Bioscope*, directed by Anindya Chatterjee, is a particularly interesting example. The film was produced and distributed by successful Bollywood film-maker Sujeet Sarkar's production house, Sun Rise Films. It enjoyed a more-than-average success at the box office. This trend perhaps hinted at the renewed interest in Bengali cinema from producers outside the domain of Bengal, and the possibility of associating or backing projects that are original in their concepts and are treated in an innovative manner. Some of the above-mentioned films are mostly directed by film-makers who have established their creative credibility not just through film direction in Tollywood, but also by involving themselves in other creative endeavours, ranging from theatre to music composition, writing, organising film festivals, and so on. For instance, film-maker Suman Mukhopadhyay has been actively associated with Bengali theatre for several years and has directed plays like *Raja Lear*, *Bisarjan*, *Samay Asamayer Britanta*, etc., earning appreciation in the press and the public sphere. Kamaleshwar Mukherjee has also directed a play and has acted in Kaushik Ganguly's 2014 film, *Khaad* (*The Abyss*) and Utsab Mukherjee's 2015 film, *Bheetu* (*Coward*). Pradipta Bhattacharya has been actively associated with a project called *Kolkata Shorts* since 2013, which acts as a platform for young and aspiring film-makers to screen their films. This project invites short feature/documentary films from young aspiring film-makers, selects films for screening in competitive sections, gives prizes, and organises talks and lectures with established film-makers. Judhajit Sarkar is involved in artistically and financially backing young experimental film-makers. Anindya Chattopadhyay is the lead singer and songwriter in the well-known Bengali band, *Chandrabindoo*, and is also a columnist for the Bengali daily, *Anandabazar Patrika*.

This in turn leads us to the concluding thoughts for this book that try to map the industrial landscape, mechanisms and dynamics of the contemporary Bengali film industry—Tollywood. An article in the *Business Standard* on 17 December 2014 claimed that as of 2014 only five to six films could be considered hits out of the total of 100 films that were produced during the year in what we know of as the Rs 150-crore worth Bengali film industry.[19] The article further refers to a report by the Confederation of Indian Industries (CII) and Indian Market Research Bureau (IMRB) and claims that although the industry releases around 100 films every year (which is almost three times higher than comparable figures in 2005), recent trends in box-office collections have not been that encouraging.[20] In this post-resurgence period, the film industry is experiencing newer problems. Contemporary film-makers and producers provide different perspectives on this crisis. Raj Chakraborty puts the blame on lack of coordination among industry players for this crisis. According to him, the state government has really been supportive of the industry, but to fully accrue the benefits, film-makers and producers have to show better collaboration. While Pradipta Bhattacharya holds the big production houses responsible for this, Suman Mukhopadhyay thinks that Tollywood has become too pro-government for it to have any alternative critical space.[21] He says, 'People were not comfortable working with me, as they would have got anti-government stamp. Some clearly told me they were scared; others sugar-coated the suggestions. In the film trade, no one wants to antagonize the government.'[22] This is the reason why he prefers theatre over films. There is no censor board, no guild, and no specific rules. It is more independent. He finds it utterly ridiculous that a Rs 40 lakh film is measured on the same scale as one made with Rs 5 crores. He rues the fact that there were times when the film industry engaged with numerous voices, but now Tollywood only promotes insularity.

Several industry sources blame chit funds operating in Tollywood for this malaise. An article published in the *Business Standard* argues:

> The industry had seen itself in the middle of a crisis, with funds drying up, as many chit-fund companies, including Sudipta Sen's Saradha Group, had been putting in their money in movie production. On an average, 80 Bengali films are produced in a year. About 30 per cent .... financed by these companies ...[23]

There are instances of the dominance of Bollywood as well, and especially, the dubbing of Hindi films and television soaps in Bengali. Here, it is relevant to refer to the turmoil caused after the release of *Gunday* (*Goons*) in 2014, directed by Ali Abbas Zafar, and produced by Yash Raj Films (YRF) in both Hindi and Bengali. The film was shot extensively in Kolkata and other parts of West Bengal, and had the star cast of Ranveer Singh and Priyanka Chopra capturing the flavour of the state in the 1970s and 1980s. The industry called for a boycott of this film, but *Gunday* was released simultaneously in Hindi and in the dubbed Bengali version in many areas of

West Bengal. The other part of the narrative is that increasingly, more and more viewers are using mobile phones for watching the latest releases. Piracy is also affecting the circulation of newly released Bengali films on mobile phones. Here it would be relevant to refer to the release of *Jamai 420* (*The Fraud Son-in-Law*) by Ravi Kinnagi in 2015. The film was produced by SVF and was released on 22 May 2015. The film could be seen on several online sites. SVF moved the court and got an interim order from Kolkata High Court that restricted 25 internet service providers and a few websites from making the film available for viewing and downloading. Advocate Soumya Ray Chowdhury, who was representing SVF, told us that they found out from their digital content provider that the version that was circulating was recorded from a cinema hall in Kolkata during the very first screening of the film, which prompted them to register an FIR.[24] Ravi Kinnagi pointed out that piracy was killing the movie business. 'Even if the print on Internet is bad, anyone watching it doesn't buy tickets again to catch the film at theatres,' he said.

Abhishek Bagaria, one of the proprietors of Regal Cinema, said that hall owners also suffer: 'The mobile phones today are extremely sophisticated and if someone captures the film on smartphones, there's no way we can stop that with our infrastructure, as frisking isn't an option. But I agree that it's a sad state of affairs.'[25]

Indranil Roychaudhury, who made his debut with *Foring* (*Dragonfly*) in 2013, however, identifies the lack of 'good original' films being responsible for the recent crisis. In an interview, he underlined the importance of producing original Bengali commercial films:

> ... millions are spent for crappy middle of the road films .... the kind of human relation drama (film) that one cannot sit even for five minutes 50s-early 70s original model Bengali films signified the golden era—original tradition, a tradition created by the Bengalis. If you want to revive Bengali cinema there is no point in replicating Rituparno Ghosh model, because it is not a viable model. It never sold. It's a myth it's a hoax. Bengalis actually never went to see a Rituparno Ghosh film. Then you'll get an industry, which is real.[26]

As mentioned earlier in this chapter, these are some of the perspectives and positions that are causing transformations in the Bengali film industry. But there are several other determining factors which are responsible for these changes. We have not been able to map all these factors and their impact on contemporary Bengali cinema, given the constraints of the scope of this book. For instance, the book does not elaborately engage in a proper study of audience reception.

However, this book has made an attempt to investigate the post-1980s scenario of the Bengali film industry with a systematic and chronological analysis of the various factors that were responsible for the 'crisis' in its cinematic tradition. The research revealed that much of the published work during this period, or for that matter, on the 'crisis narrative', was confined to the decline in cinematic values and aesthetics of a certain tradition and concept that defined Bengali cinema, so voiced by a particular class and section of the audience. The major concerns expressed were that Bengali cinema had turned into a blatant imitation of cheap Bombay formula films, and as a consequence, mainstream films had transformed into a 'crass' affair.

This was a discourse that was heavily invested in the cinematic text and gave precedence to the *bhadralok* perception or idea of 'good cinema'. In this book's exploration and observation, it stands out that the situation in the post-1980s was a complex one. On the one hand, the death of Uttam Kumar led to the fading away of a certain tradition and imagination about mainstream cinema that also caused a severe financial setback to the industry. On the other hand, one could see the rise of an alternative cinematic practice. Much of this complexity was a result of the entry of TV and VCRs into the life of middle-class city-dwellers. Consequently, the film distribution and exhibition system across West Bengal was severely affected.

Directors like Anjan Chowdhury, Sukhen Das, Swapan Saha, Haranath Chakraborty and others gained prominence, which was significantly marked by the gradual transformation and alteration in the functioning and dynamics of the film industry. However, the book has not been able to focus much on the cinematic texts of films made during the decades from the 1980s to the early-2000s, because the intention was to primarily foreground the circuits and networks that operated within the industry and how these affected production, distribution, and to a certain extent, the reception of films. Tensions that exhibition policies and the shifting of audience tastes generated over the period of more than two decades have been our major concern. Since the industrial economics of this period has been our primary focus, we have not been able to fully engage with the textual and narrative analyses of films that were being made during this period by a specific group of film-makers like Anup Sengupta, Bablu Samaddar, Arabinda Mukherjee, Biresh Chattopadhyay, etc.

It is not enough to look into the films of this phase in terms of their 'crassness' because one needs to understand that the industry at this time was in a desperate need to develop a cinematic practice that could offer something different from Hindi films and TV, and in the process, create 'a more localized form of content that could be most closely identified (with) by an audience segment which had never been directly catered to'.[27] Thus, the categories of audience and class have both been very vital for this book. The book has problematically looked at these two categories, questioning the relevance of issues related to the popularity or success of films that could form subjects of further research and analysis.

The period following liberalisation further complicated the situation and functioning of the industry. However, it also devised several new strategies for film producton, distribution and exhibition. Most importantly, the effect of corporatisation on the Bombay film industry slowly made its entry into Tollygunge. This process took almost a decade since the economic liberalisation of India in 1991. The effects of a neo-liberal market and urban lifestyle, mainly popularised by TV and Bollywood films, began to take shape and influence the overall business and economics of West Bengal. Although there was a limited and sluggish entry of big capital into the West Bengal market, it managed to create ripple effects in the entertainment scenario of the state. The proliferation of Western content through TV and the internet drastically altered public notions of image, idea, content and genre. Bengali cinema began to lose out in competition to Bollywood films and world cinema. The creation of multiplex theatres within shopping malls ushered in a revolution in terms of new spaces, mainly in cities and big towns, creating in the process, a niche audience demanding form and content that would represent this post-global life and worldview. Independent and floating producers in West Bengal had realised by then that their form of cinema was losing its audience, even among segments that they thought were their main customers.

SVF entered into film production but chose to produce films by directors who were already popular and successful in the mainstream. It took them almost a decade to change their *modus operandi* and experiment with a director who was being celebrated by the *bhadralok* for bearing the legacy of 'good cinema' and with promises of taking on the mantle of Satyajit Ray. SVF became the first fully corporatised production house of Bengali cinema and inititated the influx of increased finance into film production. They steadily adopted the vertical integration model that enabled them to create and sustain control over all the sectors of film business, from production and distribution to exhibition. Mainstream films, produced by SVF, with an increased inflow of budgets began to imitate the visual aesthetics of Bollywood and South Indian mainstream cinema. This was a visual aesthetic that represented the vision of a global world, drawing in from spaces away from the city of Kolkata. Song-and-dance sequences were shot in foreign locations and film cities.

However, the content of these films remained a subject of constant criticism for being neither completely 'Bengali' nor entirely Bollywood. This is strange. Because in reality, these very films began to reclaim the lost audience. Box-office reports and the success of these films problematised and rendered ambivalent the very segment of audience that appropriated and appreciated these films. SVF also began to diversify horizontally by tapping into the multiplex crowd cautiously, choosing directors and films that would not only give them a different market, but also elevate their reputation as a genuine production house of Tollywood. By the end of 2008, it emerged as the most powerful film business unit of Tollywood. The film industry in West Bengal experienced a resurgence. The NRI Bengali population began to grow, creating a new potential market to be taken into account. Film-makers like Anjan Dutt and Aniruddha Roychowdhury made optimum use of this segment with their 'crossover' films.

This book has also attempted to read some features of post-liberalisation Bengali parallel cinema, with a specific focus on its nostalgia discourse. At the same time, it questions this very category (parallel) as not something that is pre-given, but rather seeks to problematise the nostalgia discourse in its constructed-ness within its context. It tries to interrogate the term 'parallel' in the post-liberalisation context and tries to establish that this parallel-ness was formed because of its differentiating strategy from the mainstream and its imagined continuation of the earlier cinematic tradition. Hence, the chapter on post-liberalisation demonstrates how this cinema has formed in an intersecting plane of the idea of 'continuation' and the strategy of 'difference'. The strategy of difference worked not only in terms of the film texts' conscious use of aesthetic devices and thematic content, but also in their exhibition logic, publicity texts, promotional strategies, and even in the idea of the star director of this film culture. Rituparno Ghosh embodies this idea of a 'different' film-maker. His star director persona has a different appeal. He and his films and the 'parallel' stream post-1990s were imagined as a continuation of the tradition of the 'good' Bengali films of the past, especially of the 1950s and 1960s. The book therefore further engages with the question of the memory of 'good' old Bengali films with respect to which this parallel stream was imagined. It also explores how the *bhadralok* memory of 'good' cinema acted in shaping the post-liberalisation Bengali 'parallel' stream at different levels and in different registers.

Chapter 2 has mapped the journey of Tollywood for more than a decade, emblematically using SVF and their films as a template to look at the changing contexts and moving towards an understanding of the creation and reconstruction of Tollywood as the revamped Bengali film industry that was on its way to becoming a culture industry. This chapter focuses on aspects like budget, box-office figures, publicity and promotion strategies, new stars, and the technical upgradation of films produced by SVF in order to highlight factors that majorly effected the reconfiguration of Tollywood films.

It is interesting to note here that this entire aspect of improving the style of film production and the introduction of novelty features in the mainstream provided fodder to the English and Bengali press, which produced a voluminous discourse on this resurgence and foregrounded the new face of the industry as Tollywood.

This continuing media discourse can be labelled as being overtly celebratory. Very recently, however, alternative opinions and analyses have also emerged that critically look at the success of SVF and their films. It is now common knowledge that over the past few years (from mid-2011 to 2015), almost all mainstream films under the SVF banner have been, by and large, commercial and critical failures. Yet, SVF continues to project manipulative figures that state otherwise, so that its image of being at the top remains undented.

In spite of being touted, projected and promoted as the all-encompassing entertainment industry of West Bengal, Tollywood needs to introspect its individuality and identity seriously, that is, as being both counter-hegemonic to Bollywood and yet distinguishable unto itself. Moinak Biswas, in his 2011 work, *Neo-Bhadralok Darpan* (*Neo-Bhadralok Image*) on the 'neo-*bhadralok* cinema' (according to Biswas, this form or genre of cinema is not 'new' but rather, '*neo*', because this genre of film-making is in a process and all of its characteristics are not clearly definable or defined), talks about the emergence of a new genre of films in Tollywood. Biswas analyses some repeated motifs in these films, like interior spaces of multi-storied apartments; action sequences mostly centred in living rooms, bedroom spaces, private hospitals and highways; the centrality of marital or extra-marital relationship themes; and a depiction of mundane reality. This genre almost erases the heterogeneity of city life and urbanity, and repeatedly focuses on a homogeneous upper middle-class community and some specific signs of this community. Apart from the apartment or location spaces, two other popular spatial and locational features in these films are north Calcutta household spaces and picnic spots. While the former infests the films with a sense of nostalgia, the latter strips the spaces from confined boundaries. This new film genre and its classification initially claimed for themselves the realistic charge of earlier realisms. Strangely, however, this genre is almost silent about contemporary socio-political realities. For example, these films never react to issues like that of the 2007–08 Nandigram (East Midnapur District, West Bengal) and Singur (Hoogly district, West Bengal) agitations. These two uprisings became highly politicised movements spearheaded by the TMC party and its leader, Mamata Banerjee, as the opposition to the then Left Front government, wherein Banerjee's slogan, *Maa, Maati, Manush* (*Mother, Land, People*) became the central catchphrase for mobilising mass support and solidarity from the intellectual and film fraternity who came forward in public to demand a serious change in the dispensation, *Poriborton Chai* (*We Want Change*) becoming another popular slogan during the

2011 legislative assembly elections. Chiranjit Chakraborty and Debashree Roy, two well-known star/actors from the Tollygunge days of the Bengali film industry, contested the assembly elections and won their respective constituencies. Following this eventful election that brought in a sea change in the political climate of West Bengal with the 34-year-old Left government overthrown by the TMC, one could witness the increasing visibility of Tollywood actors and stars in several social and political events organised by the TMC government. During the 2014 general assembly elections, the TMC government provided candidature for Member of Parliament (MP) seats to veteran Tollygunge star personalities like Sandhya Roy, Moon Moon Sen, Tapas Pal, Shatabdi Roy, and the popular star figure of Tollywood, Dev. Post-2014, the TMC emerged as one of the most substantial opposition parties to the BJP-led government at the Centre. Banerjee has demonstrated a strong preference for the Tollywood film fraternity. This symbiotic association led to a significant overhaul in the political economy of media in West Bengal. However, during the 2019 general assembly elections, a section of the Tollywood industry began to form into a camp that became critical of the TMC government, eventually leading a few Tollywood personalities to officially join the BJP and win the MP seats. Nevertheless, the TMC government consistently strengthened its control and influence over the Tollywood industry, which led to the government's embroilment in a controversy around the 2019 film, *Bhobishyoter Bhoot* (*The Past of the Future*) by Anik Dutta. The film experienced a *de facto* ban immediately after its release, allegedly criticising the TMC government, creating a massive uproar within the industry and the public, and severe condemnation on the *de facto* ban from veteran actors like Soumitra Chatterjee, actor-director Aparna Sen, and others.[28]

These are discussions and analyses that perhaps do not dominantly appear within the scope of this book, but could become subjects of future research and commentary. Therefore, this book has been an attempt to trace the journey of the regional film industry from a 'period of crisis' to its present form as 'Tollywood', partly as a response to Bollywood, and to the media and public. It has tried to map the industrial changes and dynamics that enable the construction of Tollywood in the public sphere and in media discourses. The renewed interest and curiosity among film enthusiasts, cinephiles, the press and academics about Tollywood was the inspiration and motivation to try and unfold the various circuits and layers that operate within and without the film industry, which resulted in the formation and establishment of Tollywood.

Notes and References

1. Authors' interview with film-maker Raj Chakraborty, 29 March 2015, Kolkata.
2. Debaleena Sengupta and Digbijay Mishra, '*Chander Pahar* Makes Waves', *Business Standard*, 10 January 2014.
3. SVF, 'Chander Pahar Diaries', Episode 3, Columbus Vs Shankar Part 1, Dev, Kamaleshwar Mukherjee, available at https://www.youtube.com/watch?v=AaEHeEkcGaM, accessed on 22 August 2015.
4. Authors' interview with the film-maker Pradipta Bhattacharya, 31 March 2015, Kolkata.
5. Ibid.
6. Shoma A. Chatterji, '*Khashi Katha* (Bengali)/A Well Told Story', *The Indian Express*, 13 June 2014, available at http://indianexpress.com/article/entertainment/screen/khashi-katha-bengali-a-well-told-story/, accessed on 5 September 2015.
7. Aseem Chhabra, 'Review: Asha Jaoar Majhe is One of the Best Indian Films of 2015', *Rediff.com*, 29 June 2015, available at http://www.rediff.com/movies/report/review-asha-jaoar-majhe-is-one-of-the-best-indian-films-of-2015/20150629.htm, accessed on 9 November 2015.
8. Here, by Southeast Asian cinematic practice, we mean the film-makers and films of countries like Korea, Hong Kong, Taiwan, etc., which globally circulate in the contemporary international film festival forums.
9. Brent McKnight, 'We Are on the Threshold of a Great Diaster: "Gandu"', *PopMatters*, 15 January 2014, available at https://www.popmatters.com/166645-gandu-2495789067.html, accessed on 24 August 2015.
10. For details, see http://in.blouinartinfo.com/news/story/889826/cult-film-gandu-now-available-for-download#, accessed on 29 April 2021.
11. McKnight, 'We Are on the Threshold'.
12. Ibid.
13. The music of the film was produced by the band, 'Five Little Indians'.
14. See Priyanka Dasgupta, 'Pirated Copies of Gandu Go Viral in Kolkata', *The Times of India*, 30 October 2011.
15. Ibid.
16. See Priyanka Dasgupta, 'Why this Shame about Sexuality?', *The Times of India*, 11 January 2017.

17. See Priyanka Dasgupta, 'Gandu will Realign Regional Viewer to World Cinema', *The Times of India*, 15 July 2011.
18. See http://www.kaahon.com/details.aspx?ID=Wall_141120163444&title=Producer%20visualises%20`Cosmic%20Sex`%20as%20a%20mainstream%20film, accessed on 21 April 2021.
19. 'Tollywood Delivers Only Five–Six Hits a Year: A Report', *Business Standard,* 17 December 2014.
20. Ibid.
21. Zinia Sen, 'There is No Alternative Critical Space Here: Tollywood has Become Very Pro-Government', *The Times of India*, 17 July 2015.
22. Ibid.
23. 'Tollywood Delivers Only Five–Six Hits a Year'.
24. Digbijay Mishra, 'Chit Fund-hit Tollywood Gets Corporate Balm from Reliance, Viacom 18: Major Production Houses such as Reliance Entertainment and Viacom 18 have Evinced Interest in Tollywood', *Business Standard*, 6 July 2013; Zinia Sen, 'Jamai 420 Available Online, Venkatesh Films Lodges FIR against Regal Cinema', *The Times of India*, 11 June 2015.
25. Ibid.
26. Interview with Indranil Roychaudhury, *Kahon*, available at http://www.kaahon.com/details.aspx?ID=Wall_150621122309&title=Arthouse%20cannot%20survive%20w/o%20healthy20mainstream%20film%20industry, accessed on 21 April 2021.
27. Sharmistha Gooptu, 'Changing Contexts, New Texts', in Nalin Mehta, ed., *Television in India: Satellite, Politics and Cultural Change* (New York: Routledge, 2008), p. 159.
28. Express News Service, 'Bhobishyoter Bhoot: Actors, Filmmakers Take Out Rally to Protest Withdrawal of Film from Theatre', *The Indian Express,* 11 March 2019.

Index

Abar Aranye (*Again in the Forest*) 61, 111, 121, 168
adaptations 33, 117, 119, 138, 167, 188
advertisement/advertising 72, 94, 105–06, 108, 110, 114, 139, 143, 158, 160–61, 165, 168–70, 187
Anandalok 30, 39, 50, 135, 139–40, 156, 166
art cinema/film 4–6, 44, 60, 81, 132
audience 1–5, 7, 16–19, 21–25, 29, 31–36, 38–40, 43–45, 47–49, 58–59, 61–62, 65, 67–69, 71–72, 76, 79–80, 82–84, 87, 92, 94, 96, 104–05, 107–13, 115, 119, 134–35, 137, 140, 143–44, 153, 159, 162, 164–65, 171–72, 174–76, 185, 187, 189, 193, 198–200
  Bengali 1, 16, 31, 33, 48, 61, 69, 82–83, 137, 164
  diaspora 49
  educated 107–08, 115
  female 32–33
  global 176
  international 113
  middle-class 2, 62, 143, 165
  niche 48, 59, 104, 107, 134, 199
  North American 113
  rural 17, 76
  semi-urban 17, 76, 159
  urban 49, 79–80, 108–09, 115, 144, 152, 159, 164

Bakshi, Kaustav 141, 164, 175
Ballygunge Court 117, 129
Bangladesh 37–38, 46, 94, 174
Bengal 1–3, 5–6, 8–9, 15–18, 23, 26–29, 31, 35–36, 38, 41, 43–47, 49, 60–61, 64–65, 67, 70, 72–73, 81–82, 88, 92–96, 98, 107–08, 110–12, 114, 117–19, 127, 131–32, 134, 136, 150–51, 153–54, 156–57, 159–60, 174, 184–86, 188, 194–200, 202–03
  film distribution policy in 114
  literary tradition of 118
  post-liberalised 2
Bengali cinema/film 1–9, 15–20, 25–34, 36–44, 46–51, 57–58, 60–62, 67–71, 75–77, 79–84, 86–89, 92–97, 99, 104–21, 131–33, 135, 137–40, 142–44, 151–57, 159–67, 169–73, 175–77, 183–85, 187–90, 193–201, 203
  compulsory screening of 26, 28
  contemporary 49, 83, 86, 97, 105, 195, 198
  distribution and marketing of 113
  history of 32, 44, 86, 99, 115, 151
  liberalisation 1
  mainstream 7, 42, 87–88, 97, 107–08, 155, 164, 171
  post-liberalisation 1, 104, 106, 116–17, 131, 133, 143
  quality of 4, 7, 37, 49, 116
  standards of 37
  systems and practices of 1–2, 4–5, 7, 13, 15, 47, 87, 98–99, 105, 117–19, 121, 143, 198–99, 162, 185–87
  traditions of 15
  writings on 4, 6, 9, 117
Bengali film industry 1–4, 7–9, 15–16, 25, 34, 38, 42, 47, 49–51, 57–58, 60–61, 68–71, 76, 79, 87, 93, 106,

108, 110, 131, 133, 151, 154, 156, 161, 175, 177, 183, 185, 195, 198, 201, 203
condition of 17–18, 25, 29
contemporary 49, 83, 97, 105, 132, 137, 173, 195, 198
golden era 3, 17
Bengal Motion Pictures' Employees Union 29
Bengal National Chamber of Commerce 70
bhadralok 1–3, 9, 16–18, 23–25, 30–31, 34–36, 38, 45, 47, 50, 73, 98–99, 104, 107–08, 115, 127–31, 133, 135, 137, 140, 143, 162, 164–65, 167–69, 187, 198, 200–02
aesthetics 9, 73
audiences 18, 35, 38, 45, 48, 108, 115, 135, 162
belief system 127, 187
identity 128–29
sensibility 130
Biswas, Moinak 9, 97–98, 202
Biswas, Tapan 112, 114, 170
Bollywood 2, 7–9, 37–38, 44, 47, 50, 57, 63, 67, 69, 71–72, 81–82, 93, 150–51, 156–57, 162, 176, 178, 192, 196, 199–200, 202–03
Bombay film industry 7–8, 35, 37, 57, 70, 199

Calcutta Municipal Corporation (CMC) 27
Central Board of Film Certification (CBFC) 92, 153, 192
Chakraborty, Dipankar 31, 33
Chakraborty, Haranath 9, 15–16, 34, 37–40, 43–44, 48, 58, 62, 64, 73, 95, 165, 172, 198
Chakraborty, Mithun 62, 65, 71–72, 170
Chakraborty, Raj 9, 51, 73–76, 88, 95, 183–84, 196
Chakraborty, Sudipta 141, 158
Chakraborty, Utpalendu 4–5, 23–24, 37, 134
Challenge 51, 76–78
Chander Pahar 186–87
Chandrabindoo 130, 195
Charulata (*The Lonely Wife*) 86, 120
chat shows 66, 155, 161
Chatterjee, Arun 83–84
Chatterjee, Nabyendu 4, 23, 71
Chatterjee, Parambrata 62, 90, 97, 158
Chatterjee, Prosenjit 32, 42–43, 64, 71, 80–81, 83, 90, 94, 153
Chatterjee, Subhajit 97, 193
Chatterji, Shoma A. 6, 132, 134, 189
Chattopadhyay, Anindya 130, 195
Chattopadhyay, Biresh 35, 199
Chattopadhyay, Saratchandra 33
Chiranjeet 36, 80
Chokher Bali (*Sand in the Eye*) 48, 59–61, 117, 119–20, 122, 139, 144, 167, 169, 172
Choudhury, Anjan 17, 165
Chowdhury, Aniruddha Roy 65, 68, 161
Chowdhury, Anjan 15–16, 30–31, 34, 37, 43, 44, 198
Cinema/film 1–9, 15–51, 57–77, 79–90, 92–99, 104–23, 125–44, 150–78, 183–90, 192–204
aesthetics 17, 25, 122, 131, 135
alternative 5, 189
'B grade' 47
contemporary 8, 49, 83, 86, 97, 105, 132, 137, 144, 158, 172–73, 195–96, 198
experimental 5, 152, 194–95
family 36, 132, 165
foreign 71
government-financed 27
literary 118, 119, 186–88
mainstream 1, 5–7, 9, 15, 23–25, 36, 42, 44, 61, 65, 70, 87, 94–95, 97–98, 105, 107, 114, 116, 144, 155, 171, 187, 194, 198, 200, 202

cinema halls/houses 16, 18–19, 22, 24, 26–28, 31, 35, 38, 41, 44–45, 62–63, 67, 70, 92, 96, 105, 108, 115, 197
Confederation of Indian Industries (CII) 195
copyright 81–82, 178
  infringement of the act 81
  issues 82, 178
  violation 81
corporatisation 1–3, 37, 40, 48–50, 199
crisis narrative 2, 4, 7, 26, 37, 47, 49, 51, 117, 129, 152, 163, 198
culture 1–2, 5, 7, 9, 35–36, 47, 73, 99, 104, 107, 109–11, 114, 116, 119, 126–31, 141, 150, 156–58, 162–63, 168, 177, 185, 201
  Bengali 47, 119
  consumer 126, 129
  film 1, 5, 107, 114, 162–63, 185, 201
  parallel film 114, 163, 185

Dahan (*Crossfire*) 48, 112, 122, 141
Dakhal (*The Occupation*) 5
Das, Anjan 95, 108, 114, 117, 119, 125, 129, 166, 168–70
Dasgupta, Abhijit 110, 168
Dasgupta, Buddhadeb 4–5, 110, 123, 125, 130–32, 134, 137
Das, Sukhen 21, 30, 164, 198
Dekha (*Sight*) 88, 111, 122, 125
Desh 165, 168, 172, 187, 193
Dev 38, 66, 69, 72, 75–76, 79–80, 88, 158, 161, 174–75, 187, 203
Devi 116, 120
Dey, Dipankar 22, 120
Dey, Dulal 34, 37
Dhanuka, Ashok 68, 76
Dhar, Aniruddha 96, 109
Dhwani 60
diaspora 7, 38, 49, 112, 114
digitisation 67, 92
discourse 1–2, 4, 6–7, 17, 47, 49, 51, 57–58, 80, 93, 95, 98–99, 104, 108, 116, 120, 127, 131, 133–40, 142–43, 151, 155, 157, 162–64, 166, 168, 173, 177–78, 186–87, 189, 198, 200–01
  Bengali cinema 1, 3, 47, 99, 104, 120, 143
  nostalgia 2, 200
  press/media 49–50, 57, 133, 135, 140, 155, 178, 203
  taste 58, 116, 143, 163–64, 168
distribution 1–3, 5, 7, 17, 24, 34, 38, 47, 49, 57–58, 61, 67, 72, 86, 92, 96–98, 106, 108–09, 113–16, 135, 152–54, 159, 170, 173, 175–76, 178, 185, 188, 190, 194, 198–200
  innovative 175
  lack of 5, 24, 106
  obstacles 106, 135
documentary films 26, 195
Doordarshan 111, 159
Dui Prithibi 88–91, 151
Dutta, Arijit 60, 109, 115
Dutta, Jeet 51
Dutt, Anjan 49–50, 68, 71–72, 112, 200
Dutta, Salil 21, 35
Dutt, Utpal 35–36, 121
Dwitiyo Basanto (*Beyond Tomorrow*) 110, 168

Eastern India Motion Pictures Association (EIMPA) 49
Ek Je Achhe Kanya (*There is a Girl*) 108–09, 115, 164, 166, 170
Ekti Tarar Khnoje (*Stars Never Sleep*) 169
English films 27
entertainment industry 49–50, 59, 151, 157, 160, 178, 202
European films 110
exhibition 1–2, 24, 26, 28, 34, 49–50, 57, 67, 92–93, 96–98, 104, 111, 114, 116, 143, 152–53, 159, 178, 185, 188, 194, 198–201

centres/halls/houses 24, 67, 114, 188
problems of 18
systems and practices 2, 98, 152, 198

fan clubs 174
Federation of Indian Chambers of Commerce and Industries (FICCI) 60, 88
Feluda films 119–20
festivals 42, 45, 61, 88, 112, 116, 119, 132, 134, 170, 189
film clubs 110
film critic 45, 86, 162, 189–90
Film Development Board (FDB) 26
Film Export Corporation 13
Film Federation of India 110
film festivals 24, 92, 95, 170, 175, 189, 193, 195
Film Finance Corporation (FFC) 5
film industry 1–3, 9, 16, 31, 36–37, 39, 45, 49–51, 57, 60, 70, 84, 140–41, 144, 152, 155, 159, 163, 166, 175, 177–78, 189, 195–96, 198, 200, 203–04
film-makers 3–6, 16, 24–25, 29, 34–35, 37–39, 43–45, 47, 49–50, 58, 60, 64, 70, 94, 98–99, 106, 108–09, 130–38, 140–43, 153, 183, 186, 189–90, 194–96, 199, 201
film-making 3, 9, 23, 25, 37, 40, 45, 47, 70–71, 83, 105, 107, 109, 119, 120, 134, 177, 187, 190, 202
career 134
practices 177
style of 120
film production 1–3, 18, 22, 37–38, 41, 45–46, 48–49, 58, 92, 94, 96–98, 109, 111, 153, 160, 178, 188, 190, 200–01
corporatisation of 1
film projection 67
film society 2, 4, 6, 107, 110–11, 116
approach 6
culture 110–11, 116
decline in 110
movement 2, 110
screenings 110
writers 4
financing 29, 93
FM radio stations 49, 151

Gandu (*Loser*) 184, 190, 192
Ganguly, Jeet 75–76, 173
Ganguly, Kaushik 93, 112, 161, 183, 195
Ghatak, Ritwik 3–4, 132, 136, 186
Ghose, Goutam 4–5, 23–24, 37, 45, 61, 70–71, 90, 93, 108, 110–11, 121–22, 132, 134–35, 153, 168
Ghosh, Rituparno 6, 45, 48, 59, 61, 71, 86–87, 92–93, 104–05, 112, 114–15, 117–19, 122, 129, 131–38, 140–41, 143, 158, 164, 166–69, 171–72, 183, 194, 197, 201
globalisation 150–51
Goswami, Joy 125, 140, 169
Government of West Bengal 5
Grihayuddha (*Crossroads*) 5, 24
Gupta, Dinen 33, 39, 112

Herbert 131, 187
Hindi cinema/film 2–3, 7–8, 15–16, 19, 22, 25, 28, 31, 33, 35, 38, 42, 48, 58, 66, 69, 71, 81–82, 151, 172, 196, 199
Hirer Angti (*The Diamond Ring*) 105–07, 117, 119–20
Hiron 76, 158
Hollywood 8, 58, 81, 87, 108, 115, 170, 176

Icchhe (*The Desire*) 97
I Love You 66, 69, 72
Indian
censor board 192
regional films 176
Indian cinema/film 2, 4–5, 7, 69, 81, 151, 178

popular 5, 151
quality of 4
Indian Market Research Bureau (IMRB) 195
infrastructure 60, 127, 197
innovations 92–93, 152
internet 8, 93, 164, 173, 175–76, 190, 192, 197, 199
Iti Mrinalini (*An Unfinished Letter*) 86–87, 92, 94, 144
Iti Srikanta (*Yours Truly, Srikanta*) 95, 117, 119, 166–67

Jatra 3, 30–31, 37–38, 45–46, 70, 167, 183
Jeet 51, 61–62, 65, 68–69, 71, 75–76, 79–80, 88, 157–58, 173
Juddha 61–62, 65

Kar, Ajoy 118
Khan, Soha Ali 120, 166
Khela (*Game*) 171–72
Kinnagi, Ravi 58, 61, 66, 69, 76–77, 81, 197
Kolkata International Film Festival 60, 63, 190
Kumar, Uttam 3, 15–17, 20–22, 25, 29, 83, 165, 170, 183, 198

Left Front 5, 27, 107, 110, 202
liberalisation 1, 4, 8, 37, 49, 57–58, 98, 104, 106, 110–11, 114, 116–17, 126–27, 133, 137, 140, 143, 150–51, 152, 199, 201
literature 3–4, 15, 39, 48, 117–19, 128, 163
locations 69, 71–72, 75–77, 79, 93, 114–15, 120, 156, 177, 187, 200, 202

Majumdar, Tarun 5, 21, 35, 40, 51, 112, 118
marketing 1–2, 19, 50, 68, 79, 83, 93–96, 98–99, 104, 106, 112, 114, 116, 169, 171, 175
global 114
innovative 1
strategy 95
masala cinema/film 37, 41, 188
media 1–2, 8–9, 49–51, 57–58, 64–65, 67, 73–74, 79–80, 84, 86, 92–93, 96–97, 99, 104, 109, 111, 127, 131, 133, 135–37, 140–41, 143–44, 150–58, 160–63, 169–74, 177–78, 183–84, 186–87, 189, 192–93, 201, 203
audio-visual 161
Bengali 111
electronic 109, 150, 172
new 151, 170, 173, 177
print 64, 79, 86, 162, 173, 178, 187
Memories in March 86–87, 92, 94–95, 144
memory 117, 120–23, 125–26, 129–30, 139, 168, 193, 201
middle-class 2, 4, 7, 16, 30, 34, 36, 38, 48, 62, 82, 93, 98, 107–08, 111–12, 115, 118, 126–27, 129–30, 133–34, 137, 140–41, 143, 155, 162, 165, 172, 184–85, 198, 202
Bengali 2, 16, 36, 38, 48, 118, 127, 134, 137, 184–85
educated 107, 162, 172
family 34, 36, 184
households 111, 140
intelligentsia 4, 7
Minister Fatakesto 9, 65, 72–73
MLA Fatakesto 9, 64–65, 73
Mohta, Shrikant 48, 58–59, 63, 65, 67, 75, 81–82, 86–88, 96
monopolisation 92, 153, 178
movements 2–3, 23, 73, 99, 104, 110–11, 202
art cinema 3
contemporary 73
counter- 23
film society 2, 110–11
literary 90

new parallel cinema 2, 99, 104
new wave 23
Mukherjee, Qaushiq (Q) 183
Mukherjee, Srijit 83, 86, 90, 175, 183, 186
Mukherjee, Swastika 64, 68, 79, 158
Mukhopadhyay, Suman 131, 161, 169, 187, 195–96
Mullick, Koel 61–62, 69, 88, 158, 174
Mullick, Ranjit 31–33, 35–36, 40, 43, 61, 69, 158
multiplexes 48–49, 59, 83, 88, 144, 199–200
music 21, 30–32, 34, 41, 49–51, 66–67, 69, 72, 75–76, 83, 93–94, 97, 99, 130, 155–57, 171–73, 176, 189, 195
Bengali 176, 183
director 84
non-film 156, 172
release 41
sequences 151
tracks and songs 30
video 76, 97, 171, 173

Nag, Kushali 80
Namastey London (*Hello London!*) 81
Nandan 112, 114–16, 132, 188
National Awards 45, 48, 59, 106, 134
National Film Development Corporation (NFDC) 24, 60, 106–07, 110, 136, 194
Nayak (*The Hero*) 64, 83, 85
newspapers and magazines 16, 21–22, 47, 50, 99, 135, 138, 156, 158–63, 165, 168, 170, 193
Bengali 16, 159, 160, 166
English 16
New Theatres 3, 94
Nil Nirjaney (*Vacation Blues*) 164
Non-Resident Indians (NRIs) 61, 120, 200
North America 112, 154, 176
nostalgia 2, 119–20, 122–23, 128, 130, 142, 168, 200, 202

Ogo Bodhu Shundari (*O My Beautiful Wife*) 21
Open Tee Bioscope 130, 194

Pal, Tapas 30, 35, 66, 79–80, 158, 203
Pandey, Gaurav 113
parallel cinema/film 2–3, 24–25, 46, 104, 107–08, 111–12, 114, 131, 134, 163, 165, 171–72, 184, 187, 200
Paromitar Ekdin (*House of Memories*) 109, 111, 123–24
piracy 60, 193, 197
plagiarism 137–38, 178
popular cinema/film 24, 38, 47, 61, 80, 132, 172–73
Poran Jai Joliya Re 81–82
Pratibad (*Protest*) 43, 48, 58
print industry 159–62
Priya cinema hall 109
producers and distributors 2, 4, 17–19, 22, 24–25, 27–30, 39, 44–45, 47, 49, 60, 67–68, 71–72, 81–82, 86–89, 93, 95–97, 99, 108–11, 118, 153, 175–76, 178, 194–96, 199
production companies/houses 9, 47, 51, 79, 95–98, 108, 111, 153, 155, 159–61, 178, 196
Promo/promotion 2, 60–61, 63, 66, 72, 92–95, 99, 111, 140, 151, 156, 160–61, 171–72, 176, 178, 185, 190, 194, 201
digital technology 94
Facebook 94
strategies for 99, 135, 170
publicity 1, 21, 41, 50, 57–58, 61, 63, 65, 72, 76, 79, 83, 92–96, 108–09, 133, 135, 153, 158, 160–61, 163–72, 178, 187, 194, 201
pre-release 41, 66
strategy 166, 170

Rabindra Sangeet 49
Raha, Kiranmoy 5–6, 24, 117
Rai, Aishwarya 48, 120, 169
Ray, Sandip 61, 92–93, 169
Ray, Satyajit 3–5, 72, 83, 115–16, 119–20, 131–33, 136, 139, 168, 200
realism 4, 6, 15, 23, 131, 165, 189
reality shows 156
regional films 37, 153, 170, 175–76, 178, 203
rights 51, 82, 94, 109, 111, 134, 155, 158–59, 175
  cable and satellite (C&S) 158
  electronic media 109
  films 82, 134
  home video 51
  music 51
  overseas 51
  remake 82
  telecast 155
  TV 111
Royal Bengal Rashaya 92
Roychowdhury, Aniruddha 122, 169, 200
Roy, Debashree 36, 62, 125, 158, 164–65, 203
Roy, Prabhat 35, 40, 58, 62
Roy, Sudeshna 50, 63

Saha, Swapan 9, 16, 38–40, 42, 45, 47, 58, 64, 68, 73, 97, 109, 165, 198
Salil, N. K. 64–65
Samaddar, Bablu 34, 37, 199
Sananda 50, 154, 160
Sangeet Bangla 66, 69, 76, 151, 154, 156, 170–71
Saptapadi (*Seven Steps*) 94, 118
satellite television 8, 111, 153
Satyajit Ray Film and Television Institute (SRFTI) 72
screenings 19, 23, 26–29, 44–45, 49, 105, 107–08, 110–13, 155, 175, 188–90, 195, 197
Sen, Aparna 4, 6, 23, 35, 37, 45, 86–87, 106, 109, 118, 122–23, 125, 132, 140, 142, 153, 158, 164–66, 168, 170, 203
Sengupta, Rituparna 42–43, 50, 97, 185
Sen, Mrinal 3–5, 16, 23, 37, 122, 132, 137–38, 141
Sen, Sandip 108–09, 166
Sen Sharma, Konkona 87, 166, 170
Sen, Subrata 6, 26, 108, 164, 166–68
sex/sexuality 87, 192
Shami Keno Ashami (*Why the Husband is a Criminal*) 38
Shanjhbatir Roopkathara (*Strokes and Silhouettes*) 122–23, 125, 170–71
Shasurbari Zindabaad (*Hail the In-Law's House*) 41–43, 48, 58
Shatru 17, 30–34, 46
Shree Venkatesh Films (SVF) Pvt. Ltd. 2–3, 9, 16, 46–47, 51, 57–62, 65, 67–69, 71–82, 84–99, 106, 144, 152–53, 156, 169–70, 173, 186–87, 197, 200–202
  entry into Tollygunge 199
  growth of 98
  initiatives 71
  publicity and promotion 161
  standards of 67
  success of 57, 201
  television channel 69
Shukno Lanka (*Red Chillies*) 77, 113
Singh, Nishpal 68, 71, 77, 88
Sinha, Tapan 3, 16, 22, 40, 58, 112, 118
song-and-dance sequences 15, 65, 187
Soni, Mahendra 48, 58, 65, 72, 79, 81, 86–88, 92
south Indian films 81
state government 5, 21, 26, 60–61, 95, 110, 196
studio(s) 3, 16, 20, 22–23, 27–28, 36, 42, 47, 60, 76, 185

poor and deteriorating condition of 28
sound-video-film 60
Tollygunge 20, 27, 36, 47
Studio Supply Co-operative 20
superstars 16, 20, 29, 83, 85, 157–58, 161, 187

t2 50, 160–62
Tagore, Rabindranath 49, 117–18, 133, 188
Tagore, Sharmila 36, 120–22, 166
Tamil films 82, 117
Tarkovsky, Andrei 138
tax 18–19, 23, 29
benefits and rebates 23
entertainment 19, 29
subsidies and rebates 18
Team Anjan Chowdhury 34
telefilms 112, 140, 155
Television (TV) 8, 16, 24–25, 30, 36, 39–40, 46, 49, 63, 66, 69, 72, 92, 94, 97–99, 110–12, 139–40, 143–44, 150–51, 153–59, 163, 166, 168, 170–73, 175, 177–78, 188, 196, 198–99
cable 44, 49, 111, 140
channels 49, 94, 112, 143, 153–57, 163, 170
regional 105, 140
satellite 8, 111, 150, 153–55
viewership 154
Telugu films 66, 69, 76, 81–82, 88, 117
Theatres 2–3, 16, 18–19, 23, 27, 30, 32, 36, 38, 43, 48, 51, 59–60, 67, 70–72, 79, 83, 88, 92, 94–96, 110–11, 115–16, 118, 141, 156, 161, 165, 174–75, 184–85, 189, 195–97, 199
single-screen 16, 43, 60, 92, 115–16
Tiger 9, 68, 73
Tollygunge film industry 1, 16–18, 29, 33, 36, 38, 40, 45, 51, 108–09, 152, 154, 163–64
condition of 18
post-Anjan Chowdhury phase in 37
resurgence in 44
strike 29, 61, 185
studios 16, 20, 27, 36, 47
survival of 41, 96
Tollywood 1–4, 7–9, 16, 48, 50–51, 57, 59–62, 65, 67–69, 71–73, 75–76, 79–82, 85–88, 92–99, 108, 116, 133, 143–44, 150–64, 172–73, 176–78, 183–90, 194–96, 200–204
emergence of 9
experiments in 9
post- 2, 6, 9, 16, 99, 107, 109, 112, 117, 119, 122, 127, 142, 162, 164, 185, 201, 203
present situation in 31, 70
state of affairs in 153
trailers 76, 113, 176

Unishe April (*Nineteenth April*) 6, 48, 105–06, 109, 112, 125, 129, 133–34, 138, 141, 164–65
Utsab 71, 110, 112–13, 116–17, 120, 129, 140, 167, 195

Vasudev, Aruna 24, 134
Viswanathan, Ashoke 137

Washington Bangla Radio on the Internet (WBRi) Inc. 176
West Bengal Film Development Corporation (WBFDC) 5, 23–24, 110
West Bengal Film Finance Corporation (WBFFC) 18, 23
West Bengal film policy 114
westernisation 47